JOSEPH PAPP AND THE NEW YORK SHAKESPEARE FESTIVAL

GARLAND REFERENCE LIBRARY
OF THE HUMANITIES
(VOL. 793)

JOSEPH PAPP AND THE NEW YORK SHAKESPEARE FESTIVAL
An Annotated Bibliography

Christine E. King
Brenda Coven

Garland Publishing, Inc. • New York & London
1988

Library of Congress Cataloging-in-Publication Data

King, Christine E., 1954–
Joseph Papp and the New York Shakespeare Festival.

(Garland reference library of the humanities ; vol. 793)
Includes indexes.
1. Papp, Joseph—Bibliography. 2. New York Shakespeare Festival—Bibliography. I. Coven, Brenda, 1942- . II. Title. III. Series.
Z8657.4.K56 1988 016.792'0232'0924 87-25921
ISBN 0-8240-6609-X (alk. paper)

Printed on acid-free, 250-year-life paper
Manufactured in the United States of America

CONTENTS

PREFACE

This is a selective annotated bibliography on the life and career of Joseph Papp and the origins and evolution of his organization, the New York Shakespeare Festival. Periodical and newspaper indexes, subject bibliographies, government documents, reference materials and works on the New York and American theater, the RLIN, OCLC and other databases, and the extensive clippings files at the New York Public Library of the Performing Arts at Lincoln Center were among the sources that we consulted in compiling this book.

The introduction is intended to acquaint the reader with the major events in Papp's life and career and the significant contributions made by him and the New York Shakespeare Festival to the development of American theater. This is followed by a short and selective chronology of the important milestones in Papp's career and the development of the New York Shakespeare Festival.

Material authored by Papp is found in the first section of the main body of the work. Arranged chronologically, it includes newspaper columns and letters, periodical articles, testimony at congressional hearings, contributions to books, and taped interviews.

Material about Papp—monographs, dissertations and periodical articles—are arranged by author in the second section, which also includes weekly newspapers, such as the *Village Voice* and *Variety*.

Daily newspaper articles proved to be the most abundant source of information and, consequently, account for the largest section of this work. Many brief or repetitive newspaper articles have been deliberately excluded. All cited references are to the late city or final editions of newspapers. Articles from the *Wall Street Journal* and the *Christian Science Monitor* are from the eastern editions. Articles in the magazine sections of newspapers have been included in this chapter. The arrangement of this section is chronological since this seemed to be the most useful format for the reader. Anyone who knows of a specific event, and also has the date it occurred, can by-pass the subject index and go directly to the newspaper citations for that year. This section reads almost like a narrative (if a somewhat convoluted one) of Papp's career and the evolution of the New York Shakespeare Festival.

In general, the only play reviews included are the opening night reviews in the *New York Times*, which are in the productions list in the last section of this book. Reviews that contain substantial additional information on Papp or the New York Shakespeare Festival are cited in the sections on works about Papp and the Festival. The list of major productions includes not only plays produced by Joseph Papp and the New York Shakespeare Festival, but also those directed by Papp. The names of the theaters in which they were performed are listed as well. The arrangement is chronological. Productions of other companies performed at the Public or Delacorte theaters are not included. Only the first *New York Times* review is listed for each production, although some had more than one in that newspaper. If a production moved to Broadway from another location then there is an entry, with a review citation, for both its original and Broadway openings. A few productions, particularly early ones, had no *New York Times* reviews and this is indicated by the words "no review." An alphabetical list of plays by title with production dates immediately follows the chronological listing

This book has two indexes: author and subject. In both indexes item numbers of citations, not page numbers, are referenced.

Only materials that we were able to view personally and give full bibliographic citations for have been included. The annotations are intended to give an indication of the content of the references and any unique or interesting features in each work. For brevity, the New York Shakespeare Festival has been shortened to the NYSF.

We would like to thank John B. Smith and Donald C. Cook for their support and encouragement, the interlibrary loan personnel at SUNY Stony Brook for their efficient service, and our colleagues in the Frank Melville Jr. Memorial Library for their cooperation and understanding. We also want to acknowledge the assistance of the staff at the New York Public Library's Performing Arts Research Center, and the New York State/United University Professions Joint Labor-Management Committee for a grant which allowed us to take time off to finish the manuscript. Finally, we owe thanks to Jeff Coven and Nathan Baum for editorial assistance, and to Alex King for encouraging us in our efforts to master our microcomputer.

INTRODUCTION

Joseph Papp, creator, producer, and personification of the New York Shakespeare Festival has made a unique and indelible mark on the development of the American theater over the past 30 years. His theatrical domain encompasses Shakespeare in the Park, the multi-theater complex known as the Public Theater, the Mobile Theater, and numerous Broadway productions. No history of the American stage can be complete without a chapter or two on him and the Festival. "He is now unquestionably the most prominent person in the American theater," wrote theater critic Stanley Kauffmann.[1] *New York Times* critic Mel Gussow went further when he stated that "more and more he is the American theater,"[2] and Bernard Jacobs, president of the Shubert Organization, said, "I believe Joe Papp is the most important force in the English-speaking theater today."[3]

Papp's dream of bringing live drama, particularly Shakespeare, to new audiences who had never gone to the theater was realized largely because of his own personality. With his boundless energy, enormous self-confidence, fierce determination, and street-wise intelligence he has forged the largest theatrical organization and one of the most important cultural institutions in this country.

The story of Papp's life, from his poverty plagued childhood to his position as head of a multimillion dollar cultural institution, could have been written by Horatio Alger. He was born Joseph Papirofsky on June 22, 1921, in the Williamsburg section of Brooklyn; the second of four children born to Samuel and Yetta, Polish Jewish immigrants. Thirty-one years later CBS would change his name to Papp because "Papirofsky" was too long for the credits. His father was a trunk maker whose skills were in little demand, forcing him to take on a variety of menial jobs. Taking his young son along as a helper, he sold peanuts, plucked chickens, and hauled garbage. Enterprising even as a child, Papp shined shoes and hawked newspapers after school. In spite of these efforts the family found itself on home relief during the Depression. When Papp was 12 years old he began to read Shakespeare. He sometimes credits one of his English teachers with introducing him to the plays of Shakespeare. At other times he says he discovered Shakespeare's writings in his local public library, and more than one interviewer has come away from a talk with Papp believing that a free ticket to a live performance of *Hamlet* was what whetted his life long interest in the Bard. Whichever version is true, Papp's interest in Shakespeare has remained constant. "I always loved Shakespeare's work," he told a reporter. "The language captivated me, the sounds of the words and their dramatic quality."[4]

After graduating from Eastern District High School, Papp went to work at a series of low paying jobs, including delivering laundry and working as a short order cook. In 1941 he joined the Navy and was sent to the Pacific for three and a half years. He was assigned to the Special Services unit where he wrote, produced, and directed shows for servicemen, usually on the decks of aircraft carriers. He also wrote scripts and made tapes for Voice of America. Discharged in 1945, Papp headed for California and the

Hollywood Actors' Laboratory, an acting school influenced by Stanislavsky, where he studied acting and directing under the G.I. Bill. When he finished his course of study, he stayed on at the Laboratory as an office manager until 1950 when the school was closed for political reasons. While in Hollywood he taught acting part-time for about six months at the California Labor School. During the next two years he had several jobs in touring companies, including working as an assistant stage manager and understudy for the National Company's production of *Death of a Salesman.* Returning to New York City, Papp got a job as a stage manager at CBS-TV. His real passion, however, was the theater—he dreamed of directing and producing live classics. With this in mind, he and two friends, Peter Lawrence and Bernard Gersten, obtained an option on three of Sean O'Casey's plays, then found a hall to stage them in.

The two O'Casey plays Papp directed and co-produced, *Hall of Healing* and *Bedtime Story*, got a negative review from *New York Times* critic Brooks Atkinson. "Neither the director, nor the actors have any sense of genre style for Irish drama. If there were no Equity actors among them, you would assume that they are amateurs, taking a fling at something for which they have little talent."[5] Although Papp claimed to have been devastated by Atkinson's review, his self-confidence was restored when the drama critic at *P.M.* chose *Bedtime Story* as the best play of 1952.[6] His creativity and restless energy prompted him to search for a theater where he could stage plays on a continuing basis. He found the right place on the Lower East Side in the Emmanuel Presbyterian Church, a building of Elizabethan design. He purchased some seats from a defunct Bronx movie house for less than $200, borrowed lighting equipment, and persuaded a few of his friends at

CBS to help him construct a theater in the church's basement. This done, he applied for and received a provisional charter from the New York State Board of Regents to form a group that would "encourage and cultivate interest in poetic drama with emphasis on the works of William Shakespeare and his Elizabethan contemporaries and to establish an annual summer Shakespeare Festival." In September 1954 the Shakespeare Workshop was born; several years later the group would be renamed the New York Shakespeare Festival. Papp's first production in his newly constructed theater was "An Evening with Shakespeare and Marlowe." After that *As You Like It*, *Much Ado About Nothing*, *Cymbeline*, and *Titus Andronicus* trouped in rapid succession onto his basement stage. Admission to productions was free, putting into practice Papp's belief that theater must be made available to all regardless of income.

The Shakespeare Workshop's first outdoor performances were held in the summer of 1956, not far from the church, at the East River Amphitheater. With a budget of $750, Papp produced *Julius Caesar* and *The Taming of the Shrew*. The amphitheater had been built in the 1930s by Parks Commissioner Robert Moses. During the twenty years of its existence it had generally stood empty and unused; consequently, Moses was pleased to give Papp permission to use it to stage plays. It was Moses' interest in Papp's company and good reviews from critics Arthur Gelb and Brooks Atkinson that persuaded the big foundations to make some modest grants to the Shakespeare Workshop. In early 1957 the Doris Duke Foundation and the New York Foundation gave Papp a total of $30,000, which enabled him not only to pay his actors the minimum off-Broadway salary but to fulfill his wish for a mobile stage to bring free theater to the people. "I made up my mind I was going to have a Shakespeare theater that would go into congested neighborhoods. I had to reach the thousands of people who live and die in their neighborhoods."[7] Taking $2,000 from the foundations' grants, Papp bought a truck, and then had a friend construct a 45-foot platform stage on it. The truck, however, had trouble with bridges and underpasses and was continually breaking down. In July 1957 when it broke down in Central Park near the Belvedere Tower, Papp decided to stay there for the rest of the summer. Although it would be seven years before a $35,000 gift from George T. Delacorte, president of Dell Publishing, enabled the mobile theater to roll once more through the five boroughs, that fortuitous breakdown ushered in one of the great traditions of summer in New York City and of theater in America—Shakespeare in the Park. Following Papp's example, other cultural giants no less august than the Metropolitan Opera and the New York Philharmonic also began to present free concerts in the park. Papp, in effect, had transformed Central Park, the heart of Manhattan, into a summer arena throbbing with cultural activity.

At the end of the summer Papp persuade the New York City Department of Welfare to allow him to use the Heckscher Theater, a 650-seat auditorium in the Children's Center on 104th Street and Fifth Avenue, as a winter playhouse. Once again admission was free, and Papp and his company barely managed to survive on his salary from CBS and the small contributions collected after each performance.

In June 1958 Papp's career suffered a setback when he was called as a witness by the House Committee on Un-American Activities to testify on alleged Communism in the world of entertainment. Although he denied that he was a Communist Party member at the time of his questioning, he refused to say whether he had ever been a Communist and took the Fifth Amendment 12 times. He was fired by CBS the following day. The Radio and Television Director's Guild came to his defense, and in November a federal arbitrator ordered CBS to reinstate him. Even though Papp was never charged with being a Communist Party member, the issue would be raised a year later when he locked horns with the New York City Parks Department over charging admission to his plays in Central Park.

In March 1959 Stuart Constable, Robert Moses' assistant and a "passionate Red-hater,"[8] advised Papp that he would not be allowed to produce plays in the park unless he could provide funds to reimburse the Parks Department for the extra maintenance expenses incurred by the performances. Moses backed Constable and explained to Papp that at least $100,000 to $150,000 would be needed for fencing, sanitary facilities for the actors, and, most important, for paving over the lawn where the audience sat. If Papp would be willing to charge admission, Moses would reconsider the matter. Never, responded Papp, would he charge admission. "To abandon our policy of free admission would result in disenfranchising the very people we are anxious to serve."[9] Papp, with the existence of his fledgling organization in jeopardy, fought back by going to the press. The newspapers loved the story and depicted Papp as David waging a seemingly lopsided battle with his Goliath, the all-powerful Parks Commissioner Robert Moses. Although the *New York Daily News* and the *New York Mirror* ran editorials supporting Moses against Papp, whom they called a "Fifth Amendment man," most of the media came down heavily on Papp's side. The issue was finally resolved on June 17, when the Apellate Division of the New York State Supreme Court found for Papp, ruling that Moses had made "an arbitrary, capricious, and unreasonable decision." The court did, however, grant Moses the right to set "reasonable conditions" under which the NYSF could reimburse the city for any expenses. All the press coverage provided Papp and his company with so much publicity that, as one writer said of the feud, it "was one of the best things that ever happened to Joe Papp."[10] The city's liberals and wealthy patrons of the arts increased the size of their gifts and began organizing benefits for Shakespeare in the Park. As having a picnic on the great lawn while waiting in line for tickets to *Hamlet* or *The Tempest* became a rite of summer for countless New Yorkers, grants from foundations grew larger and more numerous. Even the city recognized a responsibility to give some support to an organization that had become so much a part of its cultural life.

Less than a week after the court's decision, Mayor Wagner established a committee to study the issue of financial stability for the NYSF. Moses asked the New York City Planning Commission for a quarter of a million dollars to construct a permanent outdoor theater in Central Park for Papp and his company. For Papp, who had long believed in government support for the arts, financial prospects suddenly seemed much brighter. Throughout his career Papp has always insisted that the government be responsible for arts funding. "The future of the arts in the United States lies in federal subsidy together with strong controls to insure independent and unfettered expression."[11] To plead this cause he has appeared before congressional committees, written magazine articles and letters to editors, and discussed the issue in almost every interview he has ever given.

In 1960 the city appropriated $60,000 for the NYSF's summer program. In the same year Papp was able to convince the New York City Board of Education to give him $50,000 to tour city schools with a production of *Romeo and Juliet*. In the years that were to follow, by pleading, cajoling, and haranguing the mayor and other officials, Papp managed to get some support from the city. A notable exception would occur in 1980 when the Koch administration, in the midst of a fiscal crisis, cut its usual NYSF appropriation from $323,000 to nothing. Furious, Papp refused to present any Shakespeare plays in the park that year without money from the city and demanded that the NYSF be placed on a budget line. When this demand was not met, he accepted funds from Citibank to produce the operetta *Pirates of Penzance* in Central Park. In 1981 the city, with a budget surplus, was more generous to Papp than it had been over the past several years, and Shakespeare was back in the park.

The construction of the outdoor theater in Central Park began with an appropriation of $250,000 from the Parks Department and a gift of $150,000 from George T. Delacorte in January 1961. The new theater, named the Delacorte, opened on June 18, 1962, with *The Merchant of Venice*, starring George C. Scott. The play was taped by CBS-TV and televised three days later to an audience of 800,000 homes.

There was still one more thing that Papp wanted: a permanent year-round home and theater for the Festival. "Though I was constantly struggling for funds to present Shakespeare, I still desired an outlet for shows that had concern for what was happening in the contemporary world.[12] After looking at several places in Manhattan during 1965, he was shown the old Astor Library on Lafayette

Street in the East Village. The library was named for John Jacob Astor, who in 1848 bequeathed $400,000 and a plot of land to New York City for a public library. The construction of the library in the style of a northern Italian palace of the early Renaissance period took 30 years. In 1911 the library moved to new quarters further uptown, and the building became the home of the Hebrew Immigrant Aid Society. The society had decided to sell the building, which had stood empty for many years, just at the time Papp was looking for a theater. When Papp first saw the building he thought it looked like a prison, but after a second visit he decided he wanted it. The brand-new New York City Landmarks Preservation Commission declared the building a landmark, and Papp was able to buy it for only $575,000. With an anonymous gift of $215,000 for the down payment and a bank mortgage of $360,000, Papp acquired the structure on January 28, 1966, and named it the Public Theater.

The first playhouse in the Public was completed in October 1967 and opened with a new musical called *Hair*. The response to the play was so good that David Merrick produced a much altered version of it on Broadway the following year. Admission to the Public Theater, though not free, was only $2.50 a ticket. This policy of cheap tickets has kept the theater operating at a loss since it opened. The Festival's finances were so bad in 1970 that the Public Theater was in danger of closing. In debt to the contractor for the renovation of the building, faced with a lien to foreclose on his mortgage, and unable to meet a $28,000 payroll, Papp turned to the city for help. After many stormy meetings with Mayor Lindsay and the Board of Estimate, the city agreed to buy the Public Theater for $2.6 million and lease it back to Papp for one dollar a year. Today the Public Theater contains five stages, a movie auditorium, and art galleries; and, as one critic said, it "has become institutionally the most powerful and artistically the most promising theater we have."[13]

Papp's power and influence in the theater world and the cultural life of the city continued to grow as he sought more ways to reach wider audiences. Encouraged by Merrick's success in bringing *Hair* to Broadway, Papp began to move some of his more popular plays from the Delacorte and Public theaters to Broadway theaters. By the fall of 1972 he had four productions on Broadway at the same time: *Much Ado About Nothing*, *Two Gentlemen of Verona*, *That Championship Season*, and *Sticks and Bones*. The last three of these won Tonys, and *That Championship Season* also won a Pulitzer Prize. The man who had few complimentary things to say about the Great White Way, calling it a destroyer of talent, had become a successful Broadway producer. Over the years 15 NYSF productions have been moved to Broadway, with *A Chorus Line* being the biggest hit and the longest running show in the history of the Broadway stage. It has earned over $75 million and is the most important source of support for Papp's other theatrical ventures. Earlier in 1972 he had signed a four-year contract for $8 million to produce 13 specials of CBS-TV. *Much Ado About Nothing* was the first of these and was televised in February 1973. When the contract was canceled a year later after CBS postponed its telecast of *Sticks and Bones*, a controversial drama about Vietnam, Papp signed another contract with ABC. His first production for them was *Wedding Band* by black writer Alice Childress. To date, the NYSF has made more than 20 videotapes and films for television, including *Alice at the Palace*, *Swan Lake, Minnesota*, *A Midsummer Night's Dream*, and *Rehearsing Hamlet*. The rapid growth of Papp's enterprises during the

1960s and 1970s was remarkable, and one critic observed that the Festival had become "the largest, most expensive, and farthest reaching theatrical organization in the country.[14] Another critic wrote, "The New York Shakespeare Festival theater [is] the most productive and innovative cultural institution in the U.S. today.[15]

Papp's four-year tenure at Lincoln Center was not as successful as his other undertakings. In June 1973 he signed a 25-year lease with Lincoln Center chairman, Amyas Ames, making the Festival the resident theater company at the Vivian Beaumont and Forum theaters. Since opening ten years earlier, the theaters had been plagued with artistic and financial problems. Papp, who thrives on challenges, saw an opportunity to reach new audiences and a way of making money to subsidize his Public Theater, which was, as usual, in financial trouble. He first decided to present new plays in the Beaumont Theater and classics in the smaller theater renamed the Mitzi E. Newhouse. When this policy failed he reversed himself and began producing classics with well-known actors in the Beaumont. Although audiences averaged almost 90% of house capacity, the theaters lost $3.7 million under Papp's stewardship. In 1977 he announced he would leave Lincoln Center in the fall because he believed no theater could operate there and make a profit. He planned to concentrate his energy on developing new plays for the Public Theater. In spite of his inability to make the Lincoln Center project a financial success, he could leave knowing that he had produced several artistic winners, notably *Short Eyes*, and that three of these hits—*Threepenny Opera*, *The Cherry Orchard,* and *Streamers*—had received Tony nominations.

Back at the Public Theater Papp launched one of his most successful seasons. Some of the highlights of 1977/78 were *Museum* by Tina Howe, *Runaways* by Elizabeth Swados, and Obie winner *The Curse of the Starving Class* by Sam Shepard. Richard Eder of the New York Times congratulated Papp on his "marvelous and unexpected year" and praised the Public Theater as "the single most important and flourishing theatrical institution in the country."[16] Other successful seasons followed and included such fine plays as *The Art of Dining*, *I'm Getting My Act Together and Taking It on the Road*, *For Colored Girls Who Have Considered Suicide When the Rainbow Is Enuf*, *True West*, *A Chorus Line*, *Plenty*, and *The Mystery of Edwin Drood.* By the end of 1986 Papp had produced more than 290 plays and musical works that had garnered 28 Tonys, 81 Obies, 20 Drama Desk awards, 6 New York Drama Critics' awards, and 3 Pulitzer Prizes.

Reading the list of productions at the Public, one can see that Papp favors plays dealing with contemporary problems. *Sticks and Bones*, *Dispatches*, and *Tracers* concern the Vietnam War; *No Place to Be Somebody*, *For Colored Girls . . .*, and *The Colored Museum* depict the black experience in America; and *The Normal Heart* is about AIDS. Raised during the ideological 1930s and influenced by Stanislavsky's view of the theater as a social and political mediator, Papp has always sought a socially relevant theater. "I've never separated my artistic work from the social good."[17] This is entirely in keeping with Papp's personality and private life. He has served on dozens of cultural and civic committees, has lent his name to as many charitable causes, and has demonstrated on the liberal side of political and social issues. He has been arrested at least twice for these latter efforts—in 1972 when he protested against the war in Vietnam, and in 1982 when he attempted to prevent the demolition of the Morosco and Helen Hayes theaters.

Papp's nurturing of young talent, particularly playwrights and actors, has been one of his most important contributions to the American theater. He believes that "the key ingredient of the theater [is] the living writer [and] new works by living writers must take priority over revivals, even over Shakespeare."[18] David Rabe, Tom Babe, John Guare, Sam Shepard, Ntozake Shange, Tina Howe, and Elizabeth Swados are just a few of the playwrights Papp either discovered or sponsored early in their careers. Many of our best contemporary actors also got their start via the NYSF, which has been called a cradle of acting talent. Some of Papp's most famous proteges are Meryl Streep, George C. Scott, Colleen Dewhurst, Martin Sheen, Roy Scheider, Charles Durning, Raul Julia, Kevin Kline, Richard Gere, and William Hurt.

Another of Papp's significant achievements has been as a supporter and promoter of minority theater, especially black theater. Throughout his career he has presented plays written, directed, or performed by blacks. When black theater began its emergence in the 1960s, Papp was an active participant. Adrienne Kennedy, Alice Childress, Ntozake Shange, Ed Bullins, George C. Wolfe, and Pulitzer Prize winner Charles Gordone were all championed by Papp when they were still largely unknown playwrights. On several occasions he has said that the basic elements needed to build a national theater can be found in black America because it has kept its culture intact. in 1979 he formed a black and Hispanic Shakespeare repertory company. Its two productions that year, *Julius Caesar* and *Coriolanus*, received critical reviews ranging from total rejection by John Simon to mixed praise from Clive Barnes. Papp, on the defensive, lashed out at the critics, calling them racists. One year later, after more bad reviews, he disbanded the company. In 1986 he made another attempt at a minority acting troupe. With more than $1 million of the Festival's money and half a million each from the city and *Newsday*, he formed a company of young black, Hispanic, Asian-American, and white actors under the direction of Estelle Parsons. Known as the Belasco Project, the troupe performs Shakespeare plays at city parks in the summer, and at the Belasco Theater in the winter for 200,000 city school children a year.

Thirty years ago Papp was considered by many to be a fanatic with a hopeless cause when, with messianic zeal, he struggled to bring free Shakespeare to audiences throughout the city. Today Shakespeare in the Park is an institution and along with the Mobile Theater has performed free plays before millions ofpeople. Every Shakespeare play, with the exception of *Henry VIII*, has been performed by the Festival. This revitalization of the performance of Shakespeare in America can be counted among Papp's chief accomplishments.

Today Papp, as head of one of this country's largest and most influential theatrical institutions, wields tremendous power in the theater world. With its $13 million budget and more than 150 employees, the NYSF stretches from the Public Theater in the Village to Broadway, to the Delacorte in Central Park, to improvised stages in communities throughout the city. In spite of the size of his organization, Papp continues to be an innovator. In 1983 he made an arrangement with London's Royal Court Theatre to exchange plays. The first British play under agreement, Caryl Churchill's *Top Girls*, did so well here that an American cast took over when the British actors went home. Papp's first offering, Thomas Babe's *Buried Inside Extra*, received only a lukewarm reception from the London critics. The *Guardian*, however, called the play "entertaining," and the *Daily Telegraph* thought that Papp's direction brought a "dazzling surface glitter" to the production.[19] As of this writing, the companies have each exchanged five plays.

Living just three blocks from the Public Theater, Papp's world revolves around his theater and the Festival. If he is not in his office, which is located in the Public, he can usually be found looking in on a rehearsal or a performance or just prowling the corridors of the building. When he was recently asked by students at City College why he started the NYSF he said, "I just wanted a home."[20] In fact, the Festival seems to be much more than a home to him, and he admits to worrying about its future after he is gone. Several years ago, to safeguard his organization's financial stability he created an endowment fund which now totals over $20 million. Proceeds from *A Chorus Line* and his other lucrative Broadway productions go into the fund, the interest of which is used to support other NYSF activities. Despite these plans, it is hard to imagine the Festival without Papp. Playwright Thomas Babe has said the "institution is Joe and Joe is the institution."[21]

Some years ago Papp told an interviewer that what he wanted was "to have some effect on the cultural life of the city."[22] The New York Shakespeare Festival with its numerous theatrical undertakings is a manifest testament to much more than the attainment of this goal; and its home, the Public Theater, is a living monument to the profound influence of Joseph Papp on the American theater.

Notes

1. Stanley Kauffmann, "The Stages of Joseph Papp," *American Scholar*, 44 (Winter 1974/75): 110. Item 147.
2. *New York Times*, Nov. 9, 1975, Magazine sec., 18. Item 748.
3. Ibid.
4. Joseph Papp, "The Producer and His Staff," in *The Off-Broadway Experience*, ed. Howard Greenberger (Englewood Cliffs, N.J.: Prentice-Hall, 1971), 83. Item 23.
5. *New York Times*, May 8, 1952, 35:6.
6. Papp, "Producer and His Staff," 82. We are unable to verify Papp's comment. The newspaper *PM* ceased publication in 1948.
7. *New York Times*, June 23, 1957, sec. 2, 3:1. Item 268.
8. Robert A. Caro, *The Power Broker* (New York: Knopf, 1974), 1029. Item 84.
9. Ibid, 1031.
10. Ibid, 1038.
11. *Current Biography*, (1965), 314. Item 201.
12. Papp, "Producer and His Staff," 86.
13. Stuart W. Little, *Off-Broadway: The Prophetic Theater* (New York: Coward, McCann and Geoghegan, 1972), 289. Item 163.
14. *New York Herald Tribune*, Mar. 15, 1966, 16:3. Item 522.
15. *New York Daily News*, Jan. 28, 1973, Leisure sec., 17. Item 681.
16. *New York Times*, Apr. 2, 1978, sec. 2, 22. Item 785.

17. Peter Roberts, "Not Only New York's Mr. Shakespeare," *Plays and Players*, no. 345 (June 1982): 13. Item 218.
18. *New York Daily News*, Oct. 14, 1973, 26. Item 39.
19. *New York Times*, July 2, 1983, 13:1.
20. *New York Times*, June 23, 1985, Magazine sec., 14. Item 915.
21. Ibid.
22. Roberts, "Not Only," 16.

CHRONOLOGY

1921	Papp born June 22 in Williamsburg, Brooklyn, to Samuel and Yetta Papirofsky.
1938	Graduated from Eastern District High School.
1941–45	Served in United States Navy.
1945–48	Studied at the Hollywood Actors' Laboratory.
1948–50	Employed as office manager by the Hollywood Actors' Laboratory.
1950	Job as stage manager and understudy with a road company performing *Death of a Salesman.*
1951	Returned to New York City. Directed several Off–Broadway plays. Hired by CBS–TV as a stage manager.
1953	Started Shakespeare Workshop group at Emmanuel Presbyterian Church on East 6th Street.
1954	New York State Board of Regents granted a provisional charter to Shakespeare Workshop.

	Free performances in basement of Emmanuel Presbyterian Church. First production was *An Evening with Shakespeare and Marlowe.*
1956	First outdoor performances at East River Park Amphitheater.
1957	First tour with a mobile stage. First productions in Central Park. Winter performances at Heckscher Theater began.
1958	Testified before the House Committee on Un–American Activities on June 18 and was fired by CBS the next day. In November CBS ordered to reinstate Papp.
1959	Feud with Parks Commissioner Robert Moses over charging admission for Central Park plays. Court decided in Papp's favor.
1960	In January an absolute charter was granted by the State of New York Board of Regents to the New York Shakespeare Festival, constituting an official name change from the Shakespeare Workshop.
1961	School tours began. First play was *Romeo and Juliet.*
1962	New Delacorte Theater opened June 18 in Central Park with *Merchant of Venice.*

1964	Mobile Theater tours of city began.
1966	Astor Library acquired by Papp to be the NYSF's permanent home. Became the NYSF Public Theater.
1967	The Anspacher, the first theater in the Public Theater, opened with *Hair* in October.
1969	On December 30 *No Place to Be Somebody* became the first Broadway production of the NYSF. (This was a limited engagement at the ANTA Theater.)
1970	Marathon 12-hour performance of *Henry VI* and *Richard III* in Central Park.
1971	New York City bought the Public Theater from the NYSF for $2.6 million. Leased it back to the company for one dollar a year.
1972	Papp productions won two major Tony awards: *Two Gentlemen of Verona* best musical, and *Sticks and Bones* best play. First contemporary play, *Ti Jean and His Brothers* performed in Central Park. Agreement with CBS to produce 13 plays for television.
1973	NYSF became the resident theater company at Lincoln Center. CBS canceled *Sticks and Bones* presentation in March but eventually aired the play in August without sponsors.

1975 Highly successful *A Chorus Line* moved from the Public Theater to Broadway.

1977 NYSF left Lincoln Center.

1979 Papp formed a minority repertory company.

1980 City financial crisis cut aid for summer season in Central Park. Only one production staged, *The Pirates of Penzance*.

1981 Papp produced his first film, *The Pirates of Penzance*.

1982 Papp involved in the unsuccessful fight to prevent three Broadway theaters from demolition.

1983 The NYSF began an exchange program with the Royal Court Theatre in London.
A Chorus Line became the longest running show in Broadway history.

1986 *The Mystery of Edwin Drood* won five Tony awards, making a total of 28 Tonys for the NYSF.

Joseph Papp and the New York Shakespeare Festival

WORKS BY PAPP

1. U.S. Congress. House. Committee on Un-American Activities. *Hearings on Communism in the New York Area (Entertainment)*. 85th Cong., 2nd sess. Apr. 1, 1957-June 19, 1958. Washington, D.C.: GPO, 1958. 2549-2557.

   Papp testified before the committee in New York City on June 19, 1958. Although he said he was not a member of the Communist Party, he refused to say whether he had ever been a member. He took the Fifth Amendment 12 times during his testimony.

2. "Price of this Ticket Is Responsibility." *New York Herald Tribune*, Mar. 16, 1958, sec. 4, 1:4.

   In his reply to Walter Kerr's suggestion that he charge admission, Papp says this would defeat his primary purpose which is to reach large new audiences. He is interested in a popular theater, not a theater for the few. Papp compares free theater to public libraries. Theater should be supported by the city and private donations. Financial problems do not justify compromising the principle of free theater.

3. "Creation or Destruction." *Village Voice*, June 25, 1958, 4.

   After his appearance before the House Committee on Un-American Activities and his firing by CBS, Papp was asked to comment on the issue by the *Village Voice.* He said he would have no reluctance in discussing his opinions with anybody but would not be coerced into revealing the names of innocent people. He felt it would be better for public officials to concern themselves with supporting theater rather than destroying it.

4. Joseph Papp Proposes New Arts Commission." Letter. *New York Times, Ju*ne 21, 1959, sec. 2, 3:8.

Believing that the cultural life of a community is as important to its well-being as the satisfaction of its material needs, Papp urges that a commission for the performing arts be established. He recommends that prominent educators, members of the arts, and representatives of cultural organizations serve on it.

5. "Government Aid." *New York Times,* July 24, 1960, sec. 2, 1:1.

This is Papp's response to a column by theater critic Brooks Atkinson in which he stated that government subsidies for the theater could lead to government control (*New York Times*, June 19, sec. 2, 1:1). Atkinson favors private subsidies, such as foundation assistance, but Papp believes that the government should support the arts just as it does education. "The theater, like education, needs the security...of inclusion in a government budget." Foundation assistance is unpredictable and temporary. Government aid can keep ticket prices low enough for everybody.

6. "*King Henry the Fifth* for Modern Audiences." *Henry V*. The Laurel Shakespeare. Ed. Charles Jasper Sisson. New York: Dell, 1962. 20-31.

Papp believes it is a mistake for directors to view Shakespeare's history plays as having less dramatic value than the tragedies The characters in *Henry V* are more important than the historical trappings. Instead of presenting Henry as a "static, bloodless figure," the actor should use the evident cruelty and fanaticism in the character's personality to make him more interesting. Papp argues that it is important to discover contemporary values in this play. He concludes his commentary with brief opinions on how several of the other characters should be played.

7. U.S. Congress. House. Committee on Education and Labor and Select Subcommittee on Education. *Hearings on the Economic Conditions in the Performing Arts*. 87th Cong., 1st and 2nd sess. Washington, D.C.: 1962. 109-113.

Spoke in support of a bill proposing the establishment of an Arts Council. Urged lawmakers to consider the arts essential to our nation's needs. Artists should be subsidized as they are in most European countries. The government should establish and endow permanent repertory companies. Members for the Arts Council should be chosen on the basis of genuine interest and proven ability.

8. "Sparring with the World's Champion." Review of *G.B.S. and the Lunatic*, by Lawrence Langer.

New York Herald Tribune, Dec. 22, 1963, Book Week sec., 9.

Book review of a collection of letters between George Bernard Shaw and Lawrence Langner, one of the founders of the Theatre Guild and an important figure in the development of the American theater.

9. "The Method and William Shakespeare." *Stratford Papers on Shakespeare*. Toronto: Gage, 1964. 84-98.

Papp explores the problems faced by modern actors in dealing with the demands of Shakespeare. Modern or Method acting as taught in the United States restricts the technique of American actors. Method actors often fail to understand the intent of the dramatist. Method acting cannot be applied to Shakespeare, where the language of the playwright is so important. Papp would like to see "a new style of playing that will combine the vitality and humanity of the modern actor with the discipline, grace and eloquence of the classical actor."

10. "Happy Birthday, Will, Baby!" *New York Herald Tribune*, Apr. 19, 1964, Magazine sec., 9.

Ridiculing the "hoopla" over Shakespeare's 400th birthday, Papp laments the lack of real support for the arts. Calls the planned official celebrations hypocrisy. The President's special Shapkespeare Anniversary Committee was formed to pay compliments to the playwright but what is needed is money for productions of his plays.

11. "The Shakespeare Festivals." *The Best Plays of 1965-1966*. Ed. Otis L. Guernsey, Jr. New York: Dodd, Mead & Co., 1966. 90-101.

Believes the difference between Shakespeare's audience and today's Broadway audience is extraordinary. Because playhouses were cheaper than pubs, Shakespeare was able to attract a mass audience. That Shakespeare still appeals to the masses can be seen by the rise of professional festival companies during the last 10 years. Includes a list of productions and casts of the major festival troupes.

12. "The Naked Image." Letter. *New York Times*, Sep. 11, 1966, Book Review sec., 24.

Calls Richard Schechner's review of Harold Clurman's book, *The Naked Image*, hostile (*New York Times*, Aug. 14, sec. 7, 2).

13. "Directing *Troilus and Cressida.*" *Troilus and Cressida*. Ed. Joseph Papp and Bernard Beckerman. New York: Macmillan, 1967. 23-72.

In this essay, Papp writes that his conception of Troilus as a villain incapable of love determined his direction of the play. The crux of the play is reached in act 4, scene 4 when Troilus betrays Cressida's love for him.

14. "What, No Balcony for Romeo?" Letter. *New York Times*, Sep. 15, 1968, sec. 2, 10:1.

Attacks critic Lou D'Angelo's preconceived notions about *Romeo and Juliet* (*New York Times*, Sep. 1, sec. 2, 4). The balcony scene, writes Papp, was an invention of the nineteenth century stage productions. Although a consistent tragic line was favored by the last century, the play is a "mixed bag of the serio-comic." D'Angelo's views are stale and outdated.

15. Introduction. *No Place to Be Somebody; a Black Comedy in Three Acts*. By Charles Gordone. Indianapolis: Bobbs-Merrill Co., 1969. ix-x.

For this "exciting, funny, and violent" play, the unknown black playwright received only $100. After playing to standing room only audiences at the Public Theater's small experimental playhouse, the play was moved to a larger theater.

16. *William Shakespeare's "Naked" Hamlet; a Production Handbook.* New York: Macmillan, 1969.

This is the text of the NYSF's 1968 contemporized production of *Hamlet*. Papp explains his uncoventional approach to the play. Includes stage directions and photographs.

17. "On Directing, on Playwrighting, on..." *Prompt*, 14 (1969): 13-16.

Papp's opinions on successful directing and the importance of playwrights. He thinks the audience is a form of censorship since it determines the sort of productions one stages. He gives his views on the off-Broadway theaters, and discusses the Royal Shakespeare and Stratford, Ontario companies. He regrets the demise of the Living Theatre and explains what he hopes to achieve at the Public Theater.

18. "How Shall a Critic Judge?" *New York Times*, Apr. 20, 1969, sec. 2, 1:5.

Responding to Walter Kerr's criticism of the plays at the Public Theater (*New York Times*, Mar. 30 sec. 2, 1:1), Papp insists that because Kerr was shaped by the commercial theater of Broadway he cannot understand a different kind of theater. Because the plays produced by the NYSF offer no final answers Kerr, and others like him, are made uncomfortable.

19. "Theater in the Middle." *New York Times*, Apr. 21, 1969, 55.

The first plays at the Public Theater shocked many of the 10,000 subscribers who had expected to see productions like those presented in Central Park. Even though he realizes he is challenging the status quo, Papp is determined to continue his policy of presenting modern productions as he wants to attract young non-traditional theatergoers.

20. "Needed: a Black Critic?" Letter. *New York Times*, Mar. 29, 1970, sec. 2, 6:1.

Papp is critical of Mel Gussow's review of the play *X Has No Value* by black woman playwright, Cherilyn Miles (*New York Times*, Fe. 17, 35:1). He suggests that the *New York Times* employ a full-time black critic to cover works by black playwrights because white critics are unable to fully appreciate their plays.

21. "In the Words of Joseph Papp." *Cue*, June 27, 1970, 11-12.

Papp discusses some infrequently mentioned information, such as his work in a sheet metal factory. This occurred after the Actors' Lab broke up because of accusations that its members were Communists. At another time he was an assistant stage manager for a touring production of *Death of a Salesman* in California. Back in New York, Papp directed two O'Casey plays at the Yugoslav Hall. Brooks Atkinson's negative review of these plays devastated him.

22. Letter. *New York Times*, Oct. 18, 1970, 11:7.

Refutes charges made against him by critic Martin Gottfried in *Women's Wear Daily*. Gottfried claimed producers who were board members of the American National Theatre and Academy (ANTA) used their positions to get their own shows presented at the ANTA Theater at the expense of resident theaters outside of New York. Papp regards this as an attack on him personally because the play *No Place to be Somebody* by Charles Gordone was transferred from the Public Theater to the ANTA Theater. He denies Gottfried's charge that it was done to get federal funds from the ANTA resident program. Papp says the Public Theater actually lost money on the play and the transfer, but he wanted a good play to reach Broadway. Finally, he says few regional theaters wanted to participate in the program.

23. "The Producer and His Staff." *The Off-Broadway Experience*. Ed. Howard Greenberger. Englewood Cliffs, N.J. : Prentice-Hall, 1971. 81-111.

In this account of how he became an off-Broadway producer, Papp gives a history of the NYSF. After the Actors' Laboratory closed in 1950 he returned to New York and began directing amateur groups. He reminisces that in Brooks Atkinson's review of his first off-Broadway production he told him to get out of the theater. Papp literally constructed a theater in the basement of a church at 729 East 6th Street. Papp's company took off when he persuaded Arthur Gelb, *New York Times* critic, to review a performance of *The Taming of the Shrew* at the East River Amphitheater in 1956. Brooks Atkinson did a follow-up article in the Sunday paper which gave Papp and his group further recognition.

24. "End of *The Drama Review*?" Letter. *New York Times*, Feb. 21, 1971, sec. 2, 9:1.

Papp is one of 19 co-signers of a letter to the drama editor deploring New York University's firing of the editorial staff and reorganization of the publication of the *Drama Review*.

25. "Papp Answers Free Music Store." Letter. *New York Times*, Mar. 21, 1971, 31:1.

Defends his decision to give the Music Store two weeks notice to end its free performances at the Public Theater and denies the accusation that it is because he is against free music. He cites his own free Shakespeare performances in Central Park and the free plays at the Public under the Equity Showcase code. He was forced to withdraw his support of the Music Store performances because they were costing the NYSF money they could ill afford and taking up space needed to rehearse and perform new plays. He feels that the quality of their performances was not always up to the high standard he wants to maintain in his complex.

26. "Repression in Brazil." Letter. *New York Times*, Apr. 24, 1971, 28:5.

Papp was one of the signers of a letter protesting the arrest of theater director Augusto Boal by the government in Brazil where Boal is being held without trial. The signers want the American press to inform the public of the repression and lack of human rights in Brazil.

27. "Papp's Plea for No More *Nanettes*." Letter. *New York Times*, May 23, 1971, Magazine sec., 12+.

Walter Kerr wishes that all musicals were like the revival of *No, No, Nanette* (*New York Times*, Apr. 11, sec. 6, 14). Papp objects to this influential critic's disparaging remarks about modern developments into the musical theater. Kerr failed to even mention the NYSF production *Hair*, which was so successful with young people. Papp regards the critic's views as an obstacle to progress.

28. "Is There a Fifth Column at the Forum?" Letter. *New York Times*, July 25, 1971, 4:4.

Papp condemns Amyas Ames, Richard Clurman, and their associates for what he sees as the threatened destruction of the Forum Theater at Lincoln Center.

29. "How the Artist Acts." *Cultural Affairs,* 5 (Aug. 1971): 14-16.

This essay on what it means to be an artist was adapted from a commencement address Papp delivered at the North Carolina School of the Arts. Papp sees artists as aligned with change in society and in touch with life around them. Their role is to interpret art for their audiences. When art reaches a great number of people the question of how important it is will cease to be an issue and it will get the economic support it deserves. Art needs freedom and toleration to flourish.

30. "What Happened to the Audience?" *New York Daily News*, Aug. 22, 1971, sec. 5, 3.

Laments the decline in theatergoing, which he blames in part on exorbitantly high ticket prices. The audience for Broadway shows is an elite group who prefers musicals and comedies to serious and important plays. Federal support for the arts is increasing and this will help get contemporary plays produced while keeping prices down. Works at the Public Theater will continue to be free or at low cost to the playgoer.

31. "Preposterous Quotes." Letter. *New York Times*, Aug. 29, 1971, Magazine sec., 40.

Complains that he was misquoted in Roy Bongartz's article, "Pitchman for Free (and Freewheeling) Theater" (*New York Times*, Aug. 15, sec. 6, 12). Believes he has a good relationship with his black colleagues and wants to be judged by his record on employing black actors, producing plays by black playwrights, and reaching out to black audiences with his touring theater groups.

32. Introduction. *That Championship Season.* By Jason Miller. New York: Atheneum, 1972. vii-xiii. (First published in the *New York Daily News*, Sep. 10, 1972, Leisure sec., 3.)

Papp discusses the factors leading to his decision to produce Jason Miller's play at the Public Theater. Although he was taken with the immense energy of the drama, he thought it lacked depth. A reading by five very good actors convinced him that with some script changes the play would be a winner.

33. *Twelfth Night; Opera in Two Acts.* Score by David Amram. Text adapted by Josesph Papp from Shakespeare's play of the same title. New York: C. F. Peters, 1972.

For this operatic version of the Shakespeare play, Papp condensed and modernized the original text into a libretto.

34. U.S. Congress. House. Select Subcommittee on Education. *Hearings on the National Foundation on the Arts and the Humanities Act Amendments, Part 2.* 93rd Cong., 1st sess. Washington, D.C.: GPO, 1973. 39-49.

Spoke in favor of the bills to extend the National Foundation on the Arts. Suggested that Congress create and designate several theaters across the country that would be subsidized by the federal government.

35. Letter. *New York Times*, Jan. 19, 1973, 32:4.

Papp is one of four signatories to a letter praising Wilfred Batchelder, a string bass player with the Philadelphia Orchestra, who refused to play at President Nixon's inauguration. The letter also commends those musicians in the orchestra who condemned the bombing in Vietnam. The signatories express their admiration of Air Force Captain Michael Heck for refusing to continue flying missions over Vietnam. In addition to Papp, the letter was signed by Dr. Robert J. Lifton, Richard Falk, and Andre Gregory.

36. "Much Ado about *Much Ado*." Letter. *New York Times*, Jan. 21, 1973, sec. 2, 1:2.

In this reply to an article by Harris Green (*New York Times*, Jan. 14. sec. 2, 11:5) critical of the NYSF's latest production of *Much Ado about Nothing*, Papp argues that the director A.J. Antoon was completely faithful to Shakespeare's text. Only the time, place, and interpretation were changed. Since no one knows how the plays were originally acted in Shakespeare's day, there is no "correct" way to perform them.

37. "To Break Down 'the Wall.'" *New York Times*, July 22, 1973, sec. 2, 1:5.

Papp comments on his takeover of Lincoln Center and the effect it will have on the New York theater scene. The prestige and location of Lincoln Center will serve as a magnet for both New Yorkers and suburbanites who will only venture out at night to well-lighted and well-populated areas of the city. Lincoln Center holds far less fear for the average theatergoer than Broadway. He thinks he will be able to attract a new kind of audience, including minorities, and he plans to stage new American plays for these people, using black and Hispanic playwrights and actors. He hopes his Lincoln Center productions will go on tour or become film or television productions eventually, thus reaching a much greater audience.

38. "The Theater: How Do You Get into the Act?" *Seventeen*, 32 (Oct. 1973): 91+.

Papp believes the theater has lost young audiences to movies. At Lincoln Center he is trying to win them back with his modern productions, bleacher type front seats, and low-priced student passes. Working in the theater, in whatever capacity, is very rewarding as every contribution is visible in the end product, which is always a collective effort. An increasing number of women are getting into the technical part of the the theater, including working as electricians.

39. "How Producer Picks." *New York Daily News*, Oct. 14, 1973, 26.

Defends his policy of producing new plays, rather than classics, at the Beaumont. New works by living writers will take priority over revivals, even over Shakespeare. Contemporary plays reflect our own national character and probe our place in society. The key ingredient of the theater is the living writer. There is a need to constantly infuse the body of the theater with "living intelligence."

40. The Future of the Theatre. Audiotape. Rec. 1974.

A private recording of Papp's address to the National Press Club, made by Minnesota Public Radio. The 1 hour, 13 minute cassette is available at the Tri-College Library in Moorhead, Minnesota.

41. "A Welcome Appointment." Letter. *New York Times*, Mar. 27. 1974, 30:3.

Papp's reply to an editorial in the *New York Times* (Mar. 4, 28:2), that expressed doubts about the appointment of Irving Goldman as Commissioner of Cultural Affairs because of his connection with the commercial Shubert theater organization. Papp says he welcomes Goldman and knows that he will be open-minded and receptive to new ideas.

42. Letter. *New York Times*, July 14, 1974, Magazine sec., 4.

Papp replies to Robert Brustein's article on "news theater" (*New York Times*, June 16, 7+). He believes that Brustein is as much a victim of the media as Papp, since he feels the need to write such an article. Brustein needs good reviews in the *New York Times* to raise money for the Yale Drama School. Papp thinks that the publicity the media has given to the NYSF has always been beneficial, even when it was not of his own making, as in the Moses confrontation or CBS's cancellation of *Sticks and Bones*.

43. "No 'Abandonment,' Says Papp." Letter. *New York Times*, Aug. 31, 1975, sec. 2, 5:4.

Papp denies Walter Kerr's claim (*New York Times*, Aug. 17, sec. 2, 1:6) that he is abandoning productions at the Public Theater in favor of working on Broadway at the Booth. He says that the NYSF will be producing more new works at the Public in the coming season than ever before.

44. "Bringing Back *Threepenny Opera.*" Essay on Papp's 1976 production of the *Threepenny Opera*. c[1976?]. Typescript. Microfiche available at the New York Public Library, Research Libraries.

In a handout intended for audiences of his 1976 production of *Threepenny Opera* at the Beaumont, Papp compares his version to Marc Blitzstein's of 1954. Blitzstein's lyrics sweetened and sanitized Brecht's biting and abrasive language. Much of Brecht's scatological language and many of his political leftist statements were removed in the 1954 production. Papp's version uses Ralph Manheim's and John Willett's translation, which is much closer to the original German lyrics.

45. "Modernity and the American Actor." *Directors on Directing; A Sourcebook of the Modern Theater*. Ed. Toby Cole and Helen K. Chinoy. Rev. ed. Indianapolis: Bobbs-Merrill Co., 1976. 431-33. (First published in *Theatre Arts*, 45 (Aug. 1961): 63.)

Because the NYSF's audiences are used to television and movies, they demand a Shakespeare that is believable and free of conventional stage artifices. Papp chooses actors who are natural and modern.

46. "Papp Argues against a National Theater." *New York Times*, Dec. 26, 1976, 5:1.

Papp comments on an article by Clive Barnes lamenting the lack of a national theater in the United States (*New York Times*, Dec 8, sec. 3, 19:1). He believes it is not as easy as the critic makes it seem to create such an organization. The cost of salaries and maintaining a national theater complex would be huge. He fears that if all this money were provided by the government the theater would have to show only "safe" conventional plays suitable for tourists, in order not to offend and to fill the seats. Papp feels such a national theater is unnecessary in the United States, as it has thriving theaters across the country. If a national theater was created it would probably get most of the subsidies now going to these theaters. Instead, more money should be given to existing companies.

47. "A Demurrer from Papp." Letter. *New York Times*, Mar. 6, 1977, sec. 2, 5:5.

Papp apologizes, saying he was quoted out of context in a recent article assessing the NYSF (*New York Times*, Feb. 27, sec. 2, 1:2). The article alleged he stated that he had not produced plays by Arthur Miller or Tennessee Williams because they are "disconnected in style and content to our time." Papp says he was commenting on changing styles in playwriting. He would be interested in producing new works by these playwrights if they were ever offered to him.

48. Television and Theater: A Conversation with Joseph Papp. Video-recording. Rec. 1978.

A 60 minute video cassette made by radio station WNYC. Available at the California State University Library, Chico, Ca. 95929.

49. U.S. Congress. House Subcommittee on Select Education and Senate Subcommittee on Education, Arts, and the Humanities. Joint Hearings. *White House Conference on the Arts.* 95th Cong., 1st and 2nd sess. H.J. Res. 600. Washington, D.C. : GPO, 1978. 320-22.

Papp testified in favor of a joint resolution to authorize the president to call a White House conference on the arts. Access to the arts as a principle must be discussed at the proposed conference. The conference should consider the establishment of training programs in the arts for the young and unemployed.

50. "A Good Cry, A Good Laugh." Review of *Vagabond Stars: A World History of Yiddish Theater*, by Nahma Sandrow. *New York Times*, Jan. 1, 1978, Book Review sec., 18.

After a favorable review of Sandrow's book, Papp returns to one of his favorite themes--a national theater in the United States. He writes that "we would have to look [no] further than the black population to find the basic elements on which to build a national theater." This is because the blacks in this country, like the Jews, have kept their culture intact.

51. Letter. *New York Times*, Apr. 30, 1978, sec. 2, 29:1.

Even though he has many criticisms of the NBC production "Holocaust," Papp is glad that it was shown on television to make the public aware of the atrocities that occurred in Nazi Germany.

52. "What the American Theater Needs Most." *Christian Science Monitor*, Sep. 14, 1978, 23.

Broadway lacks a social consciousness. Its musicals and comedies are forgettable, escapist fare. Broadway needs serious dramas. Government subsidies of $3-$5 million a year could support 10 or more dramas in Broadway theaters.

53. U.S. Congress. Senate. Committee on Environment and Public Works. *Hearings on Funding for the John F. Kennedy Center.* 96th Cong., 1st sess. July 20, 1979. Washington, D.C. : GPO, 1979. 39-44.

Spoke on the necessity of having the federal government contribute to the financial support of the Kennedy Center's programs and completely pay for the maintenance of the building. The center must create a resident opera company or theater group that has some permanency. In order for the Kennedy Center to become truly a "cultural center," it must develop an artistic base of its own.

54. "The American Sound of Shakespeare." Letter. *New York Times*, Feb. 28, 1979, 22:6.

Papp defends his opposition to the British Shakespeare series on public television. He says it reinforces the impression of young Americans that only British English is suitable for Shakespeare. He believes that the tougher accents of American speech are far closer to the original Elizabethan language of Shakespeare.

55. "The Shakespeare Project--A British Reserve?" Letter. *New York Times*, May 13, 1979, 32:4.

Papp replies to television critic John J. O'Connor's support of the BBC Shakespeare series on public television. He believes the critic is perpetuating the myth that only the English can perform Shakespeare successfully. An English accent is not necessary; in fact, modern British speech probably bears little resemblance to that spoken in Shakespeare's day. American theater companies can produce less conventional and more exciting productions of Shakespeare. They should have had the chance to participate in the project and show their talent.

56. Introduction. *New York's Other Theatre: A Guide to Off Off Broadway*. By Mindy N. Levine. New York: Avon Books, 1981. xi-xiv.

Off-off-Broadway is an alternative theater, both geographically and artistically. Because it is non-profit and does not have to concern itself with making money, it can take chances and stage radical plays that Broadway can never offer. It can present plays by new controversial playwrights, including black and feminist writers.

57. "Is There an Audience for Serious Drama?" Letter. *New York Times*, Mar. 4, 1984, 6:3.

Commenting on Frank Rich's article (*New York Times*, 19, sec. 2, 1:4), Papp says that he believes the lack of serious plays on Broadway is caused by the price of the tickets. Many serious theatergoers cannot afford Broadway prices, therefore, a subsidy scheme is needed. This would also attract new audiences and rejuvenate the theater.

58. "High Cost of Poor Theatre." *Advertising Age*, June 25, 1984, 20.

Papp believes the higher the price of a Broadway theater ticket, the lower the seriousness of the content of the show. Most of the expensive shows are musicals which attract investors because they are expected to be more profitable than dramas or classics. he doesn't blame the investors as there doesn't seem to be much of an audience for serious plays. This is leading to a crisis for the American theater. "The heart of the problem seems to lie in the cost of a ticket." To encourage new and serious theatergoers the price must be reduced by city, state, and federal subsidies. The city should start by acquiring those Broadway theaters in danger of demolition. "Theater subsidy is not welfare," rather, it will rejuvenate American theater and create revenues and jobs.

59. "Mayor Must Act." Letter. *New York Times*, Mar. 31, 1985, sec. 4, 22:5.

Papp attacks the Save the Theaters Committee's proposal to designate theaters as landmarks in order to save them from demolition. He believes this is inadequate protection as the landmark law permits an owner to tear down his theater if he proves hardship. The only way to protect these buildings is for the city to be ultimately responsible for acquiring any endangered theater.

60. Lucille Lortel at the Players. Audiotape. Rec. Nov. 24, 1985.

A private recording made at a dinner honoring Lucille Lortel, actress and theatrical producer, at the Players Club in New York. Papp was one of the speakers. The two sound cassettes are available at the New York Public Library, Research Libraries.

61. Foreword. *Theater in America.* By Mary C. Henderson. New York: H.N. Abrams, 1986. 8.

Papp values Henderson's book as a reminder of "the rich tradition out of which American theater sprang and developed."

BOOKS AND PERIODICALS

62. Alexander, Robert. "Return of the Prodigal Son." *City Arts Monthly*, 4 (Sep. 1982): 19.

Black playwright Ed Bullins headed a playwriting workshop at the Public Theater for seven years. After that he worked for a couple of years in the publicity and promotions section of the theater administration there.

63. Ashby, Neal. "Joseph Papp: All New York's a Stage." *Playbill*, 9 (Jan. 1972): 7+.

Papp feels that he gets help from politicians, not because they care about the theater, but because they realize his company is good for the city. That Papp is completely in control of the NYSF is emphasized. This leads to recriminations that only a favored circle of playwrights, directors and actors are patronized at the Public Theater. Papp's retort is that he is not there to help people get started, but to find the greatest talent.

64. Ashby, Neal. "Joseph Papp: Play Producer for the People." *Lithopinion*, 35 (Fall 1974): 73-78.

Papp's speed and energy are reflected in his vast organization which at this time included Broadway, television shows, Lincoln Center and the Zellerbach

Theater in Philadelphia. In this interview Papp blasts censorship after the CBS fiasco over *Sticks and Bones*. He considers critics' reviews as a form of censorship, as they can make or break a show. Papp was particularly upset by Clive Barnes' negative review of the crucially important first play at Lincoln Center. His fighting spirit has kept him going throughout his embattled career, which is described.

65. "Ballroom Imbroglio." *Village Voice*, Sep. 18, 1978, 35.

Bernard Gersten left the NYSF after a 19 year association with Papp. It is believed that the rift was caused by Papp's refusal to produce Michael Bennett's musical *Ballroom*. Papp was reluctant to have the Festival do a commercial musical.

66. "Battling Papp Berates Barnes: Bars Raidy from *Boom* Preview." *Variety*, Nov. 14, 1973, 63.

Papp had a week of brushes with critics. He telephoned Clive Barnes of the *New York Times* to complain about his review of *Boom Boom Room*, the NYSF's opening production at Lincoln Center. William Raidy of the Samuel I. Newhouse newspaper chain was asked not to attend a preview of the same show, to which he had been invited by Mrs. Mitzi Newhouse, but to wait until the press opening three nights later. Papp has also had earlier skirmishes with Martin Gottfried of *Women's Wear Daily* and Walter Kerr of the *New York Times*.

67. Bell, Marty. "A Dirge for Drama." *New Times*, Nov. 14, 1975, 57-62.

This portrait of Papp was written at a time of both great success, but also defeat for the producer. *A Chorus Line* has opened on Broadway, but he has had to consent to produce only classics at Lincoln Center. A plan to showcase new plays at the Booth Theater on Broadway has failed for lack of support from businesses and foundations. A 25 day musicians strike in September had cost *A Chorus Line* $200,000 in profits, which would also have been used to support the Booth series.

68. Berkeley, Ellen P. "Public Theater: Papp's Group Continues Rebuilding." *Architectural Forum*, 134 (Mar. 1971): 48-51.

Papp is in trouble financially because of his expansion of the Public Theater complex, which is described, and his insistence on keeping ticket prices low. Papp wants New York City to buy the Public Theater from him for $2.6 million.

69. "Best Season for Papp's Public." *Variety*, June 5, 1985, 83+.

Papp considers the 1985 season at the Public Theater the best since it opened in 1967. Box office revenue accounted for nearly 25% of the NYSF's annual income, up from an average of 10-12%. The total budget for the season, including two Central Park productions, was over $5 million. There was also income from a $20 million endowment fund from the profits of *A Chorus Line*, but the Festival needs to raise more money or the endowment will be consumed in four years. Papp hopes to receive additional income from the forthcoming film version of *A Chorus Line*, in which the NYSF has profit participation beginning when the distributor's gross profits top $30 million.

70. "Beyond Coteries; the Public Theater." *Time*, Nov. 15, 1971, 71.

Papp's life and career are recounted. Some interesting details about his youth are given. After graduating from high school he became a telegraph messenger, shoeshine boy, short-order cook and chicken plucker, before going into the navy.

71. Blank, Edward L. "Producer Joe Papp Finds Theater Subsidy Virtually a Must." *Biography News*, 2 (Jan. 1975): 168.

Papp talks about the problems of supporting his theaters financially, even though some of his productions are box office successes. Touring with even a successful play is often a money-loser. Since serious theater depends on outside support, Papp would prefer private rather than government support if he had the choice.

72. Bosworth, Patricia. "Gail Merrifield: New York Theater World's Best-Kept Secret." *Working Woman*, 10 (Nov. 1985): 199-200.

Gail Merrifield, Papp's wife, receives 4,000 manuscripts every year in her role as Director of Play Development at the Public Theater. Papp takes her advice into serious consideration whenever he is deciding whether or not he will produce a play. Merrifield joined the NYSF in 1965 and married Papp in 1976.

73. Botto, Louis. "Joseph Papp: Dynamo for All Seasons." *Intellectual Digest*, 4 (Sep. 1973): 12-15.

In this interview Papp emphasizes his commitment to new plays and playwrights, although he loves the language of Shakespeare. He looks for integrity and humanity in a play. He also thinks that the theater is more exciting than films and television because it is a "living situation." The defunct Group Theatre, Papp says, is the drama company he most closely relates to, although he does not believe in just one style of theater, the naturalistic, as that company did. He believes that the main difference between the NYSF and Broadway is that his company does not have to make a profit; and, unlike regional theaters, he does not need to keep a permanent company of actórs.

74. Brenner, Marie. "Joe Papp's Third Act." *New York*, Aug. 9, 1982, 28-32.

The history and successes of Papp and the NYSF are chronicled. The company has produced 418 works in 27 seasons. Its foundation has an endowment of $16 million. Recently Papp has been throwing himself into battles outside his theater, such as the fight to save the Morosco and Helen Hayes theaters, and his trip to Vietnam to find out about missing Americans and initiate a study of Agent Orange. He also wants a program of cultural exchange with Vietnam. The state department refuses to allow this. Papp's current battle is with Mayor Koch, who wants to cut the budget for the summer season in Central Park by 85%. He thinks Koch is doing it because he is angry with Papp for leading the fight to save Broadway theaters from demolition.

75. Breslin, Catherine. "The Hottest Show in Town Is Joe Papp!" *New York*, Nov. 29, 1971, 33-40.

A long account of one particularly exciting season for Papp and the NYSF. Papp had collected $2.5 million for the sale of the Public Theater to the city. *Two Gentlemen of Verona* had opened on Broadway. Together with the original cast record it was expected to make a lot of money for the NYSF. *Sticks and Bones* by Papp's favorite playwright, David Rabe, opened to excellent reviews. Many personal details about Papp's marriages, family and life are included.

76. "Broadway Joe." *Newsweek*, May 8, 1972, 116.

The NYSF has just won Tony awards for best play, *Sticks and Bones*, and best musical, *Two Gentlemen of Verona*. The musical is subsidizing the serious play on Broadway to the tune of $10,000 a week. There is talk of Papp going to Washington's Kennedy Center to form a national theater. He has received a Rockefeller Foundation grant to explore the possibility of setting up a national theater agency.

77. "Brooklyn's Gift to the Bard." *Theatre Arts*, 42 (Jan. 1958): 11.

Relates the early success of Papp in getting a charter from the New York State Department of Education, and securing the use of an amphitheater and later the Heckscher Theater from the city. Papp also expected to get financial aid from New York City. He had already secured aid from several foundations. After the *New York Times* started reviewing his productions and commenting on his need for funding he got help form producer Herman Levin and from Rodgers and Hammerstein, whom he had met while working on their production of *Cinderella* for CBS.

78. Brown, Les. "CBS Flunks the Papp Test." *Variety*, Mar. 14, 1973, 39+.

The writer accuses CBS of censorship for not showing *Sticks and Bones*. He believes that pressure from the Nixon administration, who didn't want political embarrassment at the time of the return of the Vietnam POWs, may have been part of the reason. He tries to analyse why CBS would risk its reputation for innovativeness, bold programming and courageous news reporting by bowing to pressure in this case. He guesses that the network's lawsuit with the Smothers Brothers, for having cancelled their show in 1969, might be another reason for cancelling the play rather than just letting individual network affiliates drop out. It would weaken CBS' argument in the lawsuit that it had a responsibility for everything it aired.

79. Brown, Les. *Les Brown's Encyclopedia of Television*. New York: Zeotrope, 1982. 321-22.

This account of Papp's venture into television deals primarily with his disastrous relationship with CBS, which ended with the row over the showing of *Sticks and Bones*. CBS finally presented the play without commercials in the light viewing month of August 1973. More than 90 affiliates refused to show it, and others delayed it to a time period around midnight. In 1973 ABC announced that it had signed Papp to produce two dramas for prime time and other shows for children and late night viewing.

80. Brustein, Robert. "The ANT and the Dragon." *New Republic*, 28 (Nov. 1983): 24-26.

Papp has outlined a $10 million plan for creating a national theater in New York. Brustein believes that Papp has the experience to undertake such a venture. He also has the support of some of the best actors, directors and playwrights in the theater. Papp is also realistic enough to know how difficult it will be to build such a company in New York.

81. Brustein, Robert Sanford. "The Anti-Hamlet of Joseph Papp." *The Third Theatre*. New York: Knopf, 1969. 64-68.

A critical, largely negative critique of Papp's controversial avant-garde production of *Hamlet* of 1968.

82. Brustein, Robert Sanford. *The Culture Watch; Essays on Theatre Society, 1969-1974*. New York: Knopf, 1975. 192-197.

Brustein discusses a 1974 letter by Papp to the *New York Times* on the way the press cannibalizes personalities. He comments on Papp's relationship to the media and wonders whether Papp has sold out.

83. Carney, Leigh. "Whom the Gods Would Humble, They Offer a Job at Lincoln Center." *New York*, July 18, 1977, 45-47.

Papp is leaving Lincoln Center four years after taking it over with great fanfare. His predecessors had failed to make it run economically and Papp found it equally difficult to do so. Finally, with a large deficit and unhappy with the plays he was forced to put on to please the subscribers, Papp decided to pull out.

84. Caro, Robert A. *The Power Broker: Robert Moses and the Fall of New York.* New York: Knopf, 1974. 1026-1039.

In his Pulitzer prize-winning book, Caro says that it was Moses' deputy Stuart Constable who was determined that Papp not be allowed to produce plays—free or otherwise—in Central Park. While Moses was on vacation, Constable, both an anti-Semite and Red hater, informed Papp that the Festival would have to reimburse the Parks Department for extra grounds maintenance. Moses, a lover of Shakespeare and a Papp admirer, was drawn into a battle he had no desire for. His policy of never publicly overruling his own men forced him to take up Constable's position.

Caro believes that Moses was glad to lose the fight. Not only did Moses not appeal the Appellate Division's ruling favoring Papp, but at the end of the Festival's 1959 season he promised Papp a permanent theater. For Papp, the fight with Moses was one of the best things that could happen to the Festival in providing it with tremendous publicity.

85. Carragher, Bernard. "Theatre USA." *Show*, Mar. 1972, 58.

Having heard that President Richard Nixon was going to attend a performance of the NYSF musical *Two Gentlemen of Verona* on Broadway, Papp hoped that the President might be interested in his idea for setting up a national theater.

86. "*Chorus Line* Sets a Record." *Fortune*, Oct. 17, 1983, 8.

A Chorus Line had just become the longest running Broadway show ever. In eight years it has grossed $260 million and netted about $38 million. The NYSF put up $1.1 million to stage the musical and has made $28 million. The proceeds have supported the free Shakespeare productions in Central Park and helped pay for new plays.

87. Churcher, Sharon. "Public Theater AIDS Play Has City Hall in a Flap." *New York*, Mar. 18, 1985, 11.

This article was written at the time Larry Kramer's play *The Normal Heart*, which is about AIDS, city hall and timid homosexual leaders, was being produced at the Public Theater. Papp denied charges that he was getting revenge against Mayor Koch for his support of the razing of theaters in order to build the Marriott Marquis Hotel. Nevertheless, city officials were upset by the allegations made against them.

88. Comtois, M.E. "New York Shakespeare Festival, Lincoln Center, 1973-74." *Shakespeare Quarterly*, 25 (Autumn 1974): 405-9.

An overall review of the NYSF's first season at Lincoln Center criticising Papp for banishing Shakespeare to the Mitzi E. Newhouse Theater, a small basement theater, rather than using the Vivian Beaumont Theater. The author also objects to using

Shakespearean plays as vehicles to comment on contemporary society.

89. "Coppola-Joe Papp May Be a Team: *Penzance* Start-Up." *Variety*, Nov. 19, 1980, 2.

Francis Ford Coppola and Papp were discussing a possible film of the NYSF's production of *The Pirates of Penzance* with Linda Ronstadt in the cast.

90. "Costumes." *New Yorker*, Mar. 3, 1973, 28-29.

Theoni V. Aldredge, the chief costume designer for the NYSF, explains how she came to work for Papp and about her role in the organization.

91. Darrach, Brad. "Indomitable Showman Joe Papp Lights Up Broadway with *A Chorus Line* and a Phalanx of New Playwrights." *People*, July 28, 1975, 64-67.

Many aspects of Papp's life and career are included in this article. The writer follows Papp through a typical day of auditions and negotiations. His stormy relations with Robert Moses, CBS television and theater critics are all mentioned. Finally Papp talks about his support of new playwrights.

92. Dewhurst, Colleen. "The Actress." *The Off-Broadway Experience*. Ed. Howard Greenberger. Englewood Cliffs, N.J.: Prentice-Hall, 1971. 81-111.

Dewhurst was an actress for 12 years before she got her first break in Papp's production of *The Taming of the Shrew* at the East River Amphitheater. After that play received good reviews she became a successful Broadway performer. She also continued to perform with the NYSF. She had first worked with Papp in the Emmanuel Presbyterian Church performing scenes from Shakespeare's plays.

93. Diesel, Leota. "Papp Brings New Theatre Here." *Villager*, June 8, 1967, 1.

The Florence Anspacher Theater is scheduled to open in the fall. This will be the first of several theaters under construction at the old Astor Library to open. The Anspacher is on the second floor and occupies what was the main reading room. The architectural detail of this landmark room is being preserved and incorporated into a thrust stage wrap-around audience theater. Papp says the first time he saw the building it reminded him of a police station, but he was taken with the beautiful interior. He will present six new plays at the Anspacher this season. Tickets will be only $2.50 each.

94. "Double-Edged Disappointment." *Time*, Mar. 7, 1983, 69.

Papp's $12 million film version of *The Pirates of Penzance*, based on his Broadway production was shown on pay-per-view cable television the same day as it opened in 91 movie houses across the country. It was the first time that a premiering film was also shown on television. Of a potential television audience of 1.2 million only 130,000, or 11%, opted to watch the show. In its first weekend the film earned only a meager $255,000.

95. Drake, Edwin Beaumont. "Non-Traditional Shakespearean Production: An Examination of

the Work of Five Directors and Nine Plays Performed at the New York and Connecticut Shakespeare Festivals." Diss. U. Colorado at Boulder, 1980. Ann Arbor: UMI, 1981. 8103089.

This study examines significant changes that occurred in non-traditional Shakespearean productions in the late 1960's in the New York area. Nine productions of the NYSF and the American Shakespeare Festival from 1968 through 1975 are looked at in detail. The director's interpretation of the text, production concept, theatrical environment, rehearsal procedures and staging techniques are all analyzed.

96. "Dramatic Rescue: the Astor Library Restored." *Architectural Forum*, 128 (Apr. 1968): 64-67.

The Astor Library, which opened in 1854, was dramatically retrieved from demolition. It was the first successful attempt by the Landmarks Preservation Commission to save a building by requesting landmark designation for it. The NYSF is now converting it into a theater complex. The first of four major performance areas is already completed in what was once the main reading room. "Giorgio Cavaglieri, the architect, has left the richness of neo-15th-century Italian Renaissance wherever possible, adding the 20th century with restraint."

97. "Ed Pressman Buys Pic Rights to *Pirates* Revival for $1.5 Mil." *Variety*, May 6, 1981, 193.

Papp has sold the film rights to *The Pirates of Penzance* to Ed Pressman Productions for $1.5 million. Linda Ronstadt will star in the film which is to be made in England. Papp will co-produce the film with Pressman. The NYSF will receive 10% of the film's profits. Wilford Leach who directed the stage version will also direct the film.

98. Faust, Richard and Charles Kadushin. *Shakespeare in the Neighborhood: Audience Reaction to "A Midsummer Night's Dream" as Produced by Joseph Papp for the Delacorte Mobile Theater; a Report by Richard Faust and Charles Kadushin of the Bureau of Applied Social Research of Columbia University*. New York: Twentieth Century Fund, 1965.

In the summer of 1964 the NYSF began its program of bringing Shakespeare to parks throughout the city. The company gave 57 free performances of *A Midsummer Night's Dream* before audiences totalling 70,000. The audience reaction was studied by the authors through methods of observation and interview. They concluded that 80% to 90% of the audiences liked the play even though many did not understand the plot. The authors observed a high level of noise at all performances and several incidents of egg and rock throwing which resulted in the cancellation of four performances.

99. Feingold, Michael. "Papp's *True West* False, Says Shepard." *Village Voice*, Dec. 10, 1980, 112.

Pulitzer Prize-winning playwright Sam Shepard repudiated the NYSF production of his play *True West*. He said that the production at the Public Theater was in "no way a representation of my intentions." His dissatisfaction included Papp's declining to use actors from the original San Francisco production. Shepard said no further plays of his would be produced at the Public Theater.

100. Flagler, J.M. "Onward and Upward with the Arts Gentles All." *New Yorker*, Aug. 31, 1957, 56+.

The writer describes a free performance of *Romeo and Juliet* in King Park in Queens by a group called the Shakespeare Workshop. The play received excellent reviews when it opened in Central Park. A detailed account is given of how Papp organized his theater company and the origins of his Mobile Theater.

101. Fox, D. "Diskman Joseph Adds 7 Songs, Drops Most Gilbert and Sullivan." *Variety*, May 19, 1982, 42.

Producer David Joseph's *The Pirate Movie* based on *The Pirates of Penzance* will be released four months before Papp's version adapted from his Broadway production. Joseph wanted to do the film with Papp, but utilize pop music. Papp did not want new music in the show so they broke off discussions. Papp's film is truer to the Gilbert and Sullivan comic opera style. It was filmed indoors at England's Shepperton Studios. Joseph predicts that Papp's version will be too operatic for a mass audience.

102. "Free Shakespeare." *Time*, Aug. 11, 1961, 36.

Audiences of approximately 3,500 watch the open air performances in Central Park each night. The Shakespeare Festival has played to more than

600,000 people in six seasons. Since Papp's battle with Robert Moses the city has supported the Festival financially and helped pay for a new amphitheater soon to be completed.

103. Freedman, Gerald. "Directing *Love's Labor's Lost.*" *Love's Labor's Lost.* By William Shakespeare. The New York Shakespeare Festival Series. New York: Macmillan, 1968. 22-69.

In a long essay on directing *Love's Labour's Lost,* Freedman explains how he based his artistic choices on his belief that this play is not an artificial comedy but a drama filled with human feeling.

104. Galantay, Ervin. "Architecture." *Nation*, Apr. 25, 1966, 500-502.

Papp explains why he chose to buy the Astor Library to house his theater company. The size, location and price were all considerations. He purchased the building for $575,000 and it will cost a further $2 million to renovate. The architect Mr. Cavaglieri proposes to preserve as much as possible of the lobby and only modernize the rest of the building.

105. Gardner, Paul. "King Papp: The Heart of American Theater May Be at 425 Lafayette Street." *Connoisseur*, 216 (May 1986): 118-19.

Papp has sent 15 plays to Broadway, which have among them collected three Pulitzer Prizes and six Drama Critics Awards. The yearly budget of the NYSF is now $11 million. Papp recently asked actress Estelle Parsons to set up and direct a company of mostly black and Hispanic actors to introduce Shakespeare to young people. Students will see the plays free during school hours.

106. Garson, Barbara. "Don't Mourn for Shakespeare, Organize." *Village Voice*, July 23, 1980, 73.

This article supports Papp's stand against Mayor Koch's budget cuts and his refusal to accept emergency funding. The writer believes that only by taking a stand now can free Shakespeare for the future be ensured.

107. Gittelson, Natalie. "Whores and Wars." *Harpers Bazaar*, 103 (July 1970): 6+.

Papp is now Professor of Play Directing at Columbia University graduate school. He has just directed a feminist musical, *Mod Donna*, an indictment of modern marriage. The author believes that Papp, for a man, has a remarkable understanding of women.

108. Goldstein, Richard. "For Colored Folks Who Have Considered Censorship." *Village Voice*, Mar. 13, 1978, 44.

Papp is planning to make the controversial play *Paul Robeson* a NYSF production. The play was attacked by a group of prominent black figures when it opened on Broadway. It closed after only 45 performances. Papp says, "There must be thousands who know nothing of Paul Robeson. This will give them a chance to be inspired by the man's life."

109. Goldstein, Richard. "He Who Steals My Turf Steals Trash." *Village Voice*, Feb. 27, 1978, 30.

A BBC proposal to televise all of Shakespeare's plays in a six year association with PBS came under attack by Papp, who "contends that the BBC productions will preclude the presence of Shakespeare on commercial television." Papp wants PBS to use American theater companies to produce Shakespeare for television. Goldstein is critical of Papp because he believes it will mean that PBS will feel obliged to mount more home-produced productions in the future whatever their quality. He objects to Papp's trying to dominate public television.

110. Goldstein, Richard. "Joe Papp's Citibank Connection." *Village Voice*, May 26, 1980, 40-41.

When New York City stopped funding free Shakespeare in the Park, Citibank stepped in with a grant of $150,000 and a further $100,000 in matching funds. The audience for the upcoming production of *The Pirates of Penzance* will pay an admission fee in order to raise the matching contributions. This should more than make up for the loss of city funding.

111. Goldstein, Richard. "The Mayor of Noho: Will Papp Expand?" *Village Voice*, Oct. 17, 1977, 47.

There is speculation that Papp is pursuing an expansion plan involving space for theater and cabaret, and an acting school in cooperation with New York University's School of the Arts.

112. Goldstein, Richard and Richard Brill. "Old Black Joe." *Village Voice*, Apr. 2, 1979, 43-44.

Critical of Papp's announced plan for a third world theater company to perform classical plays under the Public Theater's auspices. The authors believe that Papp is trying to make up a substantial portion of the Public Theater's deficit from public funding for minority projects. They think that this is unfair when black theater companies are facing financial crises.

113. Gottfried, Martin. "Now You Can See the Great Plays." *A Theater Divided: The Postwar American Stage*. Boston: Little, Brown, 1967. 142-48.

Gottfried argues that Papp's expensive plans for the expansion of the NYSF necessitated a shift to the right in his theater. He has to spend more time wooing conservative foundations and philanthropists. Gottfried gives examples of early daring interpretations of Shakespeare by the company in Central Park and more recent smoother productions.

Gottfried praises Papp's reintroduction of the Mobile Theater in 1964. He admires the quality of its performances under adverse conditions, and declares that it is " one of the few legitimately decent social things I've ever seen a theater company do."

114. Gottfried, Martin. "Shakespeare for White Liberals." *Saturday Review*, Mar. 31, 1979, 40.

Tries to analyze Papp's reasons for forming an exclusively black and Hispanic repertory company.

115. Grey, Joel. "Joe Papp." *Interview*, Apr. 1977, 16.

Papp was interviewed while he was still at Lincoln Center. He believes that writers are very important because they create theater, but audiences do not really appreciate them enough. They are more interested in seeing famous actors. He does not miss directing and is interested in giving talented directors the opportunity. He is trying to move away from traditional plays and expects the audience for his plays to change too.

116. Griffin, Alice. "New York Shakespeare Festival, 1965." *Shakespeare Quarterly*, 16 (Autumn 1965): 335-39.

After favorably reviewing the NYSF's 1965 summer season, the author discusses the Twentieth Century Fund's report on audience reaction to *A Midsummer Night's Dream*. An important conclusion of the report was that the Mobile Theater could be a force for recruiting new audiences for the professional theater.

117. Gruen, John. "Joseph Papp: The Man Who Shook American Theater from New York Streets to National Prime Time." *Vogue*, 160 (Dec. 1972): 170+.

This article includes many personal opinions of Papp. The emphasis is on his fighting spirit. He explains how his defeats have made him so angry that they gave him the impetus to carry on fighting. He also expresses his views on Americans acting Shakespeare and the social force of the bard.

118. Haller, Scot. "Broadway's #1 Bash." *People*, Oct. 17, 1983, 34-41.

A Chorus Line has become the longest running show ever on Broadway. A huge party was held to celebrate the occasion, with all the former cast members being invited to perform at the celebration. The show has earned $260 million worldwide and won nine Tony awards. The NYSF has received $28 million of the profits.

119. Harbinson, William Allen. *George C. Scott; the Man, the Actor and the Legend*. New York: Pinnacle Books, 1977. 60-66, 82-84, 92, 107-108.

In 1957 Papp offered George C. Scott, an unknown actor at the time, the lead in the NYSF's production of *Richard III*. Scott calls Papp "the original man against the elements." Scott went on to act in the Festival's productions of *As You Like It*, *Antony and Cleopatra*, and *The Merchant of Venice*. Scott credits Papp with giving him his start as an actor.

120. Harris, William. "A Man for All Seasons." *East Side Express*, Oct. 27, 1977, 9+.

In a one and a half hour taped interview, Papp reminisces about his childhood and his close relationship with his father. Music was important in his family and from age 13 he sang in a choir. He desperately wanted to play the violin but there was no money for lessons. He believes his Jewishness has helped mold his character and given him strong roots in Jewish culture. He says he does not think about success but about keeping his theater alive, which he finds a continual struggle.

121. Hashimoto, Yoko. "Joseph Papp and the New York Shakespeare Festival." Diss. U. Michigan, 1972. Ann Arbor: UMI, 1973. 7311144.

The first part of this dissertation is a chronological history of the NYSF from its inception to the purchase of the Public Theater by New York City. The second part deals with the Festival's activities at the Public Theater. The final part focuses on Papp. One chapter deals with him as a producer and discusses his philosophies and ideas. The other chapter looks at him as a director and at his theories on directing and acting. Appendices include a chronology of Papp's major productions, a list of his board and association memberships, publications by him, and newspaper citations about him and the NYSF.

122. Hatch, Robert. "Theatre: This Blessed Plot, This Shakespeare in the Park." *Horizon*, 3 (Nov. 1960), 116-18.

Papp is praised as an idealist and an optimist for giving the people of New York free theater. The NYSF has proved very successful, playing to capacity audiences every night in Central Park. It has also been popular with the press. A measure of how strong the Festival has become was its defeat of Robert Moses. Papp has plans for further expansion. He is starting a subscription program, whereby patrons contributing $7.50 will be invited to previews of Festival productions. He also wants a permanent theater in Central Park and would like to reinstitute the Mobile Theater.

123. Hatch, Robert. "Theatre." *Nation*, July 14, 1962, 17.

The NYSF survived financial problems and bureaucratic interference, because as well as being an idealist, Papp also understood politics and the use of publicity. New Yorkers, realizing the value of the free Shakespeare in the Park, also rebelled when it was threatened.

The new Delacorte Theater in Central Park is described. The first production in the new theater, *The Merchant of Venice*, raised a lot of protests in the Jewish community when it was shown on television, because of its supposed anti-Semitism.

124. Henderson, Mary C. *Theater in America; Two Hundred Years of Plays, Players and Productions*. Foreword by Joseph Papp. New York: H.N. Abrams, 1986.

In this lavishly illustrated book, Henderson surveys the last 200 years of American theater history. There are chapters on the major producers, directors, playwrights, actors, designers and architects from the late 1700's to the 1980's. Comments on Papp, the NYSF, the Public Theater, and many of the people Papp collaborated with are scattered throughout the book.

125. Herbert, Ian, et al., eds. *Who's Who in the Theatre: A Biographical Record of the Contemporary Stage*. 17th ed. 2 vols. Detroit: Gale, 1981. 1:530-31.

Although much of this entry is superseded by that in *Contemporary Theatre, Film, and Television*, edited by Monica M. O'Donnell, it does give more information about Papp's earlier awards, honors and memberships.

126. Hewes, Henry. "Broadway's Bountiful Season." *Saturday Review*, July 26, 1975, 18-19.

The musical *A Chorus Line* was first performed at the Public Theater before moving to Broadway. Papp gave the director, Michael Bennett, the necessary support, both financial and emotional, to bring the work to fruition.

127. Hewes, Henry. "A Public Theatre." *Saturday Review*, Mar. 8, 1958, 42.

This article recounts how Papp created a Shakespeare festival in Central Park. The press had strongly supported him in this endeavor. The Board of Estimate, however, had turned down Papp's request for a $45,000 a year subsidy, and Parks Commissioner Robert Moses had tabled plans for a permanent outdoor theater in Central Park until he saw evidence that the NYSF had operating funds for a minimum of five years. To comply with Moses' request, Papp mounted a campaign to raise $1 million, which included asking business and philanthropic organizations in New York to purchase plaques for $500 each, to be placed permanently on the backs of the seats in the new theater. He also hoped that people seeing performances would make contributions.

128. Hill, Errol. *Shakespeare in Sable*. Amherst: U. Massachusetts, 1984. 143-76, 187-91.

Papp's aim was to popularize Shakespeare and make his plays accessible to all New Yorkers, including the disadvantaged and ethnic minorities. To achieve this he started a school program in 1960 and a permanent summer Mobile Theater in 1964. He realized that "popular theater would need to be multiracial to have the broadest possible appeal." He employed many black actors in both principal and supporting roles. Some of their performances and the reviews that they received are described. In 1979 Papp went a step further and formed a repertory company composed entirely of blacks and Hispanics. After complaints by Asian-Americans that they should have been included, Papp announced that the company would be transformed into a "third world repertory classical acting company." The black theater community in New York objected to Papp's project. They thought that it would divert funding for minority theater from them. They also did not like the idea of whites directing Papp's productions, as it would not be truly ethnic theater.

129. Hoffman, Ted. "The Economics of Village Theatre: Box Office in Search of a Fix." *Villager*, Oct. 20, 1977, 19.

Although there are as many as 50 theater productions playing any one week in Greenwich Village, this should not be taken as an indication that theater is alive and well in the Village. Only two Village theaters survive on box office income: The Circle in the Square and the Public Theater. The irony is that it is the ticket sales at Papp's Broadway productions, such as *A Chorus Line*, that have saved and subsidized the Public. Performers and directors at other Village theaters earn little, if anything, and manage by taking jobs outside the theater. Subsidies are too small to ensure a living wage for actors. The average New York State Council on the Arts grant to a Village theater or group is $2,000 a year.

130. Hughes, Catharine. "Antic Arts." *Holiday*, 58 (Jan. 1977): 26.

Papp is changing direction for the second time in his tenure at Lincoln Center. Having switched from new American plays to classics at the Vivian Beaumont Theater because of audience disapproval, he now proposes to bring in big name stars on nine month contracts. He denies he is creating a national theater at Lincoln Center.

131. Hughes, Catharine. "An Interview with Joseph Papp." *America*, Jan. 15, 1977, 35-36.

Papp talks on various different topics including the concept of a national theater at Lincoln Center, the problem of giving subsidies to the arts in times of economic depression, the most important young American playwrights, and the lack of serious plays on Broadway.

132. Hughes, Catharine. "Joe Papp Goes Public—Full Time—with a Busy Fall Season of New Plays and Exciting Classics." *Villager*, Aug. 18, 1977, 9.

Even though Papp wants the Public Theater to be the center for new American plays, he feels that the classics are a necessary complement. In keeping with this theory, Papp will produce several new plays by such young writers as John Guare, Ntozake Shange, and Tina Howe, as well as two classics, *The Dybbuk* and *The Misanthrope*, next season.

According to Papp, today's young playwrights are "moving out of the sixties and into the seventies." That is, they are more skilled dramatists and less shocking for shocking's sake.

133. Hughes, Catharine. "New York." *Plays and Players*, 17 (Oct. 1969) : 46-48.

The quality of the NYSF productions and acting is erratic. There is a tendency to change the meaning of plays in the Central Park productions to make them crowd pleasers, and to introduce "the easy laugh at the sacrifice of the inner meaning." However, Hughes admits they are among the best productions to be seen in New York.

134. Hughes, Catharine. "Of Dolls, Dreams and Duds." *America*, Apr. 19, 1975, 303-304.

The writer admires Papp for admiting, albeit reluctantly, that the audiences at Lincoln Center did not like his "new play only" policy. She thinks that two of the factors were the poor quality of the plays and the inexperience of some of the directors. Papp's plan to form a permanent company with guest stars should raise the reputation of the theatrical component of Lincoln Center to that of the other arts organizations there.

135. Hughes, Catharine. "Poppa Papp." *Plays and Players*, 20 (Dec. 1972): 28-30.

In an interview Papp explained why he dislikes Broadway and how he decides to produce a play. He feels that his most important productions to date were the controversial 1968 *Hamlet*, David Rabe's plays and *Hair* because it revolutionized the Broadway musical.

136. Hummler, Richard. "*Chorus Line*'s Record Legit Profit: $22 Mil so far Surpasses *My Fair Lady*." *Variety*, Feb. 21, 1979, 1.

The profits from *A Chorus Line* exceed $22 million to date, a record sum for a Broadway show. The show was privately financed by the NYSF and first produced at the Public Theater in Spring 1975. Then, after wonderful reviews and sold out performances, it moved to Broadway in July 1975. The show has been "an invaluable source of revenue to the nonprofit Shakespeare Fest."

137. Hummler, Richard. "Papp Partnering with Shuberts to Move *Human Comedy* Uptown." *Variety*, Feb. 15, 1984, 107.

The NYSF and the Shubert Organization will co-produce *The Human Comedy* when it moves from the Public Theater to the Royale on Broadway. This is the first time that the NYSF is teaming up with a commercial management in the Broadway transfer of one of its shows. Papp's previous Broadway transfers, including the enormously profitable *A Chorus Line*, were all internally funded by the NYSF.

Papp is also meeting with officials of the New York City public school system in an effort to develop a subsidized program for students in city schools to attend the theater on a regular basis. He wants students to come to the theater in the evening with their families. "We've been losing the inner city audience for some time and we need them for the future," he explained.

138. Hummler, Richard. "Papp Ponders Future Sans *Chorus Line*." *Variety*, Mar. 21, 1979, 103+.

The writer anticipates the closing of *A Chorus Line* within a couple of years as audience attendence falls. The NYSF has created a $3 million endowment fund from the production. The bulk of this money has been invested in certificates of deposit. The income from the musical has also allowed Papp to retire a $2 million debt, support plays at the Public Theater and a deficit operation for two seasons at Lincoln Center, make up deficits in transfers of several Public Theater productions to Broadway, contribute to renovations at the Delacorte Theater and make internal improvements at the Public.

139. Hummler, Richard. "Pappzapoppin with Busy Sked: Sets Tandy, Ronstadt, Nelligan." *Variety*, Sep. 5, 1984, 87+.

The coming NYSF season is Papp's most ambitious in several years. Jessica Tandy, Linda Ronstadt, Kate Nelligan and Sigourney Weaver are among the stars, and Michael Weller, Edna O'Brien and David Hare are among the playwrights lined up at the Public Theater. Especially in light of the poor Broadway season, Papp's schedule looks all the more interesting. Papp is currently in London for the filming of *Plenty*, which he is co-producing with Edward Pressman.

140. Hummler, Richard. "*Pirates* New Shakespeare Fest Gusher." *Variety*, Feb. 4, 1981, 171+.

The Pirates of Penzance looks like it will be very successful financially for the NYSF, after the Broadway production opened to excellent reviews. It will give Papp the opportunity to produce some more experimental works using the *Pirates* revenue.

141. "It's Papp vs. Stevens on National Theatre." *Theatre News*, 15 (Nov. 1983): 3.

Papp and Roger Stevens, chairman of the Kennedy Center in Washington, both announced different plans to establish a national theater. Papp wanted $10 million from New York City and theater owners to launch a company called the National Theater on Broadway. The money would be used to help support smaller theaters, fund playwrights and underwrite tickets. Stevens thought that Washington was the appropriate place for a national theater, escalating the rivalry between the two cities.

142. "Joe Papp: Populist and Imperialist." *Time*, July 3, 1972, 69-70.

Describes the energy of Papp and his organization. Having gained recognition from the city, state and Washington in the form of funding, he would like to spread his net wider. He wants the federal government to establish what he calls a national theater services agency to give out money to encourage the production of new plays by American authors. He is also dabbling with the idea of television specials in order to reach an even larger audience.

143. Jones, Garth. "Joseph Papp: All the World's a Stage." *Harper's Bazaar*, 114 (Sep. 1981): 329+.

The Pirates of Penzance is about to win a Tony Award. It is an example of how Papp and the NYSF have adapted to the changes in the times. Some of Papp's earlier innovative successes are recalled: the revolutionary *Hair*(1967); Charles Gordone's *No Place to be Somebody*(1969), which became the first play by a black playwright to win a Pulitzer Prize; Miguel Pinero's *Short Eyes*(1974), the first play by a Puerto Rican to receive the New York Drama Critics Circle Award; and *A Chorus Line*(1975), which redefined the nature of the dance musical.

Papp says that he could not create the first real American repertory theater in New York. He would not be able to get the best actors in America and it would be impossible to fund.

144. Jorgens, Jack J. "New York Shakespeare Festival, Summer 1974." *Shakespeare Quarterly*, 25 (Autumn 1974): 410-14.

A summing up of Papp's accomplishments as founder and producer of the NYSF, praising him for giving a large number of actors and directors a chance to play and direct Shakespeare.

145. Kadushin, Charles. "Shakespeare and Sociology." *Columbia University Forum*, 9, no.2 (Spring 1966): 25-31.

Kadushin, a professor of sociology at Columbia University and project director at Columbia's Bureau of Applied Social Research, relates the background, methodology, and results of a sociological study of audience reaction to the Mobile Theater's presentation of *A Midsummer Night's Dream*. Kadushin and his research team attended 57 performances watched by a total of 70,000 people. In addition to observing the audiences' reactions, the team interviewed about 400 audience members in depth. Eighty to ninety percent liked the play. The chief impact of the Mobile Theater on the neighborhoods was as an "event" or a "happening." Audiences appreciated the performances more than they understood them. Kadushin defends his team's methodology which was criticized by Papp and others as using too small a sample.

146. Kass, Carole. "Papp Finds Cubans Open, Eager for Culture-Swapping with U.S." *Variety*, Feb. 15, 1984, 2+.

Papp went to Cuba for his first visit since 1958 to attend an international theater conference. Papp was surprised to find few communist companies represented. He thinks Cuban socialism is very different from East European. He says, "They make it seem as if socialism can be fun." He would like to see more cultural exchanges between the United States and Cuba.

147. Kauffmann, Stanley. "The Stages of Joseph Papp." In: *Persons of the Drama; Theater Criticism and Comment*. New York: Harper and Row, 1976. 3-28. (First published in *American Scholar*, 44 (Winter 1974/75): 110-23.)

In summarizing and appraising Papp's career Kauffmann finds that factors other than talent, intellect or creative gifts have been responsible for his success. With his strong ego and equally strong commitment to social relevance in the theater, Papp found himself in the right place at the right time. Changing demographics made New York City ripe for Papp to bring Shakespeare to all previously excluded groups. Criticizes him for grossly distorting Shakespeare's plays in the mistaken belief that they would be more accessible to black and Hispanic audiences. Says his Shakespeare productions lack artistic tone. Praises him for his openness to new young playwrights, directors, actors, and other theater people but says that the level of work has been low.

148. Kauffmann, Stanley. "Stanley Kauffmann on Theater." *New Republic*, July 9, 1977, 24-25.

Objects to one of Papp's reasons for leaving Lincoln Center, that he did not like the middle class audience. Kauffmann claims that these are essentially the same people who attend the Public Theater. He also says that it was probably the choice of new American plays at Lincoln Center not the audience that was to blame for the productions' failure.

149. Kissel, Howard. "New York Repertory Follies." *Horizon*, 23 (Dec. 1980): 41-46.

The checkered history of the Vivian Beaumont Theater at Lincoln Center is recounted. In 1964 Papp was offered the tenancy of the newly completed theater. He announced the board's offer to him in the press before a final decision was made and the invitation was withdrawn. In 1973 Papp again accepted the challenge of Lincoln Center. At first he only presented new plays. This was so unpopular with subscribers that he switched to classics with big-name stars. His revival of *A Doll's House* with Liv Ullmann was the first Beaumont production to sell out. At the same time the Shubert Organization prevailed upon Papp to support a musical by Michael Bennett called *A Chorus Line*. He reluctantly did so and the profits from the show heavily subsidized Papp's activities at Lincoln Center. However, in 1977 Papp announced that he could not afford to produce plays there any longer.

150. Koch, Stephen. "Joseph Papp: Lord of the American Theater."*World*, June 19, 1973, 44-47.

This is a portrait of Papp at an important point in his career. He is now the director of the Vivian Beaumont Theater at Lincoln Center and has a contract, though it is in jeopardy, with CBS to produce "serious theater."

Papp sees himself as a producer of theater "for the people." This is why free plays are his ideal and he writes a column in the *New York Daily News* to reach the masses. He has incredible energy in raising money and fighting for plays that he believes in. Now Papp is going to use his incredible drive to save Lincoln Center.

151. Kroll, Jack. "Theater-in-the-Home." *Newsweek*, Nov. 20, 1972, 86+.

Papp's contract with CBS is the largest the network has ever signed for theater specials. The average budget for each production will be $600,000. Papp hopes the dramas will generate interest and, consequently, increase audiences for live theater.

152. Kroll, Jack. "Visions and Revisions." *Newsweek*, May 12, 1975, 98-100.

Due to audience pressure Papp announces that he is changing his policy at Lincoln Center from an emphasis on contemporary plays to a concentration on classics. He does, however, intend to establish a black repertory company at the Beaumont "as a step toward his oft-stated plan to set up the basis for an American national theater."

153. Kroll, Jack. "Why Joe Papp Made His Exit." *Newsweek*, June 27, 1977, 57.

Papp admits that he was never happy at Lincoln Center after he announced that he is leaving. He never really pleased the conventional audiences or critics there. The deficit problems were the final straw.

154. Lee, Ming Cho. "Rebuilding a Landmark." *Theatre Crafts*, 1, no.3 (July-Aug. 1967): 18-23.

In designing a theater within the old Astor Library building, the NYSF wanted it to reflect the fact that their productions try to have a contemporary relevance even when they are traditional plays. Lee, the stage designer for the company, describes the proposed design for the first two theaters to be built. He explains how the Festival worked with the architect to produce a theater that fitted their needs and that of their audiences.

155. Lerman, Leo. "Public Theater." *Mademoiselle*, 73 (June 1971): 133+.

The history of the Public Theater up to the time it was purchased by the city is recounted. Many of the people responsible for its operation are portrayed.

156. Lewis, Theophilus. "Reviewer's Notebook." *America*, Oct. 3, 1964, 392.

The NYSF spent $784,000 on its 1964 summer season. At the end of the season it had a deficit of $38,000. This reviewer thinks the money was well spent. He cites the Mobile Theater, which performed *A Midsummer Night's Dream* at 39 locations in city parks and attracted 81,000 spectators, most of whom had never before seen live acting.

157. "Life (with Joe Papp) Is a Cabaret, Old Chum." *New York*, June 20, 1977, 7.

Papp is going to announce the formation of a theater-cabaret department at the Public Theater. The cabaret will be situated in Martinson Hall, one of the building's seven theaters. The department will be managed by Papp's wife Gail Merrifield, director of play development for the NYSF, and Craig Zadan, who will be its director.

158. "Lincoln Center's New Star." *Economist*, June 23, 1973, 46.

At the time this article was written Papp was taking over as director of the theaters at Lincoln Center. He had already demonstrated his talent for raising money for the complex. He had received a gift of $1 million from Mrs. Mitzi Newhouse, the wife of a newspaper magnate, and had been promised grants from foundations, federal and state agencies. "The biggest challenge he faces is to establish a repertory company of distinction." The writer predicts that the need to fill huge halls with paying customers will force him to bring in outside stars. While running the Lincoln Center theaters Papp must still maintain his Public Theater. He also has a 13 play contract with CBS to fulfil. He is already embroiled in a battle with the television company because his first production for them, dealing with the bitter experiences of a soldier on his return from Vietnam, was postponed and there was a possibility that the contract might be cancelled.

159. Little, Stuart W. "The City Politic: Another Opening, Another Show?" *New York*, June 29, 1970, 6-7.

The political maneuvering at the time of the NYSF's worst financial crisis is described. Mayor Lindsay strongly supported Papp, but the producer also needed the support of the mayor's political enemies on the city council and board of estimate. He failed to court the favor of the home rule committee of the city council, the group that had to approve the lease-back phase of the plan for the city takeover of the Public Theater. The committee refused to support the proposal, probably largely for political reasons since at the time the council was locked in a bitter tax bill battle with the mayor.

160. Little, Stuart W. *Enter Joseph Papp: In Search of a New American Theater*. New York: McCann and Geoghegen, 1974.

This portrait of the producer emphasizes his energetic life and battles. The work is primarily a series of flashbacks concentrating most heavily on two events: Papp's lucrative contract with CBS and subsequent fight over *Sticks and Bones*, and his takeover of the theater component of Lincoln Center. The history of the NYSF and Papp's battle with Moses are also described. Many insights are given into how Papp runs his organization and the begging he has to do to obtain funding, with one financial crisis after another. Personal details about him are sprinkled throughout the book.

161. Little, Stuart W. "Joe Papp Seeks a Bigger Stage." *Saturday Review*, Feb. 26, 1972, 40-44.

Papp's background and career are related. His latest project is to set up, with government aid and private funding, a national theater service. Its most important function would be underwriting the financial losses incurred by national tours of serious plays. Papp is also always on the lookout for new plays. He was very excited by his discovery of the playwright David Rabe. Another of his ideas is a large police chorus to improve public attitudes towards the police. He would like to form a parallel chorus of prison inmates.

162. Little, Stuart W. "Joe Papp's Biggest Real-Estate Deal." *New York*, Apr. 21, 1969, 54-55.

During the financial crisis in which it looked like the NYSF might lose the Public Theater, Papp went first to private sources for aid. An advertisement in the *New York Times* yielded $225,000. He also appealed for help from an old ally, Parks

Commissioner August Heckscher, who had headed the committee to acquire the Astor Library. Heckscher supported the city purchase of the Public Theater, and Mayor Lindsay also agreed to do so.

163. Little, Stuart W. "The Popular Theater of Joseph Papp." *Off-Broadway: The Prophetic Theater.* New York: Coward, McCann and Geoghegan, 1972. 255-89.

In 1971 Papp won his most desperate battle to date, the fight to save his theater and his company by getting the city to purchase the Public Theater. This crisis and Papp's other financial and political problems during the first 15 years of the Festival's existence are described. Papp has been consistent in his belief that government support is crucial to the theater. In a 1964 tour Papp visited several major European theater companies and was most impressed with the big government supported companies. One of his goals he said is "to build our theater on the bedrock of municipal and civic responsibility..." Little concludes that in spite of seemingly insurmountable obstacles Papp's theater has become the most artistically promising theater in this country.

164. Little, Stuart W. "The Vanishing Producer." *The Playmakers.* New York: Norton, 1970. 82-84.

Increasingly the institutional theater is becoming the theater of origination for new plays, assuming the role once played by Broadway. This is certainly true of the NYSF, and increases the importance of producers such as Papp. He has been the most successful theater head in the country in acquiring subsidies from private and public sources to keep his large company running.

165. Loney, Glenn and Patricia Mackay. *The Shakespeare Complex: A Guide to Summer Festivals and Year-Round Repertory in North America.* New York: Drama Book Specialists, 1975. 3-46 passim, 62-67.

The first six chapters of the book deal with general features of the Shakespeare festivals, such as direction, design and financing. Examples from the NYSF are frequently given. The section specifically about the NYSF concentrates on the productions staged at Lincoln Center. However, there are also descriptions of the activities at the Public and Delacorte Theaters.

166. Loney, Glenn. *Twentieth Century Theatre.* 2 vols. New York: Facts on File, 1983. 2:292 passim.

In this second book of a two-volume set, arranged chronologically by date, many Papp productions are listed. As well as the names of actors, the number of performances and other details are given. The format of the book allows the reader to see what plays were running concurrently and what important events in the theatrical world were occurring in the same year.

167. McGill, Raymond D., ed. *Notable Names in the American Theatre.* Clifton N.J.: James T. White, 1976. 255-56, 1035.

The first section contains a history of the NYSF. A comprehensive list of the company's productions is included. The biographical part of the volume has a great deal of information about Papp's life and career. It includes details about his family, memberships, awards, plays and television productions he has produced or directed, and his teaching activities.

168. Mackay, Patricia. "Jennifer Tipton: Lighting Designer." *Theatre Crafts*, 17 (Apr. 1983): 14+.

Jennifer Tipton has designed the lighting for many NYSF productions, including *The Cherry Orchard* for which she won a Tony Award. Her philosophy and work are described.

169. McMorrow, Tom. "Joseph Papp: Theatre for All Seasons." *New York Theatre Review*, 2 (Oct. 1978): 5-8.

In this detailed article about Papp and the NYSF, Papp's press agent, Merle Debuskey, who has worked with Papp since the days of the Shakespeare Workshop, describes the fight with Robert Moses and the great publicity battle that was waged in the media. Papp's astounding success in spite of his bluntness, and sometimes intemperate behavior, is analyzed. For 15 years the Ford Foundation, so generous with grants to theaters all over the country, refused to help the NYSF. Finally in 1973 it granted the Festival $1.5 million over 4 years to take over the operation of the Lincoln Center theaters.

170. Madden, John. "Papp's Theatre-Cabaret Season Takes Shape for Kick-Off in Fall." *Variety*, July 20, 1977, 106.

Papp plans to present a season of new small scale musical and play productions in the new cabaret at the Public Theater. Craig Zadan is the dirctor of the cabaret theater and Gail Merrifield, who heads the play development department, will select the shows. Papp believes it will have "a liberating effect on composers, playwrights and performers, that will not confine them to a finished product."

171. "Making of a Theater." *Newsweek*, Nov. 13, 1967, 124-25.

The Astor Library has just reopened as the Public Theater. Only one of its three theaters, the 299 seat Florence Sutro Anspacher Theater, is completed. To encourage young and blue collar audiences Papp has set the ticket price at $2.50, less than half the "break-even" rate, and limited the subscription list to half the seats. Since the NYSF's board of directors has no authority to fire Papp, he has great freedom to run his theater as he wishes.

172. Medrano, Hugo. "Latin Theater Plays New York." *Americas*, 36 (Nov.-Dec. 1984): 58-59.

Papp is the driving force behind the Latino Festival in New York. He places the resources of his organization at the disposal of the festival organizers. His moral support is also important. His patronage adds to the recognition and publicity that the festival receives as well. The 1984 festival offerings are described.

173. Meyer, Karl E. "Much Ado about Papp." *Saturday Review*, July 22, 1978, 37.

This article defends the BBC Shakespeare series on public television against Papp's attacks. It refutes his claims that the British series would make it impossible for commercial networks to produce any Shakespearean plays by American companies and that they could be done better in America.

174. Michener, Charles. "Papp's Universal Theater." *Newsweek*, July 3, 1972, 52-56.

Primarily about the great success Papp has had in this theatrical season. *Sticks and Bones* won a Tony for best play, *Two Gentlemen of Verona* won both a Tony and the New York Drama Critics' Circle Award for best musical, and *That Championship Season* won the New York Drama Critics' Circle Award for best play.

Papp has discovered several new playwrights in David Rabe, Jason Miller, Charles Gordone and John Ford Noonan. The tenacity of Papp in building up his company and his strong support for his playwrights and directors is described. Papp has over the years won the support of some wealthy patrons. Mrs. Florence Sutro Anspacher was one of the principal benefactors for the purchase of the Astor Library. Mrs. LuEsther Mertz donated the entire production costs of *Two Gentlemen of Verona* to get the show on Broadway. George T. Delacorte gave $150,000 to complete the construction of the amphitheater in Central Park. Papp's battles with theater critics, particularly Walter Kerr of the *New York Times* and John Simon of *New York* magazine, are also chronicled.

175. "Michener Talks with Joseph Papp." *James A. Michener's U.S.A.* Ed. Peter Chaitin. New York: Crown, 1981. 46-50.

In this interview with James Michener, Papp explains the influence of his background on his interest in bringing Shakespeare to minorities and the masses. He talks about how he started producing Shakespeare in the Emmanuel Presbyterian Church, which no longer exists. Most of the audience had never seen Shakespeare performed, but they loved it. Papp believes that free Shakespeare in the Park has worked better in New York than duplications in other cities because it is a strong cultural city with a theatrical tradition. Even though commercialism has pervaded films, publishing and the theater, there will always be people like Papp creating theatrical experiences without money.

176. Miller, Edwin. "What Are We Doing Here?" *Seventeen*, 27 (July 1968): 88+.

In this interview Papp reminisces about his poverty-stricken childhood and lack of education. He is now, in contrast, lecturing at Columbia, and last year he taught at Yale. He describes how he became interested in drama after seeing John Gielgud in *Hamlet*. He believes that the theater should reflect social awareness and tries to achieve this in his productions.

177. Mirsky, Mark. "The Passion of Pappovsky." *Village Voice*, Oct. 9, 1978, 49.

This is a very favorable review of Papp's first personal cabaret performance. The writer particularly liked Papp's autobiographical stories about growing up as a poor Jewish boy in Brooklyn.

178. Mitz, Rick. "America's Great White Way." *Apartment Life*, 11 (Oct. 1979): 96-105.
The best regional theaters across the United States, including the NYSF, are described. Some of the Festival's productions that have gone on to Broadway are mentioned. A list of famous actors who have performed for Papp is included.

179. Monaco, James. "Is Papp Making Peace with the Avant-Garde?" *Villager*, Nov. 11, 1976, 9.
In this unflattering portrait of Papp, Monaco calls him an entrepreneur rather than an artistic force. Blames Papp's ego for preventing him from developing lasting artistic partnerships with directors and writers. Two victims of Papp's "neurotic antagonisms" toward creative and independent-minded directors and writers were Edward Berkeley and Bill Gunn. Because of his "father-figure complex," the NYSF has failed to become a true theater company of equals. Monaco admits that Papp may be changing. In the last 18 months, for the first time in his career, Papp has hired directors, namely, Mike Nichols and Richard Foreman, whose names are as well known as his own. Papp has announced that next year *The Cherry Orchard* will be directed by the avant-garde Andrei Serban at the Beaumont.

180. Morrison, Hobe. "Papp Scrams Lincoln Center; Couldn't Lick the Economics; Board Stumped for Successor." *Variety*, June 15, 1977, 81+.

Papp announced his intention of leaving Lincoln Center. He likes to produce new plays by young playwrights and this has not been popular with the established Lincoln Center audience. He will continue producing plays at the Public Theater. "Papp is the third management to be defeated by the seemingly impossible economics of the dual theater complex of Lincoln Center."

181. Moscow, Warren. *"What Have You Done for Me Lately?"* Englewood Cliffs N.J.: Prentice-Hall, 1967. 205-206.

The author, who was Mayor Wagner's close aide in 1959, blames Moses' assistant Stuart Constable for the public battle between Papp and Moses over free Shakespeare in Central Park. Although Constable got into the fight with Papp on his own, Moses' rules called for him to support Constable at all costs.

182. "Mrs. Newhouse's $1 Mil. Gift Enables Papp to Clinch Lincoln Center Deal." *Variety*, May 30, 1973, 64.

In order to give the NYSF the financing it needed to takeover the Lincoln Center theaters Mrs. Samuel I. Newhouse donated $1 million to the company, probably the largest donation ever to a non-profit operating theater. The Festival also received a grant of $350,000 from the Rockefeller Foundation. The lease agreement between the NYSF and the Center's board of directors is for 25 years. Papp insisted that $5 million be raised, to cover two-thirds of the projected operating deficit over the first five years, when he accepted the invitation to join Lincoln Center.

183. Munk, Erika. "Cross Left." *Village Voice*, May 7, 1979, 102.

A reviewer writes about a hostile encounter with Papp after she gave an unfavorable review of the play *Dispatches*, which he produced. He has been involved in other such incidents. She believes that Papp should be more objective as these same reviewers have also given some of his productions wonderful reviews.

184. "New Acts." *Variety*, Oct. 4, 1978, 96.

Papp performed a solo cabaret act in which he talked about his life and sang songs about his childhood. As a youth he sang in a choir on high holy days. He talked about his poverty-stricken boyhood in the Williamsburg section of Brooklyn during the depression and sang songs from that era. He did not mention his current attainments in his act.

185. "New Fortress; Shakespearean Plays in Manhattan's Central Park." *Time*, June 29, 1962, 32.

Papp's first production at the new $400,000 Delacorte Theater in Central Park was *The Merchant of Venice*. The New York Board of Rabbis protested loudly because they believed that the character of Shylock gave a negative image of Jews. They were particularly upset because the production was shown on television. Papp, brought up an Orthodox Jew, refused to withdraw the production.

186. "New National Theater Plans from Papp." *Variety*, Oct. 12, 1983, 95.

Papp called for the Theater Advisory Council to designate several theaters on Broadway to stage subsidized plays on a non-profit basis. The council, which was appointed by the board of estimate to make recommendations on ways to preserve and nourish economically imperiled theaters in the Broadway district, endorsed the idea. However, funding such a massive project was thought to be extremely difficult.

187. "New Theater for Landmark Building." *Progressive Architecture*, 51 (Dec. 1970): 21.

For five years the NYSF has been in the process of converting the old Astor Library into the Public Theater. The building will eventually have two 300 seat theaters and a number of smaller halls.

188. "New York Intelligencer." *New York*, Apr. 12, 1976, 57.

Papp was negotiating with British actress Glenda Jackson to play Hamlet in a London stage production.

189. "Notes and Comment; Banning of Free Shakespeare Festival in Central Park." *New Yorker*, May 23, 1959, 31.

Critical of Parks Commissioner Moses' banning of the NYSF from Central Park. Unless the performances are free many people, particularly children, who would otherwise never see a Shakespeare play, will not come. The argument about eroding the grass is no longer applicable as the commissioner plans to coat the area in concrete. His final claim that the plays caused problems for the police is denied.

190. Novick, Julius. "Mr. Papp Sees the Light." *Village Voice*, June 2, 1975, 82.

Papp has announced that henceforth he will stage only classical plays at Lincoln Center, after two years of trying to showcase only new plays there. The audience indicated clearly what they wanted by buying up all the tickets for *A Doll's House* starring Liv Ullman before it even opened. The writer thinks that the reason the audiences did not like the new plays was not that they were too modern or shocking, but that they were bad plays. He sees this as Papp's chance to create a major classical theater in New York.

191. Novick, Julius. "Papp Goes Boom at Beaumont." *Village Voice*, Nov. 15, 1973, 74.

Since the elevation of the NYSF to Lincoln Center Papp has become one of the most powerful figures in the American theater. He will now be judged more harshly and held more accountable for his success or failure than when he was the underdog fighting for survival.

192. Novick, Julius. "Shakespeare for the People." *Nation*, Sep. 13, 1965, 146-48.

Not satisfied with his predominantly middle class Central Park audience, Papp expanded his operations last summer to include a second company which tours the boroughs and includes performances in Spanish.

193. O'Donnell, Monica M., ed. *Contemporary Theatre, Film, and Television.* 3 vols. to date. Detroit: Gale, 1984-. 1: 413-14.

In addition to personal details about Papp, includes most of the productions he has produced or directed, including television programs and films. Many of the major awards that he has won and some of his honorary degrees and memberships are listed.

194. "Open House." *New Yorker*, June 23, 1962, 19-20.

The author visited the new Delacorte Theater in Central Park. Papp talked about why he decided to present *The Merchant of Venice*, in spite of criticism from Jewish groups. He also said that the new theater fulfilled his three main requirements: a good stage, dressing rooms, and a good audience relationship to the stage.

195. "Papp Asks Higher Terms for Philly." *Variety*, Mar. 19, 1975, 77.

Papp indicated that this would be the last season of Philadelphia tryouts at the Zellerbach Theater for his Lincoln Center productions. Since he planned revivals, rather than new plays at Lincoln Center the following season, there would be no need for out-of-town tryouts.

196. "Papp Exits." *Economist*, July 9, 1977, 36.

Papp has resigned from the directorship of the Lincoln Center theaters. His tenure there was not a success. His first offerings of experimental plays were ill-suited to the huge stage and middle class audience. He then shifted to the classics, which proved more acceptable, but he still ran up a deficit of $1.5 million. Papp says that no theater company can survive at Lincoln Center without a federal subsidy.

197. "Papp Given Coe Award." *Variety*, Feb. 23, 1983, 108.
Papp was honored with the third annual Richard L. Coe Award for contributions to the development of theater. The award show at the Kennedy Center included a screening of Papp's film production *The Pirates of Penzance*.

198. "Papp Goes Pop as Vocalist in N.Y. Cafe Bow." *Variety*, Aug. 16, 1978, 79.
Papp was going to appear in his own cabaret act with a one week singing engagement at the Ballroom Restaurant/Cabaret in Gotham's Soho area.

199. "Papp Has Stars in His Eyes, Limited Runs for Names." *Variety*, Aug. 13, 1986, 1+.
Following the sellout run of *Cuba and His Teddy Bear* starring Robert De Niro, Papp is planning other Broadway productions using film stars in limited engagements. He has no specific deals arranged, but plans to approach major stars for plays that would be given 10 week runs on Broadway at ticket prices considerably below prevailing levels.

200. "Papp, Joseph." *Britannica Book of the Year*. 1973 ed. 138-39.
In 1972 the Rockefeller Foundation gave Papp a grant to explore the possibility of establishing an

agency that would tour professional companies throughout the United States.

201. "Papp, Joseph." *Current Biography Year Book.* 1965 ed. 311-14.

Relates Papp's life and career in great detail through 1965. Papp credits his poverty-stricken background and the social climate of the 1930s with forging his strong belief in "a theater for all regardless of an ability to pay." While in high school he had to work at night in a laundry to supplement the family's finances. After wartime service in the navy as a petty officer, Papp studied acting and directing at the Actors Laboratory Theater under the GI Bill of Rights. In 1950 he joined the National Company touring with Arthur Miller's play *Death of a Salesman* as assistant stage manager, and understudy for Willy Loman's two sons. The following year he returned to New York where he began to produce and direct in his spare-time, while working as a stage manager for CBS television. In 1954 he founded his own theater in the Emanuel Presbyterian Church with lighting equipment borrowed from an old Bronx movie house. Papp has continued to insist on the principle of government support "together with strong controls to insure independent and unfettered expression" as he has built up the NYSF.

202. "Papp, Kennedy Center Planning Starry D.C.—B'way Rep Company." *Variety*, Nov. 21, 1979, 2+.

Roger L. Stevens, chairman of the John F. Kennedy Center in Washington D.C., and Papp plan to form a joint repertory company of well-known performers that would perform in both Washington and New York.

203. "Papp Reacts to Reagan's Proposed Arts Budget Slash." *Variety*, Feb. 25, 1981, 105-106.

In response to the Reagan administration's proposal to cut the federal arts budget in half, Papp called for the dismantling of the National Endowment for the Arts. He suggested that all federal arts subsidy funds should be channeled directly to state arts councils. His chief reason for preferring a state agency is the greater influence that arts groups exert on the state level.

204. "Papp Seeks 100G for Street Bard in Newark, Philly, Balto and D.C." *Variety*, July 10, 1968, 47.

Papp is asking the National Council of the Arts for $100,000 to tour the cities of Newark, Philadelphia, Baltimore and Washington D.C. with the NYSF's avant-garde production of *Hamlet.*

205. "Papp Shakes Up Apple." *Down Beat*, 45 (Oct. 1978): 14.

Papp begins a "Jazz at the Public Theater" series. The Public presents a wide spectrum of under-exposed musicians. The article claims Papp is doing for jazz what he did for the theater—shaking up the establishment.

206. "Papp, Sweet and Sour." *Time*, Mar. 19, 1973, 59-60.

Papp's production of *Sticks and Bones* has been dropped by CBS, three days before it was due to be aired, because 71 of the 184 stations that carry CBS' programs refused to show it. Some would have shown it but felt this to be an inopportune time now that POWs are returning home from Vietnam. Ironically it was CBS who wanted the program to run at this time to qualify it for this year's Emmy awards. The question is raised of how much the Nixon administration was involved in the cancellation.

207. "Papp Takes Over." *Newsweek*, Mar. 19, 1973, 85-86.

Papp was originally invited to Lincoln Center as a consultant to study the ailing repertory system there. He was offered the operation of the theaters a few weeks later. He insisted on three conditions before accepting: the NYSF's board of directors replace the Repertory Theater board, the annual allowable deficit be doubled from $750,000 to $1.5 million, and Lincoln Center assume a major responsibility for raising funds to meet the increased budget. Amyas Ames, chairman of the board of the Center, baulked at the last demand. He and Papp finally compromised by agreeing to share the fund raising. Papp liked the idea of having a much bigger theater for his productions than he had at the Public Theater.

208. "Papp to Set Up Workshop Unit of Asian-Americans." *Variety*, Feb. 21, 1979, 119.

Papp met with a group of Asian-American actors and announced that he would form a workshop of

Asian-American performers next summer. He plans to enlist a strong Asian-American director to oversee artistic policy for the group. Papp's announcement was in response to a picket line set up last week in front of the Public Theater by Asian-American actors seeking employment at the playhouse.

209. "Papp's Curtain at Lincoln Center." *Time*, June 20, 1977, 66.

Papp's reasons for withdrawing from Lincoln Center are recounted: the inability to operate without a deficit, the lack of support for new or innovative productions, and finally the inflexible design of the Vivian Beaumont Theater.

210. Patterson, John. "Joe Papp Responds to Charges that a Black-Hispanic Shakespeare Company Doesn't Scan." *Villager*, Apr. 9, 1979, 9.

The author interviewed Papp with the express purpose of finding out his reason for starting a black and Hispanic Shakespearean repertory company this year. The new company has already presented *Julius Caesar* and *Coriolanus* and received reviews ranging from total rejection by John Simon to mixed reviews from Clive Barnes and Douglas Watts. Papp says that questioning the company's right to exist by some critics and other individuals is a kind of racism. He feels that the Festival's tradition of trying to create an integrated company was tokenism. "True integration comes from power where there is equal justice and opportunity and in 1979 the minorities are politically powerless." Although the new company will also include Asian actors, 75% to 80% of the troupe will be black.

211. "Phone Co. Donates 200G to Bardfest." *Variety*, June 15, 1983, 77.

New York Telephone has given the NYSF a $200,000 grant, the largest single donation for its free summer productions of Shakespeare in the city's parks. The budget for the program is over $2 million, the bulk of which comes from the Festival's Broadway and touring productions of *A Chorus Line*.

212. "The Pirates Go West." *Horizon*, 24 (July/Aug. 1981): 9-10.

Papp has formed a second company, within six months of the original Broadway opening, to perform *The Pirates of Penzance* in Los Angeles. Such a rapid expansion of a show is unusual. Like the original company, this one will consist mainly of people who have never performed Gilbert and Sullivan before and who have no theatrical background.

213. Prideaux, Tom. "*Hair*; That Play Is Sprouting Everywhere." *Life*, Apr. 17, 1970, 83-86.

The musical *Hair*, which was first produced by Papp at the Public Theater in 1967, has gone on to worldwide success. It has played in 14 countries to 3.5 million people.

214. "Public Fights for Life." *Newsweek*, Mar 22, 1971, 113-14.

The Public Theater is in danger unless the city buys it. Mayor Lindsay is the crucial figure, as his support is vital if the Board of Estimate is to vote in favor of purchasing the theater. A "Save the Public

Theater" rally was held at city hall where Papp was being presented with the Margo Jones Award "for having made the most significant contribution to the dramatic art with hitherto unproduced plays."

215. "Public Papa." *Time*, June 14, 1968, 59.
A brief history of Papp's organization at the beginning of the 12th summer season of the NYSF. Papp expresses his desire to reach younger audiences than those that usually attend theaters.

216. "Renowned Tunesmiths for New Papp Cabaret Theatre." *Billboard*, July 30, 1977, 78.
Papp is getting famous music writers, such as Marvin Hamlisch and Carole Bayer Sager, to write material for his new cabaret shows to be produced at the Public Theater. These shows will have limited runs. The more successful of them will move to other theaters within the Public complex or to Broadway.

217. Richardson, Jack. "Relevant Shakespeare." *Commentary*, 53 (Apr. 1972), 85-87.
Papp is a "relevantist," that is, he believes that "Shakespeare is the most contemporary and relevant of all past dramatists, and therefore can easily accommodate modern dress, manners and attitudes." For this reason, Papp often changes text and plots to help his audiences to understand the bard.

218. Roberts, Peter. "Not Only New York's Mr. Shakespeare." *Plays and Players*, no.345 (June 1982): 13+.

In an interview with British journalist Peter Roberts, Papp explained that he and director Wilford Leach hoped to infuse vitality into *The Pirates of Penzance* by mixing operatic singers with rock artists Linda Ronstadt and Rex Smith.

Papp does not keep up with British productions of Shakespeare, nor does he think he can learn anything from them. American actors should perform Shakespeare with American accents.

Papp brought Shakespeare to the parks because that is where the poor people go. He has always had a strong social conscience about the city and the poor of New York.

219. Rogoff, Gordon. "Knighthood in Flower..." *Village Voice*, Mar. 4,1981, 73.

At a press conference, Papp talked about the performance of *A Chorus Line* at the White House and his meeting on the National Endowment for the Arts with Reagan aide James Baker. In view of the proposed funding cuts for the NEA, Papp suggests that it be liquidated and the money distributed to individual states and municipalities who could administer it more efficiently. He thinks that the federal government should honor at least one artist each year with the equivalent of a knighthood and a stipend.

220. "Rosalind and Rosalinda; Free Play and Opera Brings Throngs to Central Park." *Opera News*, 38 (Sep. 1973):32-34.

A report on the free performances by the NYSF in Central Park, which are supported financially by the New York State Council on the Arts and New York City.

221. Rudin, Seymour. "Performing Arts: 1973-1974. Joseph Papp and Others." *Massachusetts Review*, 16 (Winter 1975): 173-77.

Found Papp's first season at Lincoln Center very disappointing. The plays at the Beaumont—*Boom Boom Room, Dance of Death*, and *Au Pair Man*—revealed Papp's "deficiency of taste." Of the three Shakespeare plays mounted at the smaller Newhouse Theater, one was a disaster and two were interesting failures.

222. Sack, John. "The Good Earth." *New Yorker*, July 4, 1959, 23-24.

A satirical article about Parks Commissioner Moses' supposed obsession with soil erosion, and the effect that NYSF audiences would have on the grass.

223. "Salute of the Week: Joseph Papp." *Cue*, Aug. 9, 1969, 1.

Papp is praised for his energy and vision in presenting free Shakespeare in Central Park and cheap drama at the Public Theater, thus attracting audiences who would never ordinarily see a play. He has managed to get help for his projects from such diverse sources as Richard Burton, Elizabeth Taylor and the City of New York.

224. Sealy, Shirley. "Papp's Progress." *Viva*, 5 (Dec. 1977): 35.

Papp "is probably the most imaginative and exciting force in the American theater today" according to this writer. He has incredible energy which he transmits to those who work for him. The seven stage Public Theater complex is always busy. Many of the plays he stages are by young playwrights. This got him into trouble at Lincoln Center where the audiences wanted to see the classics. Papp has also been accused of favoritism toward playwrights, leaving little of his energy for encouraging directors and actors.

225. Segers, Frank. "Papp Plans National Theatre." *Variety*, Nov. 10, 1971, 49.

Papp has plans for a national theater, starting by sending productions originating at the Public Theater to the Eisenhower Theater in the John F. Kennedy Center. He believes that the scheme needs government support of $10-15 million for the first five years. In order to get a pilot project going the Public Theater would apply to the Rockefeller Foundation for a $1 million grant.

226. Segers, Frank. "Road to a National Theatre: Papp's Formula for New Plays." *Variety*, Feb. 9, 1972, 1.

Papp is proposing the creation of a new federal agency to fund a national theater offering new plays by American writers. He suggests that the agency be called the National Theater Service and that it underwrite deficits at existing regional theaters and fund a national touring network. Papp has recently been working on a two-city tie-up with the Kennedy Center in Washington D.C. to present new American plays, which could be the first step towards a national theater.

227. "Shakespeare Fest Told to Fess Up." *Village Voice*, Apr. 26, 1976, 41.

The NYSF was taken to court for failing to mention in its advertising that its production of David Rabe's *Streamers* was originally produced by New Haven's Long Wharf Theater. The judge ruled in favor of the Long Wharf and Papp had to change his advertising.

228. "Showman for All Seasons." *Economist*, Sep. 2, 1972, 42.

Gives an overview of the importance of Papp in the New York theater world. Mentions the liveliness and originality of NYSF productions. The Public Theater is the training ground of many playwrights, actors and directors. Papp is at last getting the critical acclaim and financial support that he deserves. In 1971, to assure the permanence of the Public Theater, New York City purchased the building for $2.6 million, renting it back to Papp for one dollar a year. He spends over $1.6 million a year on productions, only 15% of which comes from admission fees. He has just signed a $7 million contract with CBS for the production of 13 plays on network television during the next four years. Papp sees himself as a national impresario, but he is regarded with suspicion by other theater companies who see his organization as a threat to their funding.

229. "Shubert Fund Gives $3,300,000 Grants." *Variety*, June 25, 1986, 83.

The Shubert Foundation awarded a grant of $250,000 to the NYSF. A total of 119 performing arts and service organizations will receive grants.

230. Simon, John I. "Mugging the Bard in Central Park." *Singularities; Essays on the Theater/1964-1973*. New York: Random House, 1975. 107-11. (First published in *Commonweal*, Sep. 3, 1965, 635-36.)

In this 1965 essay Simon criticizes the NYSF's summer Shakespeare productions. He calls Papp, Gladys Vaughan and Gerald Freedman monumentally untalented. He attacks Papp's use of inexperienced black performers who lack the rudiments of standard American speech and who don't look right in roles that historically demand white actors. Simon also has harsh words for the critics who in their reviews of the Central Park productions suspend their critical judgement because the plays are free.

231. Simon, John. "On Producing *Peer Gynt*." *Hudson Review*, 22 (Winter 1969-70): 675-86.

A slashing attack on the NYSF's production of *Peer Gynt*. Laments Papp's choice of artistic directors from Stuart Vaughan through Gerald Freedman.

232. Sipple, M. Noel. "New York Public Theater." *Theatre Companies of the World*. 2 vols. Ed. Colby H. Kullman and William C.Young. New York: Greenwood, 1986. 2:543.

A short history of the Public Theater that includes major productions and important actors who have appeared in them. The organization and funding of the Public are also discussed briefly.

233. Skow, John. "Hail Poetry—and Tedium Too." *Time*, Mar. 22, 1982, 71-72.

The film version of *The Pirates of Penzance* was produced by Papp on a budget of $9 million. Production problems caused by making the film in a hurry and in London are described.

234. Smith, Ronn. "Planning Ahead for Ancillary Rights, the *Haggadah* at the Public Theater." *Theatre Crafts*, 15 (Oct. 1981): 24+.

Papp has aired 12 productions on the PBS, BBC, or commercial television networks since 1963. The most recent was *The Haggadah* televised on PBS live from the Public Theater in April 1981. Since the Festival financed the project it owns the tape and distribution rights.

235. Spencer, Dean. "Shakespeare: Free for All." *Town and Country*, 17 (June 1963): 78+.

Having triumphed over adversity, in the shape of Robert Moses and the New York Board of Rabbis, Papp's free Shakespeare in the Park seems on the surface to be flourishing. However, the problem of finances continues to linger on. Since Papp regards the NYSF as a civic service, not as a show business venture, he pursues aid from public sources. He receives $50,000 a year from the city and the same amount from the board of education. The grant from the board of education requires that 80 performances be staged in schools during the winter. Papp's plans for the future, including branching out to works by other playwrights and having a year-round repertory company, are outlined.

236. Stasio, Marilyn. "Joseph Papirofsky Looks Ahead." *Cue*, Feb. 19, 1977, 23+.

Written a few months before he left Lincoln Center, Papp had just named three artistic directors, Andrei Serban, Richard Foreman and Joseph Chaikin, to guide its productions for the next five years. His long term plans include tighter links between the different theaters in his organization and with other theater companies, such as his co-productions with the Manhattan Theater Club and the New Lafayette Theater. A new 100-seat workshop space dubbed "The Old Prop Shop Theater" that just opened at the Public Theater, brings the total number of theaters there to seven. Papp is also looking for a new theater, with 500 or 600 seats where contemporary works could be moved from the Public Theater for open-ended runs.

237. Stasio, Marilyn. "Joe Papp on the Job." *Cue*, Oct. 14, 1974, 2.

Papp talks about his plans for Lincoln Center. He expects it to take about five years to create a showplace there for new American works. He admits that the disastrous production *Boom Boom Room* was not ready for the Lincoln Center stage and should have been developed at the Public Theater first. His feelings about heading the Lincoln Center Theater are ambivalent. He does not want to lose the established audience, but on the other hand he wants to attract a new clientele as well. In the ideal situation he would like to take plays developed at the Public Theater uptown to Lincoln Center.

238. Stokes, Geoffrey. "Joe Papp Crowns Himself." *Village Voice*, July 12, 1976, 128.

Describes Papp as "the street-smart survivor of an impoverished Williamsburg childhood." He was a shoe-shine boy, a chicken-plucker, and with his father a pushcart peanut vendor. The NYSF itself, like Papp, rose up from humble beginnings, starting in a church basement on the Lower East Side. Papp is its undisputed leader. His policy is expansionist. "Never get out of debt, always use any new money to grow, always have a reason to ask people for even more."

239. Sultanik, Aaron. "Diagnosis and Prognosis." *Midstream*, 24 no.1 (1978): 58-61.

Papp's championing of socially relevant plays has caught the interest of Broadway producers who, in turn, are discovering and producing plays by young writers, such as Alberto Innuarto, David Mamet and Michael Cristofer.

240. Taylor, Tim. "Shakespeare-in-the-Park." *Cue*, July 6, 1957, 10+.

The New York Summer Shakespeare Festival will be performing on a mobile stage in parks in all five boroughs this summer. The Festival is an outgrowth of the successful Shakespeare Theatre Workshop presentations at the East River Park Amphitheater last summer. That season Papp had trouble raising money for his project. This year he has asked the city for financial aid. No money has been forthcoming, but the cooperation of the New York City Parks Department and other city agencies has been promised.

Papp's employer, CBS, allows him to work either very early or very late so he can run the Festival. One of his CBS assignments was *Cinderella* by Rodgers and Hammerstein who gave him $1,000 from their foundation for his Shakespeare productions. Julie Andrews, who appeared in the show, gave him a pair of her house tickets to *My Fair Lady* each week for three months, which he offered to anyone who would give $200 to the Shakespeare Festival Fund.

241. "Theater for Everyman." *Newsweek*, Aug. 14, 1972, 42.

Papp signed an agreement with CBS to produce a minimum of 13 dramas. The whole deal is worth more than $7 million. Papp comments on whether four letter words in some of his new plays will offend television audiences or be censored.

242. "Theatre Goes Public: New York Shakespeare Festival," *Players Magazine*, 45 (Dec. 1969): 56-64.

Papp believes that he gets a greater response to his plays from his ghetto audiences than from his white middle class ones. Calling his theater the Public was indicative of a deliberate commitment to reach those people who normally never see plays. He explains how and why plays are selected for production, giving some of the plays he has done as examples. The NYSF has no permanent company of actors, but many actors work with it on an almost continual basis. This year the company got its first grant from a major foundation, the Rockefeller foundation. Papp speaks at length about the renovations to the Astor Library which created his Public Theater complex.

243. Traci, Philip. "Joseph Papp's Happening and the Teaching of *Hamlet*." *English Journal*, 58 (Jan. 1969): 75-77.

This article was occasioned by *Hamlet as a Happening* presented by Papp in Central Park. The daring nature of the production with its song and dance routines aroused much controversy. The superintendent of the New York City schools considered breaking his agreement to have the show tour the high schools. The author supports the show as an interesting and modern way to teach Shakespeare.

244. "'Try Something New' Says Papp to American Theaters." *U.S. News and World Report*, May 1, 1978, 84.

Papp calls for more originality in the theater and less reliance on the "tried and true" as this does not advance drama. He is against the idea of a single national theater but would like to see a federation of regional and ethnic theaters. He also complains about violence on television and its influence on children.

245. Tucci, Niccola. "Congress, Cowardice, and Joseph Papp." *Village Voice*, June 25, 1958, 4.

The hearings of the House Committee on Un-American Activities and particularly its investigation of Papp are condemned in this article as being unworthy of a powerful democratic country like the United States.

246. Tucker, Carll. "Can Papp's Big Three Bring Down the House?" *Village Voice*, Oct. 27, 1975, 72.

Dennis Reardon, Thomas Babe and Miguel Pinero were three of the playwrights whose work Papp planned to showcase at the Booth Theater before the musicians' strike destroyed his plans and forced him to end the season. The three writers talk about their lives, plays and working for Papp.

247. Vaughan, Stuart. *A Possible Theatre; The Experience of a Pioneer Director in America's Resident Theatre!* New York: McGraw-Hill, 1969. 33-87.

The author chronicles his work as a director with three non-profit theater companies: the NYSF, the Phoenix Theatre, and the Seattle Repertory Theatre. In 1956 Vaughan was invited by Papp to direct *Julius Caesar* at the East River Amphitheater and thus began a successful three year association between the two men. Vaughan writes that he and Papp got along so well because both of them are "volatile, quick to explode and quick to cool." The technical problems of mounting productions in the open air on a portable stage are discussed in detail.

248. Walker, Susan W. "The Play-by-Play's the Thing." *Channels of Communication*, 2 (Nov. 1982): 8+.

The NYSF and ABC Video Enterprises are collaborating on the live taping of *A Midsummer*

Night's Dream before an audience in Central Park. It is to be presented on cable during the winter season. It is being taped almost exactly as it was staged originally, using eight camera angles, instead of the usual three or four, to liven the action. Other Papp productions for television have been recreated in the studio—a much more expensive method.

249. Wallach, Susan Levi. "The 19-inch Proscenium: Plugged-in Theatre." *Theatre Crafts*, 17 (Oct. 1983): 28.

The NYSF is one of the theatrical companies featured in this article on the production of videos by theaters. The NYSF has been more successful than any other troupe in producing shows for broadcast by the network and cable channels. They have made about 20 videotapes or films altogether. In 1982 the Public Theater signed an agreement with ABC Video to provide six hours of programming over an 18 month period. ABC paid $1.5 million to produce the shows. The productions done were *The Dance and the Railroad, Swan Lake, Minnesota, A Midsummer Night's Dream* and *Rehearsing Hamlet*. The NYSF usually gets outside backers to pay for its video productions.

250. Weales, Gerald. "I Left It at the Astor." *Reporter*, Apr. 4, 1968, 36+.

The writer thinks that the new Public Theater is wonderfully designed and increases the receptivity of the audience who attend it, even if the productions seen there are sometimes disappointing.

251. Weaver, Neal. "Shakespeare, a Double Feature with Cracker-Jacks." *After Dark*, Sep. 1968, 22.

Audiences for Shakespeare in the Park seem different than Broadway audiences. Waiting in line at the Delacorte has become part of the play going experience. Central Park audiences come prepared with blankets and picnic lunches.

252. Webster, Ivan. "Joe Papp Launches First-Rate Third World Company." *Encore*, May 7, 1979, 36-37.

Papp has announced the formation of a Third World Repertory Theater Company, consisting of blacks, Hispanics and Asians, which will specialize in performing the classics. The company's composition and productions are described.

253. Weil, Henry. "Joseph Papp: An Establishment of One." *Village Voice*, Dec. 30, 1974, 96.

Now that he is at Lincoln Center Papp seems to be part of the establishment, though he still rejects its values. He refuses to present plays on the basis of their profitability and is suffering from declining audience numbers. Foundations believe that his tenure at Lincoln Center means that he no longer needs their support. The Rockefeller Foundation will probably cut back its annual grant next year. If he can continue to raise money elsewhere Papp intends to continue the same policies.

254. Weil, Henry. "Producer Joseph Papp: The New King of Broadway?"*Show*, 3 (Nov. 1972): 22-27.

The Broadway success of *That Championship Season* is the climax of an incredible season for the NYSF. The first two plays that it has ever transferred to Broadway have won Tony awards this year: *Sticks and Bones* for best play and *Two Gentlemen of Verona* for best musical. A detailed account is given of Papp's life and career to explain how he arrived at the position of Broadway producer. Particularly interesting is the account of how a wealthy Chicago theater buff, Michael Butler, made *Hair* a big hit. The NYSF earned over a million dollars for its role in the musical's creation. To Papp, Broadway is simply a collection of theaters larger than his own in the Public Theater complex, but he cannot afford to overlook the money-making possibilities of a Broadway show. Other Broadway producers comment on Papp's success. Most attribute it to his having a subsidized theater which allows him to take risks and be innovative.

255. Wetzsteon, Ross. "Let 'Em Eat Papp." *Rolling Stone*, Apr. 28, 1983, 25+.

Written at the time of the release of the film version of *The Pirates of Penzance*, the first film Papp has produced, the author believes that Papp is the most powerful figure in the American theater. Papp is disappointed by the film's poor reviews and attendance figures. The remainder of the article covers many aspects of Papp's career, such as his anger at Clive Barnes for his poor review of Papp's first production at Lincoln Center, his ability to get Hollywood stars such as George C. Scott, Meryl Streep and Richard Dreyfuss to work for him for little pay, and his wonderful ability to get money and support for his company.

256. Wetzsteon, Ross. "The Papp-Pacino Squabble: Who's Keeping Hitler from Opening in New York?" *Village Voice*, June 9, 1975,124-25.

Papp financed Al Pacino's production of Brecht's play *The Resistible Rise of Arturo Ui* which is about the rise of Nazism. Although Papp intended the work to be performed at Lincoln Center, Pacino did not want it to be performed there as a commercial play, preferring a workshop setting. The play is being staged in Boston but because of the dispute between Papp and Pacino there are no plans to bring the production to New York.

257. Woef, William. "From Shakespeare to Cinema." *Cue*, June 22, 1979, 21.

Papp's film series, which he started in March 1978, has become important to the New York cultural scene. Film program coordinator, Andy Holtzman, has recently been joined by Fabiano Canosa who previously worked for the film department of the Museum of Modern Art. Under Canosa's guidance the emphasis has broadened to include foreign films as well as new independent American films.

258. Zeigler, Joseph Wesley. "Storming the Citadel: The Theatres Go to New York." *Regional Theatre: The Revolutionary Stage*. New York: Da Capo, 1977. 227-32.

By the 1970s the NYSF "was the one institutional theater in America able to command constant attention and to make its own rules." Papp is portrayed as having a great popular touch and the promotional sense of a Broadway producer. He was so well known and successful by 1972 that the NYSF looked like a national force. Papp even called for a national theater service. The scope of the NYSF is shown to be broader than that of any regional theater, merging entertainment and art. Papp's ambitions, however, have raised hostility amongst other regional theaters.

DAILY NEWSPAPERS

1955-56

259. Calta, Louis. "Theatre: Shakespearean Workshop." *New York Times*, Oct. 29, 1955, 12:2.

A group of enthusiastic young actors calling themselves the Shakespeare Workshop performed in the auditorium of the Emmanuel Presbyterian Church at 729 East Sixth Street. They were founded two years before by Papp and chartered the following year by the New York State Department of Education. They charged no admission fee. Papp said that his mission was to build up "a love and respect for the English classics on both sides of the footlights."

260. "Open-air Theatre To Do Bard Here." *New York Times*, Mar 28, 1956, 26:4.

The Shakespeare Workshop gets the Parks Department's approval to give free Shakespeare performances in the East River Park Amphitheater. Papp, the Workshop's managing director, reports that if this season is successful the Parks Department will extend the project to other city boroughs. Papp is also chairman of a committee to give impetus to the project and raise $15,000 for actors' salaries.

261. "Stratford-on-East River Opens with *Julius Caesar* under Stars." *New York Times*, June 30, 1956, 19:6

Julius Caesar, the Shakespeare Workshop's first open-air performance, opened at the East River Park Amphitheater with an audience of 2,000. The cast of over 50 performed without pay and the admission was free.

262. Gelb, Arthur. "Theatre: Rained Out." *New York Times*, Aug. 11, 1956, 11:2.

Last night's performance of *The Taming of the Shrew* at the East River Park Amphitheater was rained out. The audience might not get a chance to see the production again because the Summer Shakespeare Festival may close due to lack of operating funds after three more performances.

263. Gelb, Arthur. "New York Shakespeare Company Maps Expansion Plan." *New York Times*, Aug. 19, 1956, sec.2, 1:3.

Herman Levin, the producer of *My Fair Lady*, rescues the Shakespeare Festival at the East River Park Amphitheater from extinction by giving it the $750 needed for its expenses. The audiences for the productions, most of whom have never seen a live play before, have been very enthusiastic. Papp is trying to raise $25,000 to maintain a permanent company of actors and build a portable stage to travel around the city from park to park.

264. Atkinson, Brooks. "*Shrew* in a Park." *New York Times*, Aug. 26, 1956, sec. 2, 1:1.

Atkinson lauds the open-air Shakespeare Workshop productions. The 2,000 seat East River Park Amphitheater has been full at every performance and the audience very enthusiastic.

1957

265. Funke, Lewis. "Time: Summer; Scene: A Park; Enter Shakespeare in a Truck." *New York Times*, Apr. 12, 1957, 27:2.

Papp says he has received permission from the Parks Department to expand his operation into all five boroughs. The plays are to be presented free of charge. A stage on a trailer will be used. Papp estimates that his nonprofit project will require a budget of $35,000.

266. "Five Cited for Work on Shakespeare." *New York Times*, Apr. 24, 1957, 30:1.

Papp is presented with an award for his contribution to Shakespearean theater by the American Shakespeare Festival.

267. "Park Curtain Call Near: Bond Posted for Actors in Shakespeare Festival." *New York Times*, May 14, 1957, 40:8.

Papp announces that he has posted a bond with Actors Equity for the performance of plays in city parks. He is still $10,000 short of the $33,000 he needs for his traveling productions.

268. Schumach, Murray. "Bard on the Green. Never-say-die Troupe to Tour the Parks." *New York Times*, June 23, 1957, sec. 2, 3:1.

The actors are busy rehearsing *Romeo and Juliet* for the opening night of the free New York Summer Shakespeare Festival in Central Park. This is basically the same troupe who brought Shakespeare to the masses last year at the East River Park Amphitheater. Papp started his Shakespeare company four years ago in a church basement. His last season was rescued from bankruptcy by producer Herman Levin. This year Papp has received enough funding from foundations to guarantee the three play season of *Romeo and Juliet*, *Macbeth* and *The Two Gentlemen of Verona*.

269. Crist, Judith. "Free Shakespeare Costs Too Much." *New York Herald Tribune*, July 21, 1957, sec. 4, 1:4.

Although the mobile theater performances in the 1957 season were a great success, the hectic schedule was too much of a technical and economic strain. It took 18 hours to set up the stage because of a lack of trained technicians. The set was damaged by being moved so frequently. The Festival has decided to make a permanent home in Central Park instead.

270. Funke, Lewis. "Park Players; Local Shakespeare Festival Achieving Place in the City's Cultural Life." *New York Times*, July 28, 1957, sec. 2, 1:1.

Papp's company has great talent and an excellent director in Stuart Vaughan. Together they mounted two wonderful productions, *Romeo and Juliet* and *Two Gentlemen of Verona*. Unfortunately, they will be unable to take the latter play on a tour through the boroughs, due to a lack of funding. Funke urges that more money should be found to support Papp's efforts.

271. "Park Troupe's Bid for Funds Lagging." *New York Times*, Aug. 5, 1957, 17:4.

The New York Summer Shakespeare Festival has a deficit of $6,500. Unless funds arrive soon Papp says that the troupe will not be able to perform beyond the opening night of *Macbeth* on August 15.

272. "Shakespeare on the Green." Editorial. *New York Times*, Aug. 15, 1957, 20:3.

The Shakespearean productions in Central Park are praised. It looked as though the season would close early because of a shortage of funds, but Papp has raised a small loan to allow it to continue until the fourth of September. The audience figures are expected to reach 100,000 before the season closes. The editor calls for the venture to be placed on a sounder footing by next summer.

273. "Human Kindness Saves Central Park's *Macbeth*." *New York Times*, Aug. 19, 1957, 22:8.

An anonymous friend lends Papp $4,800 so that the New York Summer Shakespeare Festival can continue performing *Macbeth* until the fourth of September. Papp says that Mayor Wagner will allow the group to use an unspecified city-owned theater in the fall. The free admission policy would continue there.

274. "Shakespeare Plays Get Rent-free Home." *New York Times*, Aug. 26, 1957, 19:7.

Papp's company will be given free use of the Heckscher Theater, which belongs to the city. Their tenancy will start about September 18 with *Macbeth.* Papp will find the money for salaries himself.

275. "Outdoor Shakespeare Gets Permanent Home." *New York Daily News*, Sep. 4, 1957, 64:1.

After 10 weeks of critically acclaimed performances of Shakespeare plays, Mayor Wagner and Parks Commissioner Robert Moses have promised Papp help in providing his group with permanent indoor and outdoor sites. The Board of Estimate will consider a proposal to match whatever funds Papp raises.

276. Gelb, Arthur. "Once More Unto the Breach." *New York Times*, Sep. 16, 1957, 26:3.

Howard S. Cullman will head a fund-raising committee to guarantee the continuation of the Shakespeare Workshop's free festivals in the city's parks. The indoor season will now start in November with *Richard III* at the Heckscher Theater, which has been made available rent-free by the city's Department of Welfare.

277. Moses, Robert. "Theater in the Parks - Past, Present, Future." *New York Herald Tribune*, Oct. 1, 1957, 24:7.

The Parks Commissioner states that he is "tremendously interested" in a new, young and enthusiastic Shakespeare company that has been performing free plays in Central Park. To help them play again next year, Moses has set up a committee to raise funds.

278. Calta, Louis. "English Courses Add Stage Study: High School Students to See Shakespeare as Classwork." *New York Times*, Oct. 31, 1957, 40:3.

New York city high school students can study Shakespeare by attending NYSF performances. In all 1,600 free tickets will be distributed each week and three matinees will be made available for school purposes.

279. "Stage Troupe Adds to Student Tickets." *New York Times*, Nov. 8, 1957, 22:2.

The NYSF has extended its educational program to include the allocation of free tickets to teacher groups and students from Columbia and New York Universities. Drama students from Bennington College and New York University will also work with the company. The theater group already gives matinee performances for high school students. It will also provide lectures and scenes from Shakespeare for the Board of Education's television program, "The Living Blackboard."

280. Wald, Richard C. "Papp's Shakespeare Moves Indoors and Its Admissions Are Still Free." *New York Herald Tribune*, Nov. 24, 1957, sec. 4, 3:1.

Having successfully persuaded the city to allow him to use the Heckscher Theater free of charge, Papp will open a new season tomorrow night with his production of *Richard III*. All 650 seats are reserved and free. The article goes on to chronicle Papp and the NYSF's beginnings.

281. Funke, Lewis. "City to Recreate Shakespeare Era: Elizabethan Setting Planned for Summer Productions in Central Park." *New York Times*, Nov. 28, 1957, 33:4.

The Parks Department plans to build an amphitheater at the Belvedere Tower Observatory, where the NYSF performs. The amphitheater would have seating for 2,000, an Elizabethan stage, dressing rooms and a control room.

1958

282. Funke, Lewis. "N.Y. Shakespeare Group Calls for Help." *New York Times*, Jan. 5, 1958, sec. 2, 1:3.

The NYSF is performing to 90% capacity audiences at the Heckscher Theater, but the company is in financial trouble. Papp is hoping to get funding from the city, but none has been forthcoming. Not only is the winter season in jeopardy, but the summer one too. The Parks Commissioner, Robert Moses, has been holding up the construction of a 2,000 seat amphitheater in Central Park "pending an indication of the festival's ability to endure."

283. Calta, Louis. "$1,500 is Donated for Shakespeare: Local Festival Gets Funds from Actors Equity." *New York Times*, Jan. 8, 1958, 23:3.

The Actors' Equity Association gave the NYSF $1,500 and asked other organizations to give funds to keep the Festival in existence. Equity's council also petitioned the Board of Estimate to grant the company the $40,000 it needed to survive.

284. Gelb, Arthur. "City Denies Funds for Shakespeare: Festival Troupe Will End Run Jan. 25." *New York Times*, Jan. 13, 1958, 24:1.

The Board of Estimate has turned down the NYSF's request for $40,000. A grant from Actors' Equity will allow the production of *As You Like It* to open on January 20, but it will be able to run for only five days. The plans for financing next summer's season in Central Park have also failed, because of the inability of a committee headed by Howard S. Cullman to raise the $50,000 necessary for the project.

285. "Dropping the Curtain." *New York Times*, Jan. 15, 1958, 28:3.

The Board of Estimate failed to allocate the $40,000 the NYSF needs to continue. In his inaugural address Mayor Wagner exhorted his listeners not to neglect "the social studies and the humanities, the basic strength of our civilization". The city is urged to save the Festival, which is of great cultural value.

286. Gelb, Arthur. "Donors Send Help for Free Theatre: Contributions May Extend Shakespeare Group's Run." *New York Times*, Jan. 20, 1958, 18:1.

Since the NYSF announced it would have to close down because the Board of Estimate failed to approve its funding, contributions have been pouring in. The total of $1,400 though is not enough to stop the company from closing.

287. Zolotow, Sam. "Reprieve for Revival." *New York Times*, Jan. 21, 1958, 34:1.

As You Like It has received a week's reprieve. It will stay open at least through the first of February. This was made possible by $3,000 in contributions.

288. Calta, Louis. "Bard Group Gets an Offer of Help: Rodgers and Hammerstein to Match $100 Donations." *New York Times*, Jan. 23, 1958, 22:1.

Richard Rodger and Oscar Hammerstein have offered to match every $100 contribution to the NYSF.

289. "Free Shakespeare Extended for Week." *New York Times*, Jan. 27, 1958, 22:2.

Free performances of *As You Like It* are assured for an extra week until February 8. This was made possible by a grant from the New York Foundation. This is the third contribution by the group to the NYSF. Last year the Foundation made two gifts of $10,000 each. If money continues to come in at the same rate Papp says that the production will run through February 13, and possibly until February 22.

290. Herridge, Frances. "Our Shakespeare Accepts Phily Bid." *New York Post*, Feb. 14, 1958, 40.

The NYSF has accepted an offer from the city of Philadelphia to open the season in June at the

Playhouse in the Park in Fairmont Park. The company will perform *Othello*.

291. Schiff, Bennett. "The Kids Discover a Playwright—One Shakespeare." *New York Post*, Feb. 14, 1958, 10.

About a thousand junior and senior high school students a week have been watching the NYSF perform at the Heckscher Theater. The young audiences have been overwhelmingly enthusiastic.

292. Funke, Lewis. "Help." *New York Times*, Feb. 23, 1958, sec. 2, 1:4.

Papp closes his financially troubled season at the Heckscher Theater. He will be back in Central Park in the summer. First the NYSF will appear for one week in June at the Playhouse in the Park in Philadelphia performing *Othello*.

293. Kerr, Walter. "Please, Mr. Papp, Accept that Money." *New York Herald Tribune*, Mar. 2, 1958, sec. 4, 1.

Kerr argues that Papp should charge admission because people are suspicious of anything that costs nothing. Foundations and the municipal government will soon grow weary of supporting a group that has no intention of ever being financially self-sufficient.

294. "Joseph Papps Have Child." *New York Times*, Mar. 3, 1958, 24:1.

Papp's wife, actress Peggy Bennion gives birth to a daughter, Melinda [sic], on March 2.

295. Calta, Louis. "Wanted: $1,000,000." *New York Times*, Mar. 6, 1958, 31:4.

Ralph Bellamy, President of Actors' Equity, and Howard S. Cullman, United States Commissioner General for the Brussels World Fair, submit a program to raise $1 million for the NYSF from 1,400 business firms subscribing to the New York Convention and Visitors Bureau. They will try to sell the 2,000 seats in the Belvedere arena for $500 each in order to raise an initial $50,000.

296. "Outer Circle Gives Citations." *New York Times*, Apr. 8, 1958, 34:7.

The Outer Circle, which represents reviewers from out-of-town newspapers, gives a special award to Papp.

297. "Concert Benefits Shakespeare Group." *New York Times*, Apr. 14, 1958, 21:1.

Shakespeare in Music, a program to benefit the NYSF, was held at Carnegie Hall last night.

298. Funke, Lewis. "News and Gossip Gathered Along the Rialto." *New York Times*, May 4, 1958, sec. 2, 1:4.

Papp has only $7,300 for the coming season in Central Park. He needs $50,000 for a program that would open in the park with *Othello* on July 2.

299. "Papp Wins D'Annunzio Award." *New York Times*, May 20, 1958, 39:3.

Papp is the winner of the $500 D'Annunzio Award "for the season's outstanding achievement in the Off-Broadway theater."

300. Crist, Judith. "New York Shakespeare Festival in Rehearsal." *New York Herald Tribune*, May 25, 1958, sec. 4, 1.

The NYSF has started rehearsing for its second season in Central Park. Papp has raised only $15,500 so far, which is about a third of what is needed to run the entire season. If he does reach his financial goal he will offer *Othello* and *Twelfth Night*. Philadelphia's Playhouse-in-the-Park has invited the company to open *Othello* there. The city will pay for rehearsal time and a share of the costumes and props. Boston also asked the troupe to perform at its Commons Festival, but Papp declined because of his time schedule.

301. Abrams, Norma and Neal Patterson. "'I've Got Secret' Man Keeps His, Loses Job." *New York Daily News*, June 20, 1958, 3:1.

Papp was fired by CBS yesterday after he invoked the Fifth Amendment twelve times before the House Committee on Un-American Activities when asked if he had been a Communist Party member as late as February 1955. Papp offered the Committee tapes of recordings he had made for Voice of America during the three and a half years he served in the Navy. Papp was one of nine hostile or non-responsive witnesses heard by the Committee during this session on Communist infiltration of the entertainment industry.

302. "CBS Fires Aide Who Took 5th." *New York Daily Mirror*, June 20, 1958, 2.

"Joseph Papirofsky" was fired as a CBS stage manager after he took the Fifth Amendment 12 times before a House Un-American Activities Subcommittee. Papp denied being a Communist now, but refused to say whether he had been one as late as 1955.

303. Calta, Louis, "Plays in the Park Undergo Big Cut." *New York Times*, June 20, 1958, 28:1.

Unable to raise enough funds, the NYSF has to cancel its contemplated production of *Twelfth Night* and reduce the engagement of *Othello* from four weeks to one. The Festival has been hailed by the drama critics and Mayor Wagner as a "vital and cultural contribution to the city."

304. Katz, Leonard. "'Fifth' Costs Director CBS Job - May Cost City Its Shakespeare." *New York Post*, June 20, 1958, 5:3.

Papp was fired yesterday from his job as stage manager for CBS because he took the Fifth Amendment before the House Un-American Activities Committee when asked about his Communist affiliations before February 1955.

Papp said he was most upset about the possibility of contributors to Shakespeare in the Park being afraid of all the adverse publicity he has been getting. Without contributions the Festival cannot survive.

305. Porter, Russell. "9 More in Entertainment World Refuse to Answer on Red Ties." *New York Times*, June 20, 1958, 1:4.

Papp refused to tell a House Un-American Activities subcommittee whether he had formerly been a member of the Communist Party. Papp was dismissed by CBS, where he was a television stage manager, after he had testified.

306. Calta, Louis. "No Plans in View to Bar Papp Plays." *New York Times*, June 21, 1958, 10:8.

The Parks Department does not plan to cancel the NYSF season in Central Park because of Papp's involvement with the House Committee on Un-American Activities.

The NYSF is scheduled to present *Othello* from July 2 through July 5. Its original four productions have had to be drastically curtailed due to lack of funds.

307. "Shakespeare Lures Thousands to Park." *New York Times*, July 3, 1958, 21:2.

There was a quarter-mile-long line as the NYSF opened its free summer season in Central Park yesterday. The 2,300 seats were filled and about 2,000 people turned away from the performance.

308. Shepard, Richard F. "Director's Guild to Poll Members." *New York Times*, July 10, 1958, 55:5.

The Radio and Television Directors Guild is conducting a mail referendum of its 800 members to see if it should take to arbitration the cases of Papp and Charles S. Durbin, who were dismissed by CBS and NBC respectively for refusing to answer questions by a House Un-American Activities subcommittee about former membership of the Communist Party.

309. Watt, Douglas. "Shakespeare Festival Hits Stride with Costliest Show to Date." *New York Daily News*, July 13, 1958, sec. 2, 1.

Contributions mounting into the thousands have been pouring in over the last week and a half from playgoers concerned over the Festival's threatened bankruptcy. These donations ensure that *Othello* will play out its originally alloted weeks and that *Twelfth Night* will open in August. The new production of *Othello* will cost $20,000 to put on, far more than any previous NYSF production. Much of this money is paying for new speakers, mixers and amplifiers.

310. Adams, Val. "TV Union Appeals Papp's Dismissal." *New York Times*, July 29, 1958, 49:3.

The Radio and Television Directors Guild has submitted Papp's dismissal by CBS to arbitration. They have the right to do this under the terms of their contract with the company. An arbitrator's decision is considered binding.

311. Funke, Lewis. "News and Gossip of the Rialto." *New York Times*, Aug. 3, 1958, sec. 2, 1:5.

Papp says that unless sufficient funds are available in advance next season he will not reopen the NYSF.

312. "Funds Aid Stage Fete." *New York Times*, Aug. 6, 1958, 21:4.

The NYSF has only enough funds to give free performances of *Twelfth Night* in Central Park through August 16. If sufficient donations come in, the Festival can continue as scheduled through August 30.

313. "Winter Shows Dropped by Shakespeare Group." *New York Times*, Aug. 11, 1958, 17:3.
Winter performances have been cancelled by the NYSF. They are to be replaced by concert readings at the Heckscher Theater.

314. "Spellman Is Revealed Off-Broadway Angel." *New York Times*, Aug. 22, 1958, 14:4.
Cardinal Spellman recently contributed $100 to the NYSF.

315. "One Woman's Fight for Free Shakespeare." *New York Post*, Aug. 27, 1958, 70:1..
Elisa Maury, a fan of the NYSF, voluntarily collected over $600 in contributions from friends to support free Shakespeare in the Park. Miss Maury attended every performance this summer and helped out as an usher and collection-taker.

316. "Rehire Fired TV Aide, Arbitrator Orders CBS." *New York Post*, Nov. 12, 1958, 44:1.
Federal arbitrator Emanuel Stein ordered CBS to reinstate Papp as a stage manager. Papp was fired last June after he had taken the Fifth Amendment before the House Un-American Activities Committee. Papp said he was grateful to the Radio and Television Directors Guild who submitted his case to arbitration.

317. Kaplan, Morris. "C.B.S. Is Ordered to Reinstate Papp." *New York Times*, Nov. 13, 1958, 7:1.
An arbitrator ordered CBS to reinstate Papp yesterday. Papp won only half of his back pay though because he failed to notify the company that

he had been subpoened to appear before the House Committee on Un-American Activities. Papp is now production stage manager of the play *Comes A Day* at the Ambassador Theater. Papp thanked the Radio and Television Directors Guild for challenging his dismissal. The arbitrator was Professor Emanuel Stein, chairman of the Economics Department at New York University. Papp hopes to return to work for CBS.

318. Funke, Lewis. "News and Gossip of the Rialto." *New York Times*, Nov. 30, 1958, sec. 2, 1:5.

Papp is already planning the next NYSF summer season. A newly formed board of directors is aiming to raise $100,000 for the continuance of the Festival. Papp will not undertake the venture again unless he gets the needed funds in advance. He is having a fund-raising party in honor of Sir John Gielgud, who is coming to New York to appear in *The Ages of Man.*

1959

319. Calta, Louis. "Park Troupe Told to End Free Plays." *New York Times*, Apr. 16, 1959, 35:1

Parks Commissioner Robert Moses notified the NYSF that it will no longer be allowed to operate in Central Park unless it begins charging one or two dollars a ticket, 10% of which will be turned over to the city to help defray expenses for the "erosion" caused by the plays' audiences. Papp called Moses' decision arbitrary, saying it would "remove the productions from the reach of those whom it best serves."

320. Crist, Judith. "No Free Shakespeare in Park, Moses Rules." *New York Herald Tribune*, Apr. 16, 1959, 1:3

Papp announced that he could not meet the terms set by Parks Commissioner Moses for permission to perform in Central Park. Moses wants Papp to charge admission to plays and pay the Parks Department $10,000 a year to protect the grass from erosion caused by Festival audiences. Papp said that the theatrical unions could no longer be expected to make concessions if he began charging admission and that, consequently, costs would greatly increase. Parks official Stuart Constable said that all the people he saw in the Festival audiences could well afford to pay one or two dollars.

321. "Mr. Moses Vs. Free Shakespeare." Editorial. *New York Herald Tribune,* Apr. 16, 1959, 18

Urges Moses to keep Shakespeare free. Various sports activities cause as much of an erosion problem and no one would think of charging the participants.

322. "City Aides Defend Free Park Plays." *New York Times*, Apr. 17, 1959, 27:8

Manhattan Borough President Hulan E. Jack and City Council President Abe Stark, both members of the city's Board of Estimate, oppose Robert Moses' demand that the NYSF charge admission. Mayor Wagner said he would question Moses about his decision. Moses called Papp a "fanatical, very temperamental Shakespeare producer" who has no concept of park administration. According tot the Parks Commissioner, it will take $100,000 to make the area where the plays are performed safe and sanitary.

323. Calta, Louis. "Bellamy, Lotito Hit Moses Stand." *New York Times,* Apr. 18, 1959, 19:3

Ralph Bellamy, president of the Actors' Equity Association, called Moses' action "deplorable." Louis Lotito, president of the League of New York Theatres, used the word "arbitrary" in describing Moses' position.

324. "Shakespeare in the Park." Editorial. *New York Times,* Apr. 18, 1959, 22:1

Calls Robert Moses' demand that the NYSF charge admission a "death sentence" and finds his reversal on the whole issue puzzling. Suggests that the erosion Moses is concerned about is in his own earlier appreciation of the free outdoor plays produced by the NYSF.

325. Atkinson, Brooks. "Moses and Shakespeare." *New York Times,* Apr. 20, 1959, 35:1

Prominent theater critic Brooks Atkinson urges the Parks Commissioner to allow Papp to continue his free admission policy.

326. "Plays in the Park Get Councilman's Aid." *New York Times,* Apr. 21, 1959, 37:6.

City Councilman Louis Okin is proposing a local law intended to prevent Parks Commissioner Moses from forcing the NYSF to charge admission. Okin says that if Moses prevailed, admissions could be charged for the Goldman Band concerts. Bird watchers and children playing on the grass could also be compelled to pay fees.

327. "Park Play Ruling Scored by Equity." *New York Times*, Apr. 22, 1959, 35:5

Ralph Bellamy, president of Actors' Equity, sent a telegram to Moses urging him to reconsider his demand that the NYSF charge admission to their Shakespeare plays in the park. Councilman Louis Okin introduced a bill into the City Council designed to prevent the Parks Commissioner from compelling the charging of admission.

328. "Isaacs Disputes Moses on Theatre." *New York Times*, Apr. 27, 1959, 22:5

City Councilman Stanley M. Isaacs stated, in a radio talk, that Moses should be persuaded or forced by the mayor to reverse his decision to charge admission to Shakespeare in the Park. William Thornton, founder and producer of the Shakespeare Guild Festival Company, expressed support for Moses' position saying, "there is no shame in earning a portion of one's way in art."

329. Calta, Louis. "Phoenix Begins Subscriber Drive." *New York Times*, Apr. 29, 1959, 28:4

Petitions from New York theater companies are being sent to Mayor Wagner asking him to allow the NYSF to continue to perform in Central Park free of charge. The United Parents Association has asked Moses to rescind his ban against free admission to Shakespeare in the Park.

330. Haddad, William. "Moses Sends Out Unsigned Attack on Park Producer." *New York Post*, Apr. 29, 1959, 4

An unsigned anonymous letter attacking Papp as a Communist is being circulated by Parks Commissioner Moses to those persons who oppose his ruling requiring admission be charged for Shakespeare in the Park. Papp said he was shocked by Moses' new attack.

331. "The Park—and the Gutter." Editorial. *New York Post,* Apr. 29, 1959, 45.

Charges Moses with "reckless assault" in circulating an anonymous letter that calls Papp a Communist. "No man with any claim to decency would utilize" such a letter.

332. Gelb, Arthur. "Moses Airs Attack on Play Producer." *New York Times*, Apr. 30, 1959, 1:2

Mayor Wagner criticized Robert Moses for circulating an unsigned letter referring to Papp's "socialist background." The anonymous letter writer asserted that Papp had refused to answer questions of a congressional committee about his connection with the Communist Party. Papp accused Moses of character assassination.

333. Gelb, Arthur. "Papp Supported on Play Festival" *New York Times*, May 1, 1959, 31:1

Clare C. Baldwin, assistant superintendent of schools, said that as far as he knew, Shakespeare was never a Communist. Papp told reporters that he is considering filing a libel suit against Moses for circulating a letter questioning Papp's fund raising methods.

334. Bennett, Charles G. "Mayor Plans Talk with Moses Today." *New York Times,* May 2, 1959, 25:6

Moses, fully recovered from viral pneumonia, was released from the hospital where he had been a patient for 10 days. Mayor Wagner plans to discuss with him the issue of charging admission for Shakespeare in the Park. The New York Civil Liberties Union is demanding that the mayor instruct the Parks Commissioner to apologize to Papp for circulating an unsigned letter attacking the producer.

335. Machirella, Henry. "Moses Says Bard Can't Park; He Blames Hoods in the Woods." *New York Daily News*, May 2, 1959, 3:3

Moses says he will not allow free Shakespeare in Central Park, because muggers might prey on audiences. From July 2 to September 13 of last year, the police made six arrests during performances.

336. "Tenacious Producer: Joseph Papp." *New York Times*, May 2, 1959, 47:1

Biographical article on Papp's early career and the founding of the NYSF. With actors willing to work for nothing and lighting equipment from an old Bronx movie house, Papp began to stage Shakespeare plays in the basement of a church in lower Manhattan. One of Papp's favorite comments is, "Don't tell me anything is impossible—let's try it first."

337. "Papp Sets Fall Program." *New York Times*, May 4, 1959, 36:1

Papp will produce plays in the Heckscher Theatre this fall. Aimed at high school students, these productions will be publicized in the city schools. Admission for high school students will be twenty cents.

338. Bennett, Charles G. "Wagner Hopeful on Plays in Park." *New York Times*, May 5, 1959, 35:4

Moses sent a copy of a letter to the mayor indicating a softening of his stand on charging admission for Shakespeare in the Park. He is willing to reduce the admission fee to fifty cents or one dollar if the city will put up $20,000 for fencing, ticket booths, seats, and sanitary facilities. Papp rejected this latest proposal contending that no admission fee should be charged and that the Festival should not have to pay for the use of the park. He noted that the park is free to baseball players, zoogoers, and concert audiences. In spite of this exchange, Mayor Wagner says he is confident that he can work something out between Moses and Papp

339. Crist, Judith. "Shakespeare-in-Park Feud Waxes." *New York Herald Tribune*, May 5, 1959, 1.

Papp accused Moses of singling out Festival audiences to pay for the privilege of using public facilities which are free to baseball players, zoo-goers, and concert audiences. "Mr. Moses," Papp said, "hasn't been the same since he was hit in the head by a baby carriage." Papp was referring to Moses' defeat in 1956 at the hands of a group of mothers who forced him to reverse a ruling that would have turned their children's Central Park play area into a parking lot for Tavern-on-the-Green patrons.

340. "Park Play Fight Still Unsettled." *New York Times*, May 7, 1959, 17:1

Papp announced that he is dropping one of the three plays planned for this summer's Shakespeare festival, because of the delay in giving him permission to use the park. In another development in the Papp-Moses feud, the Lexington Democratic Club in a letter to Mayor Wagner attacked Moses' position as "penny wise and pound foolish."

341. Gelb, Arthur. "Broadway Plans for Mrs. Bridge." *New York Times*, May 11, 1959, 30:5.

Murray Handwerker, executive vice-president of Nathan's (the New York hot dog king), sent a telegram to Papp offering him the use of a terrace garden of a restaurant in Oceanside, Long Island for his Shakespeare productions. The garden was used for jazz concerts last year and can accommodate 2,000 people.

342. Bennett, Charles G. "Mayor Backs Moses on Fee for Shakespeare in Park." *New York Times*, May 12, 1959, 1:2

Mayor Wagner said that under the city charter and state law, the parks commissioner had sole jurisdiction over the management of the parks. He indicated that if he did not support Moses on this issue, he would have to remove him from office. The mayor went on to say that Moses was "too valuable a public servant" to consider discharging him. Papp responded to the mayor's statement by threatening to stage demonstrations at City Hall saying, "It's an out-and-out fight—all subtleties have vanished." He indicated, however, that is is willing to try and reach an agreement with Moses.

343. Calta, Louis. "L.I. Site Proposed to Papp for Plays." *New York Times*, May 13, 1959, 39:5
Executive vice-president of Nathan's, the Coney Island hot dog restaurant, offered Papp the use of Roadside Rest in Oceanside for his productions of Shakespearean plays. Papp said he would inspect the site.

344. "Free Shakespeare." Editorial. *New York Times*, May 13, 1959, 36:2
Finds it astonishing that Moses could issue such an ultimatum to Papp when only a short time ago the commissioner was enthusiastically endorsing free Shakespeare in Central Park. Expresses the hope that "Mr. Moses will be persuaded to exercise that quality of mercy which, the Bard says, is mightiest in the mightiest, and ameliorate his original decree."

345. Fowle, Farnsworth. "Park Play Talks Break Up in Huff." *New York Times,* May 15, 1959, 31:1
Papp stormed out of a meeting with the Parks Department's executive director Stuart Constable, saying that Constable had threatened to call the police to throw him out. Papp made two offers at the meeting. One was to allow the city to collect ten or fifteen cents from each member of the Festival's audiences. The second was to allow a restauranteur to take a concession at the performances, paying

$10,000 and some of the profits to the Parks Department.

346. Machirella, Henry, and Jack Smee. "Park Shakespeare Down—and Out." *New York Daily News,* May 15, 1959, 10:1
After a stormy meeting with Papp, Parks official Stuart Constable said that there was no longer any basis for an agreement under which Papp could get a license to operate in Central Park.

347. Atkinson, Brooks. "Theatre: Sound and Fury." *New York Times*, May 16, 1959, 17:4
Says that Moses' refusal to allow free performances of Shakespeare in Central Park is devastating to the masses.

348. Robinson, Layhmond. "Mayor, Irritated, Gives Dispute over Park Plays a Low Priority." *New York Times*, May 16, 1959, 1:2
Wagner expressed disappointment over a peace meeting that he had arranged between Papp and Stuart Constable, Moses' assistant. The mayor said that the hospital strike and the city's 1959-1960 budget were higher on his list of priorities than the Papp-Moses feud.

349. Brewer, Sam Pope. "Dispute on Plays 'Closed' by Moses." *New York Times*, May 18, 1959, 1:1
On the radio program "News Closeup," Moses said that there will be no Shakespeare in Central Park this summer regardless of whether or not admission is charged. Papp, in response, made public a letter

he had sent to the mayor asking for a hearing before the Board of Estimate.

350. Robinson, Layhmond. "Moses Ordered to Court in Dispute on Park Plays." *New York Times*, May 19, 1959, 1:2

Papp obtained a show-cause order in the New York State Supreme Court directing Parks Commissioner Moses to show in court why he should not be compelled to grant the NYSF a permit to perform plays in Central Park this summer.

351. Robinson, Layhmond. "Mayor Requests Silence by Moses." *New York, Times,* May 20, 1959, 37:5

Moses has acceded to the mayor's request that he cease public statements on the dispute over Shakespeare in the Park.

352. Robinson, Layhmond. "Moses Vetoes Bid to Talks on Plays." *New York Times*, May 23, 1959, 1:1

Moses refused Justice Samuel M. Gold's offer to mediate the dispute over Shakespeare in the Park.

353. "Papp Miscasts Him, Moses Complains." *New York Times*, May 29, 1959, 25:3

Moses submitted an affidavit to Justice Gold defending his position on charging admission to Shakespeare plays in Central Park. He stated he could not ask the city to appropriate the $150,000 to $200,000 necessary for constructing a permanent stage, seating, dressing rooms, and sanitary facilities because of Papp's lack of financial responsibility and the uncertainty of his being able to produce the plays on a continuing basis.

354. Gelb, Arthur. "Moses Wins Case on Plays in Park." *New York Times*, June 3, 1959, 1:5.

Justice Gold "reluctantly" dismissed a petition by Papp to force Parks Commissioner Moses to grant a permit to allow free Shakespeare in Central Park this summer. In his decision, Gold said that the Parks Commissioner "has full discretion to determine whether or not a particular recreational or cultural activity of a special nature such as theatrical performances should be conducted in any specified area of the public parks." The city announced that a new summer theater that will charge admission will be built in Central Park.

355. "Papp Asks Court Speed." *New York Times*, June 9, 1959, 43:3.

Papp filed a notice of appeal to the Appellate Division of the New York State Supreme Court to readmit the NYSF to Central Park this summer. Papp accused the Parks Commissioner of opposing free Shakespeare plays in order to prevent competition with the new amphitheater in the park that will charge admission.

356. Calta, Louis. "Shakespeare Issue in Court." *New York Times*, June 10, 1959, 43:1.

The Appellate Division of the New York State Supreme Court will review Papp's appeal before its summer recess. Papp will present *Julius Caesar* this summer if he wins his appeal. The Actors' Equity Association is adopting a resolution asking Mayor

Wagner to set up a committee of interested citizens to study the issue of free admission.

357. Calta, Louis. "Papp Seeking Aid for Classics Tour." *New York Times*, June 13, 1959, 13:4.

Papp is hoping to enlist Governor Rockefeller's support in organizing a state-wide touring program of the classics. He envisions a "theatre-on-wheels" that would carry the actors, as well as an electric generator, lighting towers, dressing rooms, costumes, and storage room for property.

358. Kihss, Peter. "Court Bids Moses Retreat on Bard." *New York Times*, June 18, 1959, 33:1.

In an unanimous decision the Appellate Division of the New York State Supreme Court ruled that Parks Commissioner Moses had been "clearly arbitrary, capricious and unreasonable" in refusing to allow Papp to stage free plays in Central Park this summer. The court requested Moses to reconsider his decision and suggested he consider imposing "reasonable conditions" to compensate the city for any expenses it might incur because of Papp's productions. According to the Mayor's office these conditions might be that Papp would have to guarantee that the city would be paid the $20,000 necessary for fencing, seats, and sanitary facilities.

359. "As Shakespeare Said." Editorial. *New York Times*, June 19, 1959, 24:1.

Calls Moses "wrong" in dispute over charging admission to Shakespeare plays in Central Park. Says it is time for "gracious compromise."

360. Calta, Louis. "Show Will Go On If Papp Gets Bond." *New York Times*, June 19, 1959, 1:1.
Moses sent Papp a letter advising him he could produce free plays in Central Park this summer if he provides the city with $20,000 for putting "the area in condition for safe, controllable and reasonably satisfactory temporary use." Papp said he doubted he could raise the money on such short notice.

361. Bennett, Charles G. "Moses Asks Funds by City for Plays." *New York Times*, June 20, 1959, 23:1.
The Parks Commissioner asked the Board of Estimate to appropriate $20,000, the sum needed to permit free Shakespeare performances in Central Park this summer. This money would provide asphalt paving, a six foot fence around the area, and rented seats.

362. Bennett, Charles G. "Two Gifts Assure Free Parks Plays." *New York Times*, June 24, 1959, 1:1.
The Edward L. Bernays Foundation and the Louis K. Ansbacher Trust each offered $10,000 to allow free Shakespeare performances in the park this summer. Mayor Wagner announced that a committee, the Citizens Committee for the NYSF, has been formed to study a permanent Shakespeare festival.

363. Bennett, Charles G. "Papp is Assailed As Show Is Voted." *New York Times*, June 26, 1959, 27:4.
The Board of Estimate unanimously voted to accept two gifts, of $10,000 each, for free Shakespeare performances in the park. Bronx

Borough President James J. Lyons voting in favor, added that the Festival "should be conducted by someone who has not appeared before a congressional committee and taken the Fifth Amendment on communism." Lyons was referring to Papp's appearance before the House Committee on Un-American Activities on June 19, 1958. Papp invoked the Fifth Amendment when asked if he had ever been a member of the Communist Party.

364. Alden, Robert. "Papp and Troupe Return to Park." *New York Times*, July 10, 1959, 30:1.

As the first rehearsal for *Julius Caesar* began in Central Park, employees of the Parks Department prepared a platform for the production.

365. Ross, Don. "Papp's *Caesar* Free of Charge." *New York Herald Tribune*, Aug. 2, 1959, sec. 4, 1:2.

On the eve of the opening of his production of *Julius Caesar*, Papp talked to Ross about growing up in Brooklyn. When he wasn't memorizing Shakespeare, he was in gang wars using bottles and BB guns. His formal education ended with his graduation from high school. He is dedicated to bringing Shakespeare to the masses, and thinks there is a big difference between English and American Shakespearean actors. While the English actor places his emphasis on the sound of the words, the American actor emphasizes the emotion and vitality.

366. Gelb, Arthur. "Papp and Troupe Return to Park." *New York Times*, Aug. 4, 1959, 30:1.

About 2,400 people watched the NYSF production of *Julius Caesar* under a fair sky in Central Park. Robert Moses, who was offered a reserved seat for the performance, declined to attend. Papp still needs $7,000 to run the play for the planned three week stand.

367. "Shakespeare Loss Cancelled by Gift." *New York Times*, Aug. 19, 1959, 31:4.
Public relations man Edward L. Bernays offered the NYSF the $4,600 needed to cover the deficit for the free Shakespeare productions in Central Park this summer.

368. "Moses Asks City for $250,000 for Park Shakespeare Theatre." *New York Times*, Aug. 20, 1959, 1:5.
The Parks Commissioner asked the New York City Planning Commission for a quarter of a million dollars to construct a permanent theater in Central Park for the NYSF. Moses' request was prompted by his desire to avoid a dispute similar to the one he engaged in this year with Papp.

369. "Shakespeare in the Park." Editorial. *New York Times*, Aug. 22, 1959, 16:2.
Urges the city to give a sympathetic hearing to Moses' request for $250,000 for a permanent theater for the NYSF.

370. "Moses-Papp Storm Brewing for 1960." *New York Times*, Oct. 16, 1959, 33:1.
Papp reported that he had recently written to Moses requesting a permit to produce Shakespeare

plays in Central Park next summer. Moses said he would issue a permit if the city appropriates $250,000 for the construction of a permanent theater, and if Papp provides "definite, reliable, written assurance" that he has the funds necessary to produce the theater program.

371. "Shakespeare in the Park." Editorial. *New York Times*, Oct. 20, 1959, 38:1.

An editorial supporting the plan for a permanent free NYSF in Central Park.

372. "Trustees Proposed for Park Theatre." *New York Times*, Oct. 20, 1959, 45:2.

Robert W. Dowling, chairman of the Citizens Committee for a NYSF, appeared before the New York City Planning Commission and suggested that the proposed Shakespeare theater in Central Park be administered by a board of trustees, similar to the one for the Metropolitan Museum of Art. Dowling supports the Parks Department's proposal to allocate $250,000 for the construction of a permanent theater in the park.

373. Bennett, Charles G. "Miss Hayes Plays City Hall's Stage." *New York Times*, Nov. 19, 1959, 41:2.

Actress Helen Hayes appearing before the Board of Estimate, pleaded with its members to appropriate $250,000 for a permanent Shakespeare theater in the park. She was accompanied by Papp.

374. "News and Gossip Gathered on the Rialto." *New York Times*, Nov. 29, 1959, sec. 2, 1:6.

Marking the fifth anniversary of the founding of the NYSF, Papp announced his plans to launch a campaign to sign up 15,000 Festival supporters. Charging each supporter $7.50 would guarantee an annual income that could comfortably assure a Shakespeare program in the park.

1960

375. Atkinson, Brooks. "Bard in the Park: Plans for Fifth Season of Free Shakespeare." *New York Times*, Jan. 10, 1960, sec. 2, 1:1.

Although the city has agreed to appropriate $250,000 to build a permanent site for the NYSF, Parks Commissioner Robert Moses is requiring that Papp prove he has sufficient funds for a 10 week season. A committee, headed by Helen Hayes, is attempting to raise the necessary $110,000. Papp is hoping to raise most of this money through public subscriptions of $7.50 each. Atkinson urges friends and supporters of the NYSF to subscribe.

376. Calta, Louis. "Papp Is Planning 3 Plays in Park." *New York Times,* Jan. 23, 1960, 15:4.

Papp announced that he will present *Henry V*, *Measure for Measure,* and *The Taming of the Shrew* this summer in Central Park. So far has has raised only $28,000 of the $110,000 needed to run this year's program.

377. "Unit Sought to Aid Park's Shakespeare." *New York Times*, Feb. 2, 1960, 39:6.

A conference was held at City Hall to address the NYSF's financial problems. Concerned parties, including Papp and New York City Deputy Mayor O'Keefe, agreed to work on establishing a permanent committee to handle the Festival's economic difficulties. Papp reported that $35,000 of the $110,000 required to produce three plays this summer has been raised.

378. Calta, Louis. "Wagner Supports Free Park Shows." *New York Times*, Mar. 9, 1960, 39:4.

Mayor Wagner hosted a reception to seek the support of prominent New Yorkers for the NYSF's outdoor productions. The mayor promised that his administration would do all it could to encourage the successful completion of a new $250,000 amphitheater.

379. "Ian Keith Fund Established." *New York Times*, Mar. 31, 1960, 30:4.

An annual memorial award of $1,000 was established by George C. Scott to honor Ian Keith, an actor who died last Friday. The award will go to a NYSF player who is "most deserving of aid and encouragement toward a career in the theatre."

380. "Park Association Objects to Cafe." *New York Times*, Apr. 8, 1960, 33:5.

The directors of the Park Association of New York City adopted a resolution opposing the construction of a cafe and a permanent open-air theater in Central Park. The resolution is based on the association's belief that all "further encroachment" on the park must be resisted.

381. Gelb, Arthur. "Papp Signs Guthrie for a Park *Hamlet*." *New York Times*, Apr. 11, 1960, 1:5.

Tyrone Guthrie, one of the world's foremost directors, accepted Papp's invitation to direct a modern dress version of *Hamlet* in Central Park in June 1961. Guthrie will receive the customary $300 the NYSF pays its directors. This will be the first production at the new theater. Papp reported that he had resigned his stage manager's job at CBS to devote himself entirely to the Festival. He went on to accuse Broadway of being "froth, with very little cultural or social value."

382. "Shakespeare Aided." *New York Times*, Apr. 15, 1960, 26:2.

Four labor unions contributed $1,200 to the NYSF for its free Central Park plays.

383. "April 23-30 to Mark Free Shakespeare." *New York Times*, Apr. 20, 1960, 45:1.

Mayor Wagner proclaimed April 23 to April 30 as Free-Shakespeare-in-the-Park Week. He urged New Yorkers to "support this wonderful cultural undertaking."

384. "20,000 Is Raised for Papp Festival." *New York Times,* May 9, 1960, 32:3.

A dinner and entertainment held at the Commodore Hotel raised $20,000 for the NYSF's free outdoor productions. A total of $110,000 is needed by May 30 in order for Papp to produce three plays in the summer. To date, $78,000 has been raised.

385. "Broadway Held Barbaric by Papp." *New York Times*, May 10, 1960, 45:5.

Papp, speaking before the Women's City Club of New York, attacked Broadway as a "talent destroyer." He accused Broadway of cutting off 90% of the city's population with its high ticket prices. Auditions for Broadway productions are "barbaric, undignified and intolerable."

386. "Joe Papp's Regards to Broadway." Editorial. *New York Herald Tribune*, May 11, 1960, 26.

Agrees with Papp that the whole issue of theater economics, from ticket prices to ticket availability, needs examination. Papp, in a speech before the Women's Civic Club, said that 90% of the city's population cannot afford to go to the theater. He said that he wished the city saw theater less as show business and more as an art form, and urged that the Department of Commerce and Public Events change its name to Department of Culture, Commerce and Public Events.

387. "$25,000 Offered to Fete in Park." *New York Times*, May 18, 1960, 48:1.

The New York Foundation announced it was prepared to give $25,000 to the NYSF, if an equal amount was raised from the community at large.

388. Gelb, Arthur. "Papp Offers Plan to Avert a Strike." *New York Times*, May 23, 36:1.

Responding to the deadlocked contract negotiations between the Actors' Equity Association and the League of New York Theatres, Papp proposed that ticket prices be raised in order to immediately satisfy actors' demand for higher wages, even though he believes the government must ultimately subsidize any increases. He stated that it is necessary to "take the serious theatre out of the sphere of business enterprise."

389. "Shakespeare Tour of City is Sought." *New York Times*, Aug. 10, 1960, 25:2.

Papp announced before an audience of 2,500, gathered to watch *Measure for Measure* in Central Park, that he would ask the New York City Board of Education for money to support a touring company that would perform free Shakespeare plays in city parks next summer.

390. "Levitt Casts Bard in Mayoral Race." *New York Times*, Aug. 29, 1960, 23:4.

State Comptroller Arthur Levitt, candidate for mayoral nomination, said he was refused permission to appear at the opening of the NYSF's production of Richard II. Levitt feels it was unfair that Mayor Wagner was invited to speak. Parks Commissioner Newbold Morris said that "anybody can go to the theatre."

391. Calta, Louis. "Mayor to Pay Bill for Shakespeare." *New York Times*, Aug. 30, 1960, 24:1.

Mayor Wagner personally guaranteed to raise the $11,000 that the NYSF needs to complete its current season.

392. Murphy, Agnes. "At Home with Mrs.Joseph Papp." *New York Post,* Sep. 11, 1960, Magazine sec., 15.

An interview with Peggy Bennion Papp. The Papps, with their two year old daughter, live in an apartment on the upper West Side near Central Park. Mrs. Papp is studying for an M.A. in social work. On an ordinary evening the Papps read plays aloud. Article includes a recipe for Mrs. Papp's chicken and wild rice.

393. Gelb, Arthur. "Music and Ballet as Well as Plays Planned in Park." *New York Times*, Sep. 30, 1960, 1:3.

Although New York City officials once opposed free plays in Central Park as a nuisance, new Parks Commissioner Newbold Morris is one of the Festival's biggest supporters. He would enlarge the Festival to include concerts, ballet, operas, and children's entertainment. Believing that the Festival has made the park safer on summer evenings, he is attempting to raise $1.5 million for floodlights to illuminate an even wider area of the park. Mr. Morris also supports Papp's plans to take his Shakespeare troupe on a tour of the city schools between October and March.

394. Zolotow, Sam. "Papp Shifts Scene: Park to Schools." *New York Times*, Oct. 4, 1960, 45:1.

City Hall announced that $50,00 will be made available for the NYSF to tour the city high schools for six months beginning in January. Papp estimated that the Festival would cost $140,000 in 1961. Mayor Wagner promised to support Papp's request for $60,000 from the city. The remaining $80,000 will come from private donations and benefits.

395. "Watch This Guy, Men." Editorial. *New York Daily News*, Oct. 5, 1960, 43.

Warns Mayor Wagner and the Parks Commissioner against giving Papp money for Shakespeare in the Park. Reminds them that he refused to tell the House Un-American Activities Committee whether he had ever been a Communist. Papp's "political past is still shrouded in mystery."

396. Taubman, Howard. "Green Oases." *New York Times*, Oct. 9, 1960, sec. 2, 1:1.

Proposes that free Shakespeare plays should be presented at parks throughout the city. Suggests the repertory be enlarged to include classics of all periods. Praises Parks Commissioner Newbold Morris' idea to use the new theater in Central Park for concerts, opera, and ballet after Papp's season is over.

397. Calta, Louis. "Papp Still Plans Plays in Schools." *New York Times*, Nov. 5, 1960, 27:1.

Three members of the New York City Board of Estimate are refusing to approve the $50,000 necessary for the NYSF's tour of the city schools because Papp invoked the Fifth Amendment before a congressional committee in 1958.

398. Benjamin, Philip. "Donors Solicited for Shakespeare." *New York Times*, Nov. 11, 1960, 36:4.

At a luncheon honoring Brooks Atkinson, Papp opened a drive for "audience sponsors"—a euphemism for cash contributors—for the NYSF. Papp praised Atkinson for his early and constant support of the Festival, as well as of Off-Broadway theater. The designs for the new Central Park amphitheater, scheduled for construction next year, were exhibited by the architect Eldon Elder. Other speakers at the luncheon, which was held at Tavern-on-the-Green, included Parks Commissioner Newbold Morris and George C. Scott.

399. "Shakespeare Set for School Tour." *New York Times,* Dec. 2, 1960, 31:1.

After a stormy session the New York City Board of Estimate voted 12 to 10 to give Papp $50,000 to stage performances of *Romeo and Juliet* in city high schools beginning in January. Spokesman for the opposition, Controller Lawrence E. Gerosa, said he was not voting against Shakespeare but against Papp. Children should not be exposed "to a man who took the Fifth Amendment many times before a congressional committee investigating Communism."

400. "Sound and Fury." Editorial. *New York Post*, Dec. 4, 1960, Magazine sec., 8.

Criticizes Controller Gerosa and borough presidents Clancy, Lyons, and Cashmore for opposing Papp's request for $50,000 to fund a tour of the city's high schools with *Romeo and Juliet.* When Papp invoked the Fifth Amendment before a congressional committee, he was exercising his constitutional rights.

401. "Shakespeare in Schools." Editorial. *New York Times*, Dec. 5, 1960, 30:1.

Calls the decision of the Board of Estimate to fund the NYSF's performances of *Romeo and Juliet* in city schools "reasonable and enlightened." Says there is no danger that children watching one of these performances will be subverted.

402. "Martinson Heads Festival." *New York Times*, Dec. 7, 1960, 56:7.

Joseph B. Martinson of Martinson's Coffee has been elected chairman of the board of trustees of the NYSF.

403. "School Hearing Divided on Papp." *New York Times*, Dec. 23, 1960, 40:1.

Fifteen speakers appeared before the New York City Board of Education to address the issue of whether the NYSF should be allowed to perform *Romeo and Juliet* in city schools. Nine speakers directed their opposition against Papp because he invoked the Fifth Amendment two years ago before a congressional committee when asked if he had ever been a member of the Communist Party. The board voted to continue its discussion of this issue at the next meeting in January.

404. Calta, Louis. "Papp Sees Threat to Troupe's Plans." *New York Times*, Dec. 24, 1960, 9:1.

The delay by the Board of Education on allowing the NYSF to present *Romeo and Juliet* in the city schools could cause serious financial problems, according to Papp. In anticipation of a $50,000 appropriation for the school tour, the Festival has gone ahead and spent $9,000 for production costs. This money was originally earmarked for the troupe's summer productions in Central Park. Lashing back at his opponents, whom he called "procrusteans who yearn for the return of the thumbscrew and the rack," Papp said that he invoked the Fifth Amendment "to protect myself and others from unjust abuse and persecution."

405. Morisseau, James J. "Papp's Reply to Accusers: 'Not a Red'." *New York Herald Tribune*, Dec. 24, 1960, 5:1.

After listening to a number of speeches on the issue of the NYSF's tour of city high schools with its production of *Romeo and Juliet*, the Board of Education voted to delay its decision for a month. Papp, who was accused by several speakers of being a Communist, called his critics "self-appointed super patriots" who want to destroy his school project.

406. "Board Votes to Let Students See *Romeo* in City's High Schools." *New York Times*, Dec. 30, 1960, 15:2.

At a special meeting the Board of Education approved the use of $50,000, earlier appropriated by the Board of Estimate, to finance the production of *Romeo and Juliet* in the city schools. Approximately 120,000 students are expected to watch the play, which will be performed from January through April.

407. "Park Theatre Bids 50% above Budget." *New York Times*, Dec. 31, 1960, 15:3.

The New York City Department of Parks reported that the lowest bid for the amphitheater to be built in Central Park was for $370,820. The Board of Estimate has budgeted only $225,000 for the theater.

408. "Strange Eruption." Editorial. *New York Daily Mirror,* Dec. 31, 1960, 11.

Attacks the Board of Education for giving Papp $50,000 to present *Romeo and Juliet* in 80 city high schools. Calls Papp a "Fifth Amendment man" who should not be rewarded. Objects to board members giving away money without first having seen Papp's production.

1961

409. Little, Stuart W. "Papp to Present *Romeo* Out of Town." *New York Herald*, Jan. 2, 1961, 8:1.

For the first time, Papp will present a Shakespeare play, *Romeo and Juliet,* at colleges and community centers outside of New York City. Ten engagements at theaters from Trenton, New Jersey, to Stamford, Connecticut, are scheduled on weekends through April. The money received for these performances will be used for the Festival's school program.

410. Bennett, Charles G. "$150,000 Gift from Publisher Assures Central Park Theatre." *New York Times*, Jan. 26, 1961, 1:4.

George T. Delacorte, president of the Dell Publishing Company, has offered the New York City Parks Department $150,000 for the construction of a 2,500 seat outdoor theater in Central Park. This gift will make up the difference between the

$225,000 appropriated by the Board of Estimate, and the amount quoted by the lowest acceptable bidder. Parks Commissioner Newbold Morris is hopeful that the theater can be completed by the start of the Festival's season in June.

411. Zolotow, Sam. "*Romeo and Juliet* Begins Tour of 12 City Schools at Taft High." *New York Times*, Feb. 8, 1961, 24:5.

The NYSF began its tour of city high schools with its presentation of *Romeo and Juliet* at Taft High School in the Bronx. The tour, which is expected to continue into May, is being subsidized by a municipal appropriation of $50,000.

412. Calta, Louis. "Papp Tells Plans for New Theatre." *New York Times*, Feb. 28, 1961, 38:4.

Papp announced the NYSF's program for this summer, the sixth season of free Shakespeare in Central Park. The plays scheduled to be presented are *Much Ado About Nothing, Midsummer Night's Dream,* and *Richard III*. Papp said his company would need $160,000 to operate this summer but that only $38,000 had been pledged so far.

413. "Temporary Stage Planned in Park." *New York Times*, Apr. 13, 1961, 30:6

Because of bad weather and contract delays, the new permanent theater will not be ready in time for the start of this year's Shakespeare in the Park. Papp has proposed to Parks Commissioner Newbold Morris that a temporary theater be constructed at a cost of $7,000.

414. Gelb, Arthur. "600 Pay $50 to Aid Park Play Season." *New York Times*, Apr. 24, 1961, 31:8.

A $50 a plate dinner, held at the Hotel Commodore, raised $35,000 toward the $160,000 needed to underwrite the production of three Shakespeare plays in Central Park this summer. This amount, added to the $40,000 contributed over the past several months, means that $85,000 must still be raised. Papp called on Mayor Wagner to honor the promise he made last year to ask the Board of Estimate for $60,000.

415. "Papp Plans Move to Wollman Rink." *New York Times*, May 4, 1961, 41:2.

The New York City Parks Department will erect a temporary stage in Wollman Skating Rink for this summer's productions by the NYSF. The permanent $400,000 theater, that is presently under construction in Central Park, will not be completed in time for this year's program. Mayor Wagner has agreed to ask the Board of Estimate for $60,000 to help underwrite the cost of the three plays the Festival will present beginning in July.

416. "Shakespeare in the Park." Editorial. *New York Times*, June 22, 1961, 30:2.

Urges the Board of Estimate to appropriate $60,000 to insure free Shakespeare in the Park this summer.

417. Gelb, Arthur. "News of the Rialto: In the Park." *New York Times,* Aug. 6, 1961, sec. 2, 1:3.

Papp has decided to open the NYSF's 1962 season with *The Merchant of Venice.* This will be the first play to be performed in the new amphitheater in Central Park. George C. Scott will play Shylock. The Festival will also present *The Tempest* and an operatic version of *Two Gentlemen of Verona.*

418. "Topics: Shakespeare in the Park." *New York Times*, Aug. 7, 1961, 22:3.

A brief history of Shakespeare in the Park from the first season in the summer of 1956 at the East River Park amphitheater. The very first production had only 45 cast members, now there are almost 100 actors in the troupe. Approximately 120,000 people attended the free performances in Central Park in 1960. Last winter, the NYSF played before 100,000 students during its tour of the city high schools.

419. "Funke, Lewis. "News of the Rialto." *New York Times*, Oct. 22, 1961, sec. 2, 1:5.

Papp has signed a contract with the Macmillan Company to edit a series of books on the productions of the plays performed by the NYSF. An introduction by the play's director, along with his comments on each scene, will be included in each volume. Papp will write a commentary for each play.

420. "$200,000 Is Sought for Park Festival." *New York Times*, Dec. 4, 1961, 5:2.

Papp announced the beginning of a campaign to raise $200,000 for next summer's free Shakespeare performances. The new 2,300 seat amphitheater is expected to be completed by the end of April.

421. Esterow, Milton. "School Will Endow a Chair." *New York Times*, Dec. 9, 1961, 21:1.

Students at Sheepshead Bay High School in Brooklyn will have a plaque in their school's name attached to a seat in the new amphitheater in Central Park. For $500, a group or an individual can have a plaque in his name attached to a theater seat. The high school students' offer to contribute $100 a year for five years has been accepted by Papp.

422. "Shakespeare Fete Gets $50,000 Grant." *New York Times*, Dec. 19, 1961, 37:7.

The New York City Board of Education has approved a $50,000 appropriation for the NYSF's production of *Julius Caesar*, which will be performed in city high schools this winter.

423. Zolotow, Sam. "Fountain Slated for Park Theater." *New York Times*, Dec. 20, 1961, 39:1.

George T. Delacorte, president of Dell Publishing, will donate $50,000 for a lighted fountain, which will be installed in the lake next to the new amphitheater in Central Park. Mr. Delacorte is chairman of a committee to raise money for next summer's free Shakespeare performances.

1962

424. Zolotow, Sam. "Shakespeare Tour Planned." *New York Times,* Jan. 2, 1962, 24:3.

The New York State Council on the Arts has invited Papp to prepare two shows for a ten week tour of the state. Papp has decided on *Julius Caesar* and *Antony and Cleopatra*, which he will both produce and direct.

425. Zolotow, Sam. "Festival in Park Gets Mayor's Aid." *New York Times*, Feb. 19, 1962, 23:1.

Mayor Wagner and his wife have invited 500 prominent New Yorkers to a meeting at Gracie Mansion on March 14 to plan a drive to raise money for the NYSF. Papp estimates that $212,000 will be necessary to produce three plays this summer. The city is expected to appropriate $100,000.

426. Esterow, Milton. "Student Audiences See Staging of Shakespeare's *Julius Caesar*." *New York Times*, Feb. 22, 1962, 19:6.

The NYSF's production of *Julius Caesar* will play at the Heckscher Theater through March 2. It will then tour the city high schools in all five boroughs through June 1. The New York City Board of Estimate has appropriated $50,000 for the tour, but another $18,600 is needed. Papp is asking foundations and individuals for this additional sum.

427. "$285,000 Fund Drive Begins to Assist Shakespeare Festival." *New York Times*, Mar. 15, 1962, 28:2.

One hundred fifty prominent New Yorkers attended a meeting at Gracie Mansion to plan a campaign to raise money for the NYSF. R. Peter Straus, president of radio station WMCA, was named chairman of the Mayor's Committee for the NYSF.

428. Calta, Louis. "Prisoners Warm to *Julius Caesar*." *New York Times*, Mar. 20, 1962, 34:3.

The NYSF's production of *Julius Caesar* was presented yesterday before 1,400 inmates of Rikers Island Penitentiary.

429. Atkinson, Brooks. "Critic at Large: New Shakespeare Theatre in Central Park No Surprise to Papp, Its Director." *New York Times*, Mar. 30, 1962, 30:4.

Shakespeare in the Park has become a permanent institution primarily because the productions "glow with vitality." Many of the actors who appear in these productions are among New York's best. The budget for the Festival in 1957 was $33,845. This year it will be $263,466.

430. "Shakespeare Festival Light Tower Stirs Complaints." *New York Times*, Apr. 6, 1962, 24:4.

A newly erected 55 foot aluminum tower is being attacked for marring the beauty of the Belvedere Lake area in Central Park. Papp says the tower is essential for lighting his productions.

431. "...In Central Park, for Instance." Editorial. *New York Times*, Apr. 7, 1962, 24:1.

Attacks the 55 foot lighting tower built for the NYSF, calling it "hideous." Urges Parks Commissioner Newbold Morris to not allow the tower to remain a "permanent disfigurement to the park."

432. Zolotow, Sam. "Funds Voted to Festival." *New York Times*, May 14, 1962, 35:3.

The Board of Estimate appropriated $100,000 for the NYSF on May 10. So far, including this appropriation, $194,000 has been raised for this summer's productions. Another $91,000 is still needed.

433. Esterow, Milton. "Portia Pleads, Hammers Pound and Papp Gets Season Started." *New York Times*, May 19, 1962, 29:2.

Yesterday was the first day of rehearsal for the NYSF in its new theater in Central Park. The Festival will open June 19 with *The Merchant of Venice*.

434. Calta, Louis. "Tower Is Shifted at Park Theatre." *New York Times*, May 23, 1962, 37:1.

The 55 foot lighting tower, which so upset local residents, was moved from the center area of the amphitheater to the back. Papp denies that the tower was moved to placate angry residents.

435. Kandel, Myron. "The Bard's New Home in the Park." *New York Times,* May 27, 1962, sec. 2, 1:5.

Except for some finishing touches the new, as yet unnamed, 2,300 seat amphitheater in Central Park is completed. Papp is pleased with the theater, which meets his basic demands. One is that the audiences sit around the stage, and the other is that the seating consist of permanent raised seats.

436. "Papp Troupe Plays to Its Benefactors." *New York Times*, May 29, 1962, 21:1.

The Mayor's Committee for Free Shakespeare met for the last time yesterday in George T. Delacorte's apartment. Delacorte, president of Dell Publishing, contributed $150,000 last year toward the $400,000 needed to construct an amphitheater. The Festival's board of trustees reported to the committee that only a small amount was left to be raised for this season's operating budget of $285,000.

437. Adams, Val. "TV Will Record Park Merchant." *New York Times*, June 7, 1962, 27:8.

CBS will tape the NYSF's Central Park preview performance of *The Merchant of Venice* on June 17. The drama, starring George C. Scott, will be televised on June 21. Parks Commissioner Newbold Morris said that sponsorship of the program will not be permitted.

438. Gelb, Arthur. "Rabbis Protest Showing of *Merchant of Venice* on TV." *New York Times*, June 15, 1962, 17:2.

The New York Board of Rabbis met with Parks Commissioner Newbold Morris and Papp to request that *The Merchant of Venice* not be televised because it is an anti-Semitic play. Papp, who does not think the work is anti-Semitic, said he was bound by contract to allow CBS to televise the play locally. He said he would ask CBS not to release the tape to stations outside of New York.

439. Shepard, Richard F. "Rabbi is Hopeful on TV *Merchant*." *New York Times*, June 16, 1962, 47:5.

Rabbi Israel Mowshowitz, president of the New York Board of Rabbis, said that he hopes CBS will substitute another play for *The Merchant of Venice*, scheduled to be televised on June 21. The rabbi voiced his belief to reporters that Shylock is an anti-Semitic stereotype.

440. Little, Stuart W. "Papp and His New Amphitheater." *New York Herald Tribune*, June 18, 1962, 10:1.

Interviewed at the brand new Delacorte Theater, Papp said that he did not think *The Merchant of Venice* was anti-Semitic. The play, which will be the first offering at the new theater, stars George C. Scott. Papp also discussed the problem of raising $50,000 more for this season.

441. Gardner, Paul. "Central Park's Shakespeare Amphitheatre Dedicated." *New York Times*, June 19, 1962, 28:1.

At a benefit performance of *The Merchant of Venice* last night, Parks Commissioner Newbold Morris announced that the new theater would be named the Delacorte Theater. The dedication is in honor of George T. Delacorte who contributed $150,000 toward the construction of the $400,000 amphitheater.

442. Mowshowitz, Israel et al. "*Merchant* on TV Protested." Letter. *New York Times,* June 19, 1962, 34:5.

Letter from the president of the New York Board of Rabbis, and other concerned citizens, protesting the televising of *The Merchant of Venice.* Calls the character of Shylock "an amalgam of vindictiveness, cruelty and avarice." Says that a mass television audience, which includes impressionable young children and teenagers, will believe Shylock to be a typical Jew.

443. Shanley, John P. "*Merchant* Tape Has Moon as Prop." *New York Times*, June 19, 1962, 71:3.

CBS's television crew had perfect weather for the taping of *The Merchant of Venice*, which will be televised on June 21. The telecast will include filmed scenes of the dedication of the new open-air theater.

444. "CBS Picketed in Protest Against *Merchant* on TV." *New York Times*, June 22, 1962, 15:1.

One hundred fifty pickets, representing the Jewish War Veterans, demonstrated against the televising of *The Merchant of Venice.* They said they objected to the anti-Semitic aspects of the play.

445. "TV *Merchant* Viewers Are Put at 1,600,000." *New York Times,* June 23, 1962, 47:5.

CBS reported that its telecast of *The Merchant of Venice* had reached 800,000 homes. It outdrew all other New York stations from 8:30 p.m. to 11:00 p.m.

446. Gould, Jack. "TV: A Vivid Demonstration of Contrasting Media." *New York Times*, June 25, 1962, 51:2.

Author found that watching the live version of *The Merchant of Venice* was more pleasurable than seeing it on television.

447. Atkinson, Brooks. "Critic at Large." *New York Times*, June 26, 1962, 30:2.

Atkinson is puzzled by the New York Board of Rabbis' opposition to the televising of *The Merchant of Venice*. Because of the play's "make-believe" quality, he doesn't understand all the controversy it provoked. He puts it in the same category as *Twelfth Night* and *As You Like It*.

448. Atkinson, Brooks. "Critic at Large." *New York Times*, July 3, 1962, 20:7.

In responding to a flood of protests opposing his stand on the televising of *The Merchant of Venice*, Atkinson states that "one must trust the good sense of Americans." He believes that more openness is a counter-measure to bigotry.

449. Gardner, Paul. "Shakespeare in Park Draws Lines of Patrons." *New York Times*, July 18, 1962, 19:2.

Every night in Central Park thousands of people line up in hopes of securing seats in the 2,249 amphitheater for a free performance of a Shakespeare play. On the average, 2,000 prospective theatergoers get turned away.

450. Esterow, Milton. "State Arts Unit to Aid Theatres." *New York Times,* Aug. 17, 1962, 10:1.

The New York State Council on the Arts will send professional directors, actors, writers, and other theater personnel to some 400 non-professional community theaters to provide them with expert guidance for their local productions. The council will also sponsor a tour of 176 high schools by the NYSF with its production of *Much Ado About Nothing*.

451. Zolotow, Sam. "Festival in Park May Be Expanded." *New York Times*, Sep. 27, 1962, 32:1.

The NYSF may present free performances in the Bronx and Brooklyn next summer, as well as in Central Park. Authorization by the New York City Parks Department would be required. It is estimated that it would cost between $75,000 and $100,000 to bring free Shakespeare to the Bronx and Brooklyn. An additional $300,000 is needed for the 1963 Central Park productions.

452. Calta, Louis. "Ford Fund Grants Attacked by Papp." *New York Times*, Nov. 10, 1962, 17:1.

Papp has charged the Ford Foundation with hurting the NYSF by granting money to the Stratford Theater in Connecticut for an actor's training school. This grant has enabled Stratford to offer $100 a week salaries to actor trainees, thus luring away young actors from the NYSF. Papp said that both the Rockefeller and Ford Foundations turned down his requests for grants because of his policy on free admission.

453. Esterow, Milton. "Theatre: A Gift to Pupils." *New York Times,* Nov. 17, 1962, 16:2.

The NYSF's production of *Macbeth* is being presented at the Hechscher Theater for school children during the day and for adult audiences in the evening through November 30. In December the troupe will begin touring the four other city boroughs. In April of next year the Festival will make an eleven city tour of the state under the auspices of the New York State Council on the Arts.

1963

454. Adams, Val. "Festival in Park Plans a Telecast." *New York Times*, Apr. 2, 1963, 95:2.

The NYSF's production of *Antony and Cleopatra* will be taped by WCBS-TV and televised June 19. Papp says that CBS will solicit contributions to the Festival through on-the-air announcements.

455 Gelb, Arthur. "Integrated Cast Will Act in South." *New York Times*, Apr. 11, 1963, 28:5.

The NYSF will tour 20 cities in the South next year performing *Antony and Cleopatra* with a cast including about 10 black actors. Diana Sands, a black actress, has already been cast as Cleopatra. The U.S. State Department is considering sponsoring the Festival on a 12 week tour of Africa, Asia, and Europe.

456. Zolotow, Sam. "Delacorte to Add Stage Equipment.": *New York Times,* Apr. 24, 1963, 39:1.

The New York City Board of Estimate has approved an appropriation of $198,610 for a sound system, dimmer board, and direct power lines for the open-air Delacorte Theater.

457. Zolotow, Sam. "Park Shakespeare Grants." *New York Times,* May 7, 1963, 47:3.

The NYSF is only $80,000 away from the $300,000 needed to produce this summer's free performances in Central Park. The $220,000 raised so far includes $100,000 appropriated by the city. The rest is from grants and gifts from individuals and businesses.

458. Zolotow, Sam. "Theater Sought for Civic Center." *New York Times*, May 17, 1963, 26:4.

The New York City Planning Commission is considering a request by Papp to build a 1,000 seat theater in the proposed civic center, which is to be constructed in lower Manhattan. The estimated cost of the theater is $2.5 million. The civic center will cost over $168 million.

459. Calta, Louis. "Papp and Troupe Begin Rehearsal." *New York Times*, May 18, 1963, 29:2.

The NYSF has begun rehearsing *Antony and Cleopatra* in the 2,300 seat Delacorte Theater in Central Park. The play will open June 20.

460. Esterow, Milton. "Papp Gives Would-Be Sponsors $9,000 Refund, But No Tickets." *New York Times*, June 26, 1963, 33:1.

The NYSF has returned contributions to 1,200 would-be sponsors. By the beginning of June, the

Festival had received $90,000 from 12,000 sponsors and the decision was made not to accept any more. Since each sponsor, for a contribution of $7.50 is entitled to one free ticket for each of the Festival's three plays, too many sponsors could eliminate every free seat in the theater.

461. "Integrated *Antony* Won't Tour South." *New York Times*, Aug. 24, 1963, 10:6.

The NYSF's planned six week tour of southern cities with its production of *Antony and Cleopatra* was cancelled for lack of funds. Papp was able to raise only $11,250 of the $50,000 needed for the tour.

462. Zolotow, Sam. "U.S. Decides Against Sending Shakespeare Troupe Abroad." *New York Times*, Aug. 24, 1963, 11:2.

The cultural advisory committee of the U.S. State Department has decided not to send a NYSF Shakespeare production to Europe, Africa, and Asia because European competition is "too keen." Papp contends that his company is experienced enough to compete. The State Department has been sending American artists and entertainers on tours throughout the world since 1954.

463. Zolotow, Sam. "Papp Gets $50,000 from City for *Twelfth Night* School Tour." *New York Times*, Aug. 27, 1963, 27:2.

The New York City Board of Education has allocated $50,000 to the NYSF to tour city schools with its production of *Twelfth Night*. Another $20,000 is needed to make the tour possible. Papp's plan to tour the South with an integrated cast playing *Antony and Cleopatra* has been canceled because of lack of funds.

464. Zolotow, Sam. "Open-Air Shakespeare Is Urged for All Boroughs." *New York Times,* Sep. 4, 1963, 34:21.

Papp's plan to tour the city's parks performing free Shakespeare plays has the support of Parks Commissioner Newbold Morris. The plan calls for $156,000, which includes the money needed to construct a portable stage. A play would start its tour after its engagement in Central Park.

465. Little, Stuart W. "Explicit Scenes for the Bard?" *New York Herald Tribune,* Sep. 9, 1963, 12:3.

Papp will use a new elaborate stage set, designed by Ming Cho Lee, for his school production of *Twelfth Night.* The set is a big change from the bare platform staging of most contemporary productions of Shakespeare plays. The new stage set has a very large picture panel book at the rear center of the stage. Every panel has a literal representation for each scene.

466. Zolotow, Sam. "*Electra* Chosen by Park Festival." *New York Times*, Dec. 5, 1963, 58:3.

Next summer the NYSF will present Sophicles' *Electra*, its first non-Shakespeare drama. The Festival's tenth season will also include *Hamlet, The Merry Wives of Windsor,* and an operatic version of *Twelfth Night.* Papp has announced that he needs $350,000 for next year's program.

1964

467. "Joseph Papp Wins Jersey Bias Fight." *New York Post*, Jan. 2, 1964, 51:1.

The New Jersey State Division of Civil Rights announced a settlement of a complaint brought by Papp against a motel for refusing to provide accommodations for his black housekeeper last summer. The motel has agreed to cease discrimination and has invited the Papps and their housekeeper to return at any time.

468. Zolotow, Sam. "Mayor Seeks Funds for Tour of Shakespeare in City Parks." *New York Times*, Jan. 6, 1964, 1:3.

Mayor Wagner will recommend to the Board of Estimate that it appropriate $170,000 to the NYSF for its tour of 25 city parks this summer. The Festival will present free performances of *A Midsummer Night's Dream.* It is expected that the mayor will also recommend that the board approve a permanent NYSF theater in the civic center, which will be constructed in lower Manhattan. The proposed theater, which would cost more then $5 million, would seat 1,000 and be air-conditioned. The mayor will also ask the board to again appropriate $100,000 for free Shakespeare in Central Park this summer. George T. Delacorte, president of Dell Publishing, has donated a mobile stage costing $35,000 for the parks tour.

469. "Plays in 25 Parks Approved by City." *New York Times*, Jan. 15, 1964, 28:2.

Mayor Wagner announced that the Board of Estimate unanimously supports the proposed tour of city parks by the NYSF. The tour, which will take place in the summer, will present free open-air performances of Shakespeare plays beginning with *A Midsummer Night's Dream.*

470. Zolotow, Sam. "Festival in Park Assisted by City." *New York Times*, Mar. 20, 1964, 26:1.

The New York City Board of Estimate approved an appropriation of $325,000 for the NYSF. Of this sum, $225,000 is for the Festival's tour of city parks this summer and $100,000 is for the free performances in Central Park. Morningside Park, Inwood Hill Park, and Highbridge Park are some of the parks that will be included on the tour.

471. Adams, Val. "WCBS-TV to Show *Hamlet* June 16." *New York Times,* Mar. 31, 1964, 71:1.

A tape of the NYSF's production of *Hamlet* will be shown without commercial interruption on June 16. On the same evening the Festival will open its new season at the Delacorte Theater. The NYSF's productions of *The Merchant of Venice* and *Antony and Cleopatra* have previously been televised on CBS.

472. Zolotow, Sam. "Park Players to Travel." *New York Times*, Apr. 20, 1964, 35:7.

The NYSF will present *Hamlet* and *Othello* in Philadelphia's Playhouse in the Park, a municipally controlled theater, after its Central Park program ends. Papp said that the Festival will receive $6,000 for each play for props, costumes, and other production costs.

473. Little, Stuart W. "Shakespeare Day—Just Humdrum to Papp." *New York Herald Tribune,* Apr. 24, 1964, 14:4.

A day in the life of Joe Papp. The author followed him on a typical work day from morning through late afternoon. Papp's days are spent meeting with benefactors, actors, playwrights, and directors. Much of his time is given to raising money for the Festival.

474. Watts, Jr., Richard. "Saving Shakespeare from Pedantry." *New York Post*, May 3, 1964, Entertainment sec., 2.

Applauds Papp for showing Shakespeare as a living dramatist with something fascinating to say to all of us.

475. Zolotow, Sam. "Papp Gets $21,250 for Borough Tour." *New York Times*, May 4, 1964, 36:1.

Business and labor groups have donated $21,250 to the NYSF to tour city parks this summer performing free Shakespeare plays. The Taconic Foundation has agreed to make a matching grant once Papp raises $35,000.

476. Little, Stuart W. "Shakespeare Tour Climax: World's Fair." *New York Herald Tribune*, May 8, 1964, 12:7.

After its school tour, the NYSF will set up its mobile stage at the World's Fair for the last weekend in August. It will give two performances of *A Midsummer Night's Dream* with an integrated cast.

477. Weissman, Paul. "Park Impresario." *New York Post,* May 15, 1964, 39.

Summarizes Papp's life and career on the eve of the 11th season of Shakespeare in the Park. He started the NYSF in 1954 with $200 and borrowed lighting equipment. Actors worked for free and Papp supported himself as a CBS stage manager. Today, his budget is $731,738, he employs 250 people, and the actors are paid salaries ranging from $75 to $250.

478. Zolotow, Sam. "Delacorte Plans Play Every Night." *New York Times*, May 15, 1964, 41:1.

Actors' Equity has granted the NYSF permission to perform on Monday evenings in addition to all other evenings. This ruling applies to the free Shakespeare productions at the Delacorte Theater and to the Festival's tour of city parks with *A Midsummer Night's Dream.*

479. Zolotow, Sam. "Mobile Theater Set Up for Parks." *New York Times,* June 16, 1964, 46:1.

A mobile theater costing $35,000 has been set up in Central Park for rehearsals of *A Midsummer Night's Dream,* which will be presented by the NYSF this summer at 39 city parks. The mobile stage was designed by Ming Cho Lee and paid for by George T. Delacorte. It is an Elizabethan stage patterned after the one at the Stratford Festival in Ontario.

480. Zolotow, Sam. "Festival in Park Gets New Hamlet." *New York Times*, June 18, 1964, 28:1.

Robert Burr, understudy for Richard Burton who is playing Hamlet on Broadway, appeared as the lead in the NYSF's production of the play. He is substituting for Alfred Ryder, who has laryngitis.

481. "Robert Burr Hailed by Critics for His Hamlet in Central Park." *New York Times*, June 19, 1964, 36:1.

Robert Burr, substituting for Alfred Ryder in the title role of the NYSF's production of *Hamlet*, has received "unstinting critical praise" for his performance.

482. "The Return of Ryder as Hamlet Blocked." *New York Times*, June 25, 1964, 26:2.

Papp will not allow Alfred Ryder to resume his lead role in the NYSF's production of *Hamlet*. When Ryder was unable to continue in the role after his opening performance because of laryngitis, Robert Burr took his place. Papp and Ryder have had a falling out because of an alleged remark by Papp that he was "sorry to have engaged Mr. Ryder."

483. "Portable Stage Set Up in Mount Morris Park." *New York Times*, June 26, 1964, 32:1.

A crew of 18 people set up the NYSF's mobile theater stage in Mount Morris Park at Fifth Avenue and 120th Street. The first production will be *A Midsummer Night's Dream*.

484. Calta, Louis. "Bottom, Puck & Co. at Harlem Park." *New York Times*, June 27, 1964, 15:1.

The NYSF presented *A Midsummer Night's Dream* on its new mobile stage at Harlem's Mount Morris Park last night, the first of its 58 performances to be given at 39 city parks this summer. Seating for 1,600 was provided.

485. Zolotow, Sam. "Mobile Theater Rallies Neighborhoods." *New York Times,* July 2, 1964, 25:2.

Sophronus Mundy, a senior at Hunter College, has been directing a campaign to win the support of neighborhood organizations for the NYSF's free Shakespeare performances. Mundy, who is paid $85 a week by the Festival, recruits neighborhood talent to entertain audiences before the play begins. He also finds volunteers to act as ushers.

486. Zolotow, Sam. "Mobile Theater to Visit Longer." *New York Times*, July 10, 1964, 17:1.

Papp plans to have his company perform for one or two weeks, instead of two days, next summer at selected city parks. This summer, in addition to *A Midsummer Night's Dream*, the NYSF will present two plays in Spanish. Irving Maidman, chairman of the Mayor's Festival Committee, disclosed that the cost of the Festival's entire operation this year is $750,000. Sixty thousand dollars of this amount still needs to be raised.

487. Taubman, Howard. "A New Audience." *New York Times,* July 12, 1964, sec. 2, 1:1.

With his new mobile theater, Papp is seeking out audiences that do not go to see Shakespeare in the Park. The NYSF is traveling through the city and performing before audiences that have rarely, if ever, seen a live play.

488. "Audience Reaction Studied on Shakespeare Tour Here." *New York Times*, July 22, 1974, 36:1.

The Twentieth Century Fund is sponsoring a study to investigate what the audiences experience when they watch *A Midsummer Night's Dream* being performed in their neighborhoods in the open-air.

489. Shepard, Richard F. "Harlem Festival of Arts Proposed." *New York Times*, Aug. 22, 1964, 13:4.

Papp, impressed by the audience turnout for *A Midsummer Night's Dream* in Mount Morris Park, has suggested that a Harlem cultural festival of music, dance, and drama be held next summer. A committee, headed by Actors' Equity president Frederick O'Neal, has been set up to explore this proposal.

490. "Vandals Assault Theater in Park." *New York Times*, Aug. 29, 1964, 9:4.

For the fourth time in nine weeks, egg-throwing vandals have forced the closing of the NYSF;'s production of *A Midsummer Night's Dream.* The attack took place in Chelsea Park at Tenth Avenue and Twenty-eighth Street. Cast member David C. Jones estimated that there had been scores of incidents involving eggs, rocks and firecrackers during the company's tour.

491. Ashforth, Albert. "Papp Presents Mobile Theater in Spanish on Central Park Mall." *New York Times,* Sep. 3, 1964, 23:2.

Papp's Spanish theater, an extension of the Mobile Theater that toured city parks this summer, is touring New York's Spanish speaking communities with two Garcia Lorca plays.

492. Zolotow, Sam. "Papp Is Planning Expansion in '65." *New York Times*, Sep. 7, 1964, 10:1.

Papp is hoping to obtain $1 million from the federal government, New York City, foundations, and provide sources for the NYSF's expanded program next year. In addition to three Shakespeare plays at the Delacorte, the Mobile Theater's tour would be longer, and a cultural festival would be held in Harlem. Papp plans to produce a Spanish version of *Romeo and Juliet* for Spanish speaking neighborhoods. The Festival's activities this summer cost $784,000. This fall the troupe will perform *A Midsummer Night's Dream* in city schools.

493. "Shakespeare Fete Licenses Its *Othello* to 2 Producers." *New York Times*, Sep. 28, 1964, 21:4.

The NYSF will receive a licensing fee of $250 a week for 10 weeks for allowing its production of *Othello* to be shown at the Martinique Theater. Gladys Vaughan will again direct.

494. Little, Stuart W. "Papp Taking Trip to Europe, to See Bard's Birthplace." *New York Herald Tribune*, Oct. 14, 1964, 18:6.

Papp and his wife will travel to Europe this month to see several Shakespeare companies on their home ground. The Papps will be accompanied by Joseph B. Martinson, chairman of the board of the NYSF, and Bernard Gersten, associate producer.

495. "City College Presents Finley Award to Papp." *New York Times*, Nov. 11, 1964, 34:2.

City College honored Papp with its annual John H. Finley Award for significant service to the city. Papp has also received the Tony Award for Distinguished Service to the Theater and the Shakespeare Club of New York City Award for bringing Shakespeare to the city.

496. Little, Stuart W. "Papp's European Tour Strengthens His Convictions." *New York Herald Tribune*, Nov. 17, 1964, 17:3.

After a month in Europe where he saw more than 30 productions, Papp is convinced of the necessity of a permanent theater company. He was most impressed with the Royal Shakespeare Company and the Brechtian Berliner Ensemble.

497. "Gerald Freedman to Join Papp as Festival Director." *New York Times*, Nov. 23, 1964, 52:1.

Director and composer Gerald Freedman will share the position of artistic director of the NYSF with Papp.

498. Funke, Lewis. "Patient Recovering." *New York Times*, Nov. 29, 1964, sec. 2, 1.

Papp received a check for $94,000 from the Ford Foundation. When he called the foundation he learned that the check should have been sent to the American Shakespeare Festival of Stratford Connecticut.

499. Little, Stuart. W. "Papp's Shakespeare Plans—Three Plays in Park and Five on Tour." *New York Herald Tribune,* Nov. 30, 1964, 15.

The NYSF's 11th season will include three plays at the Delacorte Theater and five plays by the Mobile Theater. This ambitious schedule requires 110 actors and a budget of $825,000. Papp is asking the city for $400,000.

500. Zolotow, Sam. "$825,000 Budget Proposed by Papp." *New York Times*, Nov. 30, 1964, 43:1.

Papp estimates that $825,000 will be needed for the NYSF's 1965 season. Four hundred thousand dollars will be requested from the city and the rest will come from contributors. In addition to the three plays at the Delacorte Theater, two Shakespeare plays will be performed by the Mobile Theater. The Mobile Theater will also present a children's play and a play in Spanish. The company will tour the schools next year with *Henry V*. Papp has applied to the board of ANTA to occupy their Washington Square Theater next summer when the Lincoln Center's repertory company moves to its permanent home, the Vivian Beaumont Theater.

1965

501. Zolotow, Sam. "Papp Approached for Kazan's Post." *New York Times*, Jan. 12, 1965, 32:1.

The position of artistic director of the Lincoln Center Repertory Theater has been offered to Papp by the repertory's board. Elia Kazan resigned last month from the post. Papp is willing to accept the assignment if the NYSF can perform in the Vivian Beaumont Theater during the winter seasons until the construction of a permanent home in the proposed downtown civic center.

502. "Repertory Offer to Papp Disowned." *New York Times*, Jan. 13, 1965, 36:2.

Robert L. Hoquet, Jr., president of the Repertory Theater of Lincoln Center, denied reports that Papp has been offered the post of artistic director of the company. Papp's discussions with board member Michael Burke were only exploratory, according to Hoquet.

503. Zolotow, Sam. "Specialist Added to Play Program." *New York Times*, Jan. 13, 1965, 37:1.

Papp announced a three part program aimed at bringing theater to poor neighborhoods, at the annual meeting of the Mayor's Committee for Free Shakespeare. A series of lecture demonstrations, designed by theater education specialist Esther Jackson, will be given in Brooklyn's depressed communities. Apprentices will be picked from poor neighborhoods and trained as performers and administrators for the Festival. Free bus service will be provided from poor neighborhoods to previews at the Delacorte Theater.

504. Zolotow, Sam. "$200,000 Pledged for Papp Theater." *New York Times*, Feb. 4, 1965, 24:1.

Papp announced that he has been promised $200,000 to operate a 299 seat repertory theater. Papp will not name the donor or the theater until the gift arrangements are completed. The first productions at the year-round theater will be *The Wild Duck, Blood Wedding*, and *Edward II*. Admission will be charged at the playhouse.

505. Shepard, Richard F. "Papp Disagrees with Fund Study." *New York Times*, Apr. 13, 1965, 32:2.

A report of a study of NYSF's audiences concluding that lower class audiences differed from middle and upper class audiences in their responses to *A Midsummer Night's Dream* drew some negative comments from Papp. The study, which was paid for by the Twentieth Century Fund and conducted by the Columbia University Bureau of Applied Social Research, had two researchers observe audiences' reactions at 57 free performances given by the Festival's Mobile Theater. Papp said that his company had not noticed any "essential differences between Negro and white, between middle and lower income audiences."

506. "ANTA Honors Papp at Annual Meeting." *New York Times*, Apr. 26, 1965, 39:2.

The American National Theatre and Academy presented Papp with an award for his "outstanding contribution to the art of the living theater."

507. "Dinner to Provide Funds for School." *New York Times*, May 3, 1965, 40:1.
The Center for New York City Affairs of the New School for Social Research will present its first Medallion for Distinguished Service to New York City to Papp at the Plaza Hotel.

508. Zolotow, Sam. "$224,285 Is Raised by Park Festival." *New York Times*, May 13, 1965, 31:4.
Although the NYSF has received $224,285 in contributions from some 7,700 donors, it still needs an additional $679,715 for this year' season. The Board of Estimate will vote on an appropriation of $400,000 later this month.

509. "Spanish Theater Expanding in City." *New York Times*, June 1, 1965, 42:5.
Argentinian actor and director Osvaldo Riofrancos founded the El Primer Teatro Espanol several years ago with $750. Using teenagers from the Spanish-speaking communities in New York City, Riofrancos has been presenting a dozen street productions every summer since 1962. Papp saw one show in 1964 and arranged for the Spanish Mobile Theater to become part of the NYSF. This summer a Spanish version of *Romeo and Juliet* will be presented in Central Park.

510. "Quality of Mercy Is Shown to Park Festival Audiences." *New York Times*, June 7, 1965, 49:3.

Tickets for free Shakespeare plays at the Delacorte Theater will now start to be distributed at noon, rather than at 6:00 p.m. This should eliminate the long wait prospective theatergoers had to endure in previous summers.

511. Fremont-Smith, Eliot. "Poets Take Over Actors' Domain." *New York Times*, June 22, 1965, 26:7.

"An Evening of Poetry in the Park" played before 1,000 people last night at the Delacorte Theater. It was the first in a series of experimental programs to be presented Monday evenings when the theater is not presenting a Shakespeare play.

512. Barthel, Joan. "Who Threw the Rocks?" *New York Times*, June 27, 1965, sec. 2, 1:1.

In discussing the Festival's tour of city parks, Papp denies that his purpose is to enrich the lives of the poor. Instead, he is attracted by the different kind of audience that constantly challenges the actor. He agrees with the part of a report published by the Twentieth Century Fund that blames last year's rock throwing on teenage gangs resentful of the takeover of their territory by the Mobile Theater. In hopes of cutting down on this kind of incident, two people have been hired to make contact with neighborhood groups including the police and gangs.

513. Calta, Louis. "Shakespeare Rolls into Chelsea Park." *New York Times*, July 3, 1965, 10:5.

The NYSF's Mobile Theater is presenting an improvisational teenage show, as well as *The Taming of the Shrew*, on its tour of the five boroughs. Last night the company played to a crowd of several hundred people at the Chelsea Park Playground. The teenage show, called "We Real Cool," is an attempt to attract children to live theater.

514. "Islanders Songs Pack a Theater." *New York Times,* Aug. 24, 1965, 26:2.

Last night the NYSF presented "An Evening of Puerto Rican Poetry and Folk Music" to an enthusiastic audience of over 2,300 people. The Spanish language show was performed at the Delacorte Theater.

515. Calta, Louis. "Students Enjoy Touring *Henry V.*" *New York Times*, Oct. 19, 1965, 50:1.

The NYSF will present 70 performances of *King Henry V* at 38 city schools during the next 10 weeks. This is the fifth season of the school tour and will cost about $82,000. The New York City Board of Education will pay $50,000 of this amount.

1966

516. Huxtable, Ada Louise. "A Landmark Is Saved." *New York Times*, Jan. 6, 1966, 29:6.

The old Astor Library is the first building to be declared a landmark under New York City's 18 month old landmarks law. The building, which was destined for destruction only six months ago, was saved by the Landmarks Preservation Commission when it persuaded Papp to buy the library for a permanent home for his company. The building, which was completed in 1854, has not been used since 1911.

517. Little, Stuart W. "Astor Library to House Papp's Festival." *New York Herald Tribune*, Jan. 6, 1966, 17.

Beginning in March, the 113 year old Astor Library will become the headquarters for the NYSF. During the winter the group will perform modern plays and classics in the two theaters that are to be constructed inside the Astor Library. The capital funds needed for the acquisition and conversion of the landmark building come to $2,375,000. August Hechscher, executive director of the Twentieth Century Fund, has agreed to head a select committee to assist in the planning and fund raising for the theater. The three story building, which had been earmarked for demolition by a real estate developer who planned to erect a modern apartment building, was saved by the Landmarks Preservation Commission.

518. Shepard. Richard F. "Shakespeare Festival to Acquire Old Astor Library for a Theater." *New York Times,* Jan. 6, 1966, 29:2.

The NYSF is in the process of buying the 112 year old Astor Library at 425 Lafayette Street for its permanent home. The company expects to pay about half a million dollars for the building, which is owned by the United Hebrew Sheltering and Immigrant Aid Society of America. Papp estimates that $1.8 million will be needed to renovate the building, which will include two theaters, a children's stage, rehearsal halls and offices. The first phase of construction, a 200 seat theater, should be completed in time for the first season of performances in October. Admission prices of $2.50 to $3.00 will be charged, but the Festival's plays in Central Park and other neighborhood sites will remain free. The city is being asked to appropriate $100,000 toward the $320,000 needed to build the first theater. This is in addition to the $400,000 it provides annually for the Festival's other programs.

519. Calta, Louis. "Park Troupe Sets $1.3 Million Goal." *New York Times*, Jan. 12, 1966, 29:4.

The NYSF celebrated its 12th anniversary with 100 Festival supporters at the Harkness House for the Ballet Arts. The troupe's 1966 budget includes expenditures of $1.3 million. Part of this sum is earmarked for establishing the company at the 112 year old Astor Library. A total of $1.8 million will be needed to renovate the Victorian structure.

520. Taubman, Howard. "Arts Conference Begins in Chicago." *New York Times*, Jan. 28, 1966, 47:1.

Representatives from the States, Puerto Rico, and Canada gathered in Chicago for a conference on public patronage of the arts. Papp, one of three representatives from New York, will address the group.

521. Little, Stuart W. "Shakespeare Festival Takes Title to Astor Library Home." *New York Herald Tribune,* Feb. 10, 1966, 15:4.

The NYSF has taken title to its new winter home in the old Astor Library. The total purchase price of the 113 year old building was $575,000. The Festival has put down $115,000 and expects the rest will come from a proposed three year capital fund of $2,375,000 for the purchase and conversion of the building. The architect is Giorgio Cavaglieri, best known for his conversion of the Jefferson Market Courthouse into a branch library.

522. Little, Stuart W. "$12.5 Million, 5-Year Plan." *New York Herald Tribune*, Mar. 15, 1966, 16:3.

A five year program budgeted at $12.5 million will make the NYSF the largest, most expensive, and farthest reaching theatrical organization in the country. For the first time, Papp plans to extend Festival activities beyond city limits. He is planning a 20 week annual tour of some of the 58 upstate New York universities.

523. "Papp Productions Face Budget Cut." *New York Times*, Apr. 16, 1966, 30:4.

Mayor Lindsay's budget for this year includes only $300,000 for the NYSF, $100,000 less than the city's appropriation last year. Papp had asked for $500,000. The mayor hopes to raise additional funds for the Festival from philanthropic sources. Papp advised the mayor by letter that if the city's appropriation is not raised, the Spanish language presentation and the children's plays will have to be eliminated. The length of the school tour will be cut in half and one production will be dropped from the Central Park program. Parks Commissioner Hoving expressed his unhappiness with the amount allocated to the Festival.

524. Strongin, Theodore. "Lindsay Proposes Arts Foundation." *New York Times,* Apr. 21, 1966, 41:1.

In a speech at a dinner celebrating the beginning of the second decade of Lincoln Center for the Performing Arts, Mayor Lindsay proposed the establishment of a city foundation for the arts and humanities. Concerning the $100,000 reduction in city funds for the NYSF, Lindsay said, "We are making progress toward the replacement of the budget cut with private funds."

525. "Papp Asks Lindsay to Restore Funds." *New York Times*, Apr. 26, 1966, 54:1.

Papp appealed to Mayor Lindsay for 65 minutes to persuade the city to appropriate half a million dollars for the NYSF, rather than the $300,000 proposed by the Board of Estimate. The mayor reiterated his promise to raise the additional money from private sources. Papp plans to appeal to the Board of Estimate in early May.

526. "Shakespeare Group Plans Dance Show." *New York Times*, June 4, 1966, 18:2.

A one hour song and dance show for children will tour the city this summer along with the Mobile Theater's production of *Macbeth*. The children's show, called *Potluck!*, contains works by such major choreographers as Bob Fosse and Lotte Gosler.

527. "Energetic Impresario Gets His Own Repertory." *Times* [London], June 6, 1966, 14:1.

In November Papp will begin running his own repertory theater. It will be heavily subsidized, but for the first time he will have to charge admission—half of the cost of each seat. His top price will be three dollars. Papp is also working on an arrangement to take a touring company around the campuses of the State University of New York. This would supplement the other services Papp offers the community: the Mobile Theater that tours the city, a troupe that tours city schools, and the summer productions of Shakespeare in Central Park. The city's donation to these projects has just been cut, but Papp will probably succeed in raising the funds elsewhere.

528. Zolotow, Sam. "Amplification for Shakespeare." *New York Times*, June 7, 1966, 53:3.

Fifteen thousand dollars of new sound equipment was installed at the Delacorte Theater in response to complaints that dialogue could not be heard in certain parts of the theater whenever planes flew by. The cost of the new system will be paid for by the New York City Parks Department, George T. Delacorte, and the NYSF.

529. Bender, Marilyn. "Society Dresses Up, but Just Barely, à la Shakespeare." *New York Times*, June 14, 1966, 40:2.

Five hundred people attended a benefit supper dance for the NYSF at the Plaza Hotel last night. The proceeds will go toward the conversion of the old Astor Library into a permanent theater for the company.

530. "Shakespeare's Characters Enrich Outside of Theater." *New York Times*, June 17, 1966, 37:3.

Twenty-four foot square panels depicting major Shakespearean characters in black and white silhouette were installed on the exterior of the Delacorte Theater. The installation of the art works was paid for by George T. Delacorte.

531. Zolotow, Sam. "$25,000 Granted to Papp Festival." *New York Times*, June 27, 1966, 40:1.

The Old Dominion Foundation's contribution of $25,000 to the NYSF is the largest single gift so far this year. The money will be used for the conversion of the Astor Library to a permanent theater. Papp estimates that $1.3 million is needed this year for the Festival's various productions and projects.

532. "Papp to Teach at Yale." *New York Times*, July 28, 1966, 22:6.

The dean of the Yale School of Drama named Papp adjunct professor of play production. In addition to supervising student workshop productions, Papp will teach a course on acting.

533. Ickeringill, Nan. "A Loaf of Bread, a Jug of Wine, and Free Entertainment in Central Park." *New York Times*, Aug. 1, 1966, 31:1.

Theatergoers lining up at the Delacorte Theater for the distribution of free tickets to begin, generally pass the time by picnicking. One reporter's survey found chicken to be the most popular food.

534. Raymont, Henry. "$1.8 Million Given by Arts Council." *New York Times*, Aug. 30, 1966, 1:7.

The National Council on the Arts has made a $100,000 grant to the NYSF. The grant requires that it be matched by other funds.

535. Zolotow, Sam. "Library to House Small Theaters." *New York Times*, Aug. 31, 1966, 37:1.

Papp has cancelled his plan to build a 800 seat theater in the old Astor Library because of time and money. Instead, two smaller auditoriums will be built—one with 300 seats and one with 150 seats.

536. "Papp Advises Los Angeles." *New York Times*, Nov. 1, 1966, 33:2.

Papp left for California to advise a Los Angeles civic group on setting up a free Shakespearean program similar to that of the NYSF.

537. Zolotow, Sam. "Papp to Present $2 Million Budget." *New York Times*, Dec. 5, 1966, 66:1.

The NYSF's budget for 1967, which is $786,000 more than this year's budget, will be presented to Mayor Lindsay and Thomas P.F. Hoving, head of the New York City Recreation and Cultural Affairs Administration. The city will be asked to appropriate half of the $2 million, while the remainder will be raised by donations. Half a million dollars will be used for the construction of two theaters in the old Astor Library. The opening of these two theaters has been delayed until September 1967.

1967

538. Zolotow, Sam. "Planning for Shakespeare." *New York Times*, Jan. 10, 1967, 33:1.

Mayor Lindsay's Committee for Free Shakespeare will meet today at Gracie Mansion to start the drive for funds for the NYSF. This year's budget of $2,086,032 is the highest in the Festival's 12 year history. Papp is planning productions in the two theaters in the Astor Library in addition to three plays in Central Park, a tour of the five boroughs by the Mobile Theater, and a tour of the city schools.

539. "Lindsay Solicits Funds for Free Shakespeare." *New York Times*, Apr. 11, 1967, 50:5.

Mayor Lindsay spoke to a group of businessmen and show business representatives at a fund raising luncheon at the Harvard Club.

540. Taubman, Howard. "Papp on Lafayette St." *New York Times*, Apr. 25, 1967, 40:1.

In addition to all his other NYSF responsibilities, Papp is supervising the creation of two theaters in the Astor Library. The first theater, whose name will be the Anspacher Theater, will seat 300 in three tiers around a thrust stage. A second theater, a music hall, a dance hall, a children's theater, and a picture gallery are also being planned. Prices at the theater will be kept to a maximum of $2.50.

541. Shepard, Richard F. "City Arts Groups Meet for a Chat." *New York Times*, Apr. 19, 1967, 24:4.

Papp and other Festival staff people met with 30 representatives from city, community, and social agencies to discuss the handling of children at the Mobile Theater shows. Suggestions included involving more neighborhood groups, using more ushers, and better preparing of audiences. No one advised barring children from attending shows.

542. Bender, Marylin, "Some Social Butterflies Are Turning into Industrious Moths." *New York Times*, May 7, 1967, 90:3.

New York socialites have taken up the cause of the NYSF. Several gala benefits last year raised thousands of dollars for the Festival. A benefit opening of *The Comedy of Errors* and a supper dance at the Astor Library are just two of many fund raising activities planned for this year. Papp estimates that these kinds of parties raise 20% to 25% of his budget.

543. Zolotow, Sam. "Summer Dramas Curtailed by City." *New York Times*, May 24, 1967, 54:1.

The New York City Board of Estimate has appropriated $151,000 less for the NYSF than the $524,000 Papp had requested for this year's budget. If Papp cannot get the necessary funds from the city he will cancel the Spanish production of *Volpone*, the public school production of *Hamlet*, and reduce the Mobile Theater's season from ten to eight weeks. Last year, after the Board of Estimate failed to come through with sufficient funds, the National Council on the Arts came to the rescue with an emergency grant of $100,000.

544. "Papp to Get $27,000 More for Free Shakespeare." *New York Times,* May 25, 1967, 57:4.

Hechscher announced that the city will give the NYSF an additional $27,000 for its summer programs. This money will come from the funds originally allocated to the Metropolitan Opera for six operas in the park.

545. "Foundations Give Mobile Theaters Funds for Season." *New York Times*, June 5, 1967, 52:1.

The Rebekah Harkness Foundation has given the NYSF $40,000 for its production of *Lallapalooza*, a children's play.

546. "Tickets to Be $2.50 at 2 Papp Theaters." *New York Times*, June 9, 1967, 50:2.

Tickets for the two 300 seat theaters in the old Astor Library will cost $2.50. The Florence Sutro Anspacher Theater is scheduled to open October 26 with *Hair*, a new musical. The Estelle R. Newman Theater will open with *The Memorandum* in March of next year. Only new plays concerned with modern themes will be produced at these theaters.

547. Calta, Louis. "3 Troupes Share $695,000 Grants." *New York Times*, July 11, 1967, 27:1.

The National Council on the Arts has awarded the NYSF $250,000 in partial support of its 1967-68 season of contemporary plays in the newly acquired Astor Library.

548. Shepard, Richard F. "In Central Park Sholom Aleichem Is Also a Bard." *New York Times,* July 18, 1967, 29:1.

The NYSF presented an evening of Yiddish poetry, readings, and folk music to a crowd of 2,300 last night. The program was directed by Bernard Gersten.

549. Lask, Thomas. "Poems and Songs by Negroes in Park." *New York Times*, Aug. 15, 1967, 32:1.

The NYSF presented a program entitled, "Poetry and Folk Music of American Negroes," at the Delacorte Theater last night as part of its special Monday night series.

550. "Papp Eliminates a *Volpone* and Cuts Schools' *Hamlet*." *New York Times*, Aug. 16, 1967, 46:5.

The NYSF was forced to eliminate its Spanish version of *Volpone* from its mobile tour due to lack of funds. In order to save additional money, *Hamlet* will be performed in schools this autumn with 12 actors instead of 20.

551. Zolotow, Sam. "Subscription Sales Encourage 4 Theater Producing Troupes." *New York Times*, Oct. 5, 1967, 46:4.

The NYSF's new Public Theater, which has limited its subscriptions to 10,000, has already sold 9,648 season tickets.

552. Van Gelder, Laurence. "'Village' Theater Nearing Reality." *New York Times*, Oct. 6, 1967, 33:1.

The Anspacher Theater, the first of three planned theaters in the old Astor Library, will open on October 17 with a new musical, *Hair*. Papp hopes that all three theaters will be in operation within 18 months. A hall for chamber music and dance programs is also planned.

553. Shepard, Richard F. "Multidedications Open Papp House." *New York Times*, Oct. 11, 1967, 39:1.

The box office of the new Public Theater opened yesterday and sold twenty tickets for $2.50 each. The first production will be *Hair*, which will open October 17. Numerous plaques were unveiled throughout the building dedicating specific areas of the complex.

554. Sullivan, Dan. "'Papp Is a Love Person.'" *New York Times*, Oct. 15, 1967, sec. 2, 1:6.

The new Public Theater is a merger of three buildings designed between 1849 and 1881. The center building, formerly the Astor Library's main reading room, is now the Anspacher Theater, a 299 seat thrust stage theater.

555. "Papp Interpretation of 5 by Shakespeare Put in Book Series." *New York Times*, Oct. 17, 1967, 52:1.

Macmillan Company will publish two books a year by Papp on his interpretation, scene analyses, and rehearsal details of five plays by Shakespeare. The first book in the series, *Troilus and Cressida,* was published last July. Royalties from the sale of these books will go to the NYSF for its productions.

556. Huxtable, Ada Louise. "The Theater: *Hair,* a Love-Rock Musical, Inaugurates Shakespeare Festival's Anspacher Playhouse." *New York Times*, Oct. 30, 1967, 55:4.

The Anspacher Theater, the first of three planned theaters, opened last night with a new musical, *Hair*. The new playhouse is an architectural hit. Huxtable calls it "one of the most delightful small theaters in New York." The cost of converting the Astor Library's main reading room into the Anspacher was $445,000. The original hall has been left virtually intact. Victorian balustrades and columns have been restored to their original splendor.

557. Esterow, Milton. "Papp Says Crisis Threatens Fete." *New York Times*, Dec. 2, 1967, 48:1.

Papp accused Mayor Lindsay of being responsible for the NYSF's financial problems. The mayor, according to Papp, would prefer to have the Festival supported by private enterprise. Under the former mayor, Robert Wagner, the city's allocation to the Festival rose from $60,000 in 1961 to $402,000 in 1965. In 1966 and 1967 with Lindsay as mayor, the city allocated only $400,000 each year.

558. Zolotow, Sam. "Lindsay Upheld on Theater Fund." *New York Times*, Dec. 5, 1967, 59:1.

George T. Delacorte, president of Dell Publishing and one of the NYSF's major contributors, defended Mayor Lindsay against Papp's recent charges. Delacorte said that considering the greater financial difficulties confronting the mayor, he has done as much for the Festival as former Mayor Wagner.

1968

559. "Mayor Backs Drive for Papp's Theater." *New York Times*, Jan. 16, 1968, 25:1.

Papp held a meeting yesterday at the Public Theater to begin his annual fund drive for the NYSF. Mayor Lindsay spoke at the meeting and urged New Yorkers to be generous in their contributions. The Festival needs $1,575,000 for its 1968 programs.

560. Wardle. Irving. "*Hamlet* in Central Park." *Times* [London], Jan. 20, 1968, 19:1.

After reviewing Papp's life and career and the history of the NYSF, Wardle comments on the troupe's controversial rock version of *Hamlet*.

561. Zolotow, Sam. "School Aides Object to Papp's Modern *Hamlet*." *New York Times*, Jan. 22, 1968, 33:1.

Officials of the New York City Board of Education are objecting to the NYSF's controversial modern dress, rock music version of *Hamlet* that will be performed at city schools this year. Papp claims that the board has no right to censor the Festival's production. The issue will be decided after a special matinee of the play next week when several members of the board will serve as judges. They will be advised by 10 persons selected by the Festival and the board's Bureau of Audio-Visual Instruction.

562. Calta, Louis. "Papp Says City Aide Suggested a Fee for Shakespeare in the Park." *New York Times*, Jan. 24, 1968, 38:1.

In a talk at the Woman's City Club, Papp said that a high city official suggested that the NYSF charge admission to its free plays in Central Park to help defray some of the operating costs. The Festival's budget this year for its Shakespeare in the Park program is $525,000.

563. Severo, Richard. "Papp Gives *Hamlet* to Catch Conscience of School Board." *New York Times*, Jan. 31, 1968, 43:1.

The NYSF gave a special matinee performance of a controversial version of *Hamlet* yesterday for an audience composed of school officials, teachers, and students. Certain members of the audience had been chosen to act as judges in deciding whether this avant-garde production is suitable for touring city schools this year. In this modern dress version of Shakespeare's play, Hamlet is dressed in only his underwear, while his ghost father wears sneakers and Ophelia sports a miniskirt. The play opened at the Public Theater last month and received mixed reviews. Clive Barnes called it "incompetent" and "aimless." Walter Kerr wrote in his review that this production is "exactly like the shows idiot children used to put on in their basements."

After the play, Papp acted as moderator of a discussion among members of the audience on the production's merits. He cut short teachers' criticisms, saying he did not want their advice on directing.

564. Zolotow, Sam. "*Hamlet* Cleared for School Tour." *New York Times*, Feb. 8, 1968, 39:1.

Over objections of Board of Education officials, Bernard E. Donovan, superintendent of schools, authorized Papp to tour 50 to 60 city schools this year with his avant-garde production of *Hamlet*. In a letter to Papp, Donovan said his decision was based on reports from a committee of 10 judges representing teachers, students, and parents.

565. Zolotow, Sam. "Negro Will Play Hamlet for Papp." *New York Times*, Feb. 13, 1968, 49:1.

Black actor Cleavon Little has been picked to play the lead in Papp's avant-garde production of *Hamlet*. The play will be performed for high school students beginning in March.

566. "It's Spring, When Shakespeare Festival Casts for Summer." *New York Times*, Apr. 2, 1968, 52:1.

Artistic director of the NYSF. Gerald Freedman, is auditioning actors for parts I and II of *Henry IV*, which will be performed at the Delacorte Theater this summer.

567. "Whitney Museum Wins Bard Prize." *New York Times*, Apr. 26, 1968, 39:5.

The NYSF received a special landmarks preservation award from the Albert S. Bard Civic Award Trust Fund for its rehabilitation of the old Astor Library. Awards for excellence in architecture and urban design were given to the Ford Foundation, Whitney Museum, and vestpocket Paley Park.

568. Zolotow, Sam. "$400,000 for Papp Season." *New York Times*, May 8, 1968, 40:3.

According to Papp, the city plans to allocate $400,000 to the NYSF instead of the $600,000 he requested. The Festival's budget this year is $1.2 million.

569. Sullivan. Dan. "Papp Shakespeare Company Returns Tonight with *Henry IV*. *New York Times*, June 11, 1968, 52:2.

The NYSF is $270,000 in the red this year for its summer programs. *Henry IV*, part I, opening tonight at the Delacorte Theater, will be followed by *Henry IV*, part II, and *Romeo and Juliet*. The controversial pop-black-rock version of *Hamlet* will be performed at several city parks by the Mobile Theater.

570. Zolotow, Sam. "Mobile Theater on Way." *New York Times*, June 25, 1968, 31:2.

The NYSF's Mobile Theater begins its tour of the city parks tonight at Tompkins Square Park with an avant-garde production of *Hamlet*. Cleavon Little, a black actor, will portray the prince.

571. Lahr, John. "Rolling Along on Love—and Hope." *New York Times*, July 14, 1968, sec. 2, 1:7.

In spite of unruly audiences and financial problems. the Mobile Theater is still rolling along in the five boroughs. The troupe is performing *Take One Step*, a musical for children, in the afternoons, and Papp's controversial *Hamlet* in the evenings. Hamlet is being played by black actor Cleavon Little dressed in basketball shorts and knitted scarf. Much of Shakespeare's language has been replaced by street slang.

572. Klemesrud, Judy. "Everything's Coming up Roses for Romeo." *New York Times*, Aug. 11, 1968, sec. 2, 1:3.

An interview with actor Martin Sheen, who starred in Papp's productions of *Romeo and Juliet* and *Hamlet*. Sheen calls Papp a "marvelous man" and says that his theater is "the only one that has anything to give" in this country.

573. Zolotow, Sam. "Public Theater to Reopen Nov. 2." *New York Times*, Sep. 5, 1968, 54:1.

Papp will present three new American plays this season: *Huui, Huui* by Anne Olson Burr, *Cities in Bezique* by Adrienne Kennedy, and *Invitation to a Beheading* by Russell McGrath. A new policy of offering tickets at reduced prices to those under 25 will be introduced.

574. Barnes, Clive. "Papp's Enterprises: Sound Art and Shaky Finances." *New York Times*, Dec. 7, 1968, 62:1.

Despite the NYSF's $300,000 a year deficit, Papp vigorously defends the creation of the Public Theater, which he calls "an absolute and undeniable artistic necessity" for his company.

575. "Theatrical Beggars." Editorial. *New York Times*, Dec. 11, 1968, 46:2.

Urges the National Endowment for the Arts, private foundations, and the public to support the NYSF and the APA-Phoenix Repertory Company.

576. "Music Series Arranged by Shakespeare Festival." *New York Times*, Dec. 20, 1968, 63:4.

Four free concerts will be presented by the NYSF and radio station WBAI at Martinson Hall in the Public Theater. As there are no seats in the hall, those attending are encouraged to bring pillows.

577. Shepard, Richard, "Pupils Exhibit Poignant Art on Teachers' Strike." *New York Times*, Dec. 24, 1968, 12:1.

Drawings, sculpture, compositions, and poetry created by school children depicting the teachers' strike are on display in the lobby of the Public Theater. Between 600 and 800 children participated in the art project, which was organized by the Center for Urban Education.

1969

578. Calta, Louis. "City Plans to Buy Papp's Playhouse." *New York Times*, Jan. 16, 1969, 47:2.

Mayor Lindsay announced that New York City is negotiating to buy the Public Theater from the NYSF for $3.5 million and then lease it back to the company. This purchase would provide enough capital to complete the renovation and restoration of the building.

579. Funke, Lewis. "Langella—Shakespeare to Hamlet." *New York Times*, Feb. 23, sec. 2, 1:3.

Frank Langella will play the lead in *Hamlet* at the Delacorte Theater this summer. The NYSF will also present *Twelfth Night*, directed by Papp. Papp intends to set the play in the 1890s. A third play, *Peer Gynt*, will star Stacy Keach.

Papp announced that the city seems serious about buying the Public Theater from the NYSF. It will cost $2.5 million to complete the Estelle R. Newman Theater and a small recital hall.

580. Kerr, Walter. "Were You There All the Time?" *New York Times*, March 30, 1969, sec. 2, 1:1.

Kerr believes that the productions at the Public Theater fail to recognize their audiences. Every play has the same fundamental tone with "a metallic look, sound and feel to it." Audiences are never drawn into the plays.

581. Calta, Louis. "Papp to Curtail Festival Season." *New York Times*, Apr. 21, 1969, 58:1.

The NYSF will offer two plays rather than the usual three at the Delacorte Theater this summer because of city budget cutbacks and a decline in private donations. The troupe will also eliminate the Mobile Theater's children's show to save more money.

582. Zolotow, Sam. "Papp to Produce *Cressida*, Rock Opera." *New York Times*, Apr. 23, 1969, 40:1.

Papp and Galt MacDermot are collaborating on a rock opera based on Shakespeare's *Troilus and Cressida*, which will be presented at the Public Theater next season. According to Papp, operatic singing usually obliterates Shakespeare's words while rock makes them "stand out."

583. Calta, Louis. "Summer Outs and Ins." *New York Times,* April 28, 1969, 36:2.

Although the NYSF is cutting its summer program because of financial problems, it is adding a fourth play *No Place to Be Somebody*, to its indoor season at the Public Theater. The play is by a young black writer, Charles Gordone, who was discovered by Papp.

584. Nemy, Enid. "For Men: A Mixture of Fashion and Fantasy." *New York Times*, May 13, 1969, 36:1.

The NYSF's annual benefit, a supper dance at the Public Theater, raised more than $47,000. The featured entertainment was a men's fashion show of fantasy costumes by some four dozen designers.

585. Riley, Clayton. "O' Blacks, Are We Damned Forever?" *New York Times*, May 18, 1969, sec. 2, 22:1.

Black critic Clayton Riley discusses the difficulties of having white producers and directors present plays by black writers. More specifically, Riley attacks Papp and director Ted Cornell for the problems with the play *No Place to Be Somebody.*

586. Calta, Louis. "Public Theater Given $400,000 by Rockefellers." *New York Times*, June 6, 1969, 32:4.

The Rockefeller Foundation awarded the NYSF the largest grant in the company's 15-year history. The $400,000 will be used for the operation of the Public Theater over a three year period. In addition to its use for covering the costs of producing new plays, the grant will help to subsidize ticket prices.

587. Bosworth, Patricia. "From Nowhere to 'No Place.'" *New York Times*, June 8, 1969, sec. 2, 1:1.
Biographical article on black playwright Charles Gordone whose play *No Place to Be Somebody* is currently at the Public Theater. At age 43, Gordone became an overnight success when his play received rave reviews.

588. Berg, Beatrice. "'Find Me a Judy Collins.'" *New York Times*, July 6, 1969, sec. 2, 1:1.
An interview with folk singer Judy Collins about her acting debut in the NYSF's production of *Peer Gynt*.

589. Shepard, Richard F. "Papp Digging Theater Below Festival Building." *New York Times*, July 9, 1969, 32:1.
A new 300 seat amphitheater, which will be named the Newman Theater, is being constructed this summer at the Public Theater at a cost of $1.1 million. A 100 seat film auditorium is also being built. The two new playhouses will join the 300 seat Anspacher Theater and a 108 seat experimental theater which will open next month.

590. "ANTA Elects Officers." *New York Times*, Aug. 6, 1969, 29:2.
Papp was elected president of the American National Theatre and Academy.

591. Dennis, Landt. "Public Theatre: 'Art for People's Sake'." *Christian Science Monitor*, Oct. 6, 1969, 15:2.

Even though $1 million in debts is due in January on the Public Theatre, Papp refuses to let it bother him. He says "the problem of money has always been too enormous to worry about continually," in this article about the financing of the NYSF. With a top admission price of $3.50, the Public Theatre loses at least $1,000 a week. Fortunately, dividends from current Broadway, London, Los Angeles, and Sydney, Australia, productions of *Hair* lessen the losses. Papp's philosophy is to present only the best in dance, film, music, theater, and art. Believing this can best be achieved by his maintaining artistic control, he hires his board of directors whose role it is to support him.

592. Gussow, Mel. "On the Stage or Off, Troupe is United." *New York Times*, Oct. 31, 1969, 32:1.

A group of 23 white, middle class college students from the South are the performers of *Stomp*, a protest rock musical, that will open at the Public Theater next week.

The group and the show got started last winter at the University of Texas in Austin. Papp discovered *Stomp* last month in a basement theater at the Atlanta Arts Center.

593. "Communities Urged to Find Dramatists." *New York Times*, Dec. 12, 1969, 55:1.

At its third annual meeting, the National Theater Conference awarded Papp its 1969 citation for distinguished services.

1970

594. "Papp Resigns ANTA Posts, Citing Festival's Demands." *New York Times*, Jan. 23, 1970, 31:2.

Papp has resigned as president of the American National Theater and Academy, as well as from its board of directors. He was president of ANTA for a year. He cited as his reason for resigning the demands of the NYSF—its expanding program and the heavy debts he has to deal with.

595. Calta, Louis. "*Wars of Roses* Set for Staging in Park." *New York Times*, Mar. 6, 1970, 30:1.

The NYSF is planning to present Shakespeare's *Henry VI* and *Richard III* in its Central Park season. The plays together cover the Wars of the Roses, the fifteenth century English civil wars. This will be the costliest season yet of Central Park productions. The program will cost $500,000. The director for the productions will be Stuart Vaughan, who will be directing his first play for the NYSF since 1959.

596. Bender, Marilyn. "Women's Liberation Taking to the Stage." *New York Times*, Mar. 26, 1970, 60:1.

Two women have written and composed the first feminist musical, *The Mod Donna*, which opens May 1 at the Public Theater. It is being directed and produced by Papp. Myrna Lamb wrote the play and Susan Bingham composed the music.

597. Calta, Louis. "*Hair* Producer Wins *Stomp* Rights." *New York Times*, Apr. 10, 1970, 50:1.

The NYSF will take the protest musical *Stomp* on a four month tour of Europe. The tour begins May 21 in Paris, where it will be presented for nine days as the American entry at the Festival of Nations.

598. Kisselgoff, Anna. "Students Benefit in Rush-Ticket Plan." *New York Times*, Apr. 10, 1970, 50:1.

The Public Theater is one of several New York theaters participating in a rush program that allows students to pay lower prices for unfilled seats half a hour before performances. The NYSF feels that this is in keeping with its aim of reaching out to young, minority and poor audiences.

599. Gent, George. "*Applause* and Bacall Win Tonys." *New York Times*, Apr. 20, 1970, 47:1.

The NYSF and Papp won a special award at the 24th annual presentation of the Tonys.

600. Calta, Louis. "Arts Centers Urged to Rent Some of Their Space." *New York Times*, May 8, 1970, 37:1.

Papp is one of the nine members of the Twentieth Century Fund Taskforce on Performing Arts. It was established by the fund to recommend methods for planning and managing the facilities of the nation's art centers in light of their growing economic problems. The taskforce has just published a report which says that performing arts centers should rent part of their space to commercial ventures in order to improve their shaky financial situation.

601. Calta, Louis. "Cutback Imperils Park Shakespeare." *New York Times*, June 10, 1970, 38:1.

Because of New York's financial crisis the NYSF's summer season in Central Park may have to be cancelled. The Festival is too low on funds to meet its payroll and the city may not make up the shortfall. The City Council also refused to go along with Mayor Lindsay's request that the city acquire the old Astor Library and lease it back to the company. The NYSF needs capital funds to complete the renovation of the building. The purchase price requested is $3.5 million.

602. Calta, Louis. "Lien Threatened on Papp's Theater." *New York Times*, June 17, 1970, 38:1.

The Yorke Construction Company threatens to place a lien on the NYSF's Public Theater unless a bill of more than $400,000 for work on the Newman Theater is paid within a few days. This means that foreclosure proceedings for the sale of the theater building could be started. The performances in Central Park and the Mobile Theater are also threatened by a cut in city funds for those programs from $500,000 to $350,000. Papp has sent a telegram to Mayor Lindsay, who is attending the United States Conference of Mayors in Denver, to inform him of the gravity of the situation.

603. Calta, Louis. "City Seeks to Take Over Shakespeare Theater." *New York Times*, June 19, 1970, 26:1.

Deputy Mayor Richard Aurelio says that the city will attempt to take over the NYSF's Public Theater, but would not provide additional funds for the free Shakespeare performances in Central Park or the Mobile Theater that tours the city. Papp says that the summer festival will close after one week if he does not receive $200,000. Aurelio says that Papp was told two months ago that the extra funding would not be forthcoming. Papp denies that he learned about it before last week.

604. Calta, Louis. "State Promises $250,000 to Aid Papp Theater Plan." *New York Times*, June 20, 1970, 22:1.

Governor Rockefeller has offered $250,000 in state matching funds if the city acquires the NYSF's Public Theater. Dr. Louis C. Jones, the chairman of the New York State Historic Trust has notified Papp that the state can provide matching funds for the preservation or restoration of municipally-owned historic sites under the Municipal Grant-in-Aid Program. Deputy Mayor Richard Aurelio has already said that the mayor's office will ask the Board of Estimate and City Council for about $5 million to purchase the Public Theater.

605. "Shakespeare Marathon Is now Set for Saturday." *New York Times*, June 23, 1970, 38:1.

The NYSF will perform its dusk-to-dawn production of *Henry VI* and *Richard III* in Central Park on Saturday June 27 instead of July 25 as originally planned, because Papp believes that the cutback in city funds may close the season early.

606. "Shakespeare Festival Alarums." Editorial. *New York Times*, June 26, 1970, 40:2.

The fact that there may be no more free Shakespeare in Central Park after next week, unless more funds are forthcoming from the city, state and private sources, is lamented. The entire NYSF operations, including the Public Theater, are in jeopardy.

607. Clark, Alfred E. "All-Night Shakespeare Enthralls 3,000." *New York Times*, June 29, 1970, 1:1.

The NYSF gave a marathon performance of *Henry VI* and *Richard III* at the Delacorte Theater. The plays were put on to dramatize the NYSF's serious fiscal plight. The company needs another $200,000 to finish the current season in Central Park. The show started at 7pm and lasted 12 hours. At the end of the performance the actors received a 10 minute standing ovation.

608. Calta, Louis. "City Asks Funds to Buy Papp's Theater." *New York Times*, June 30, 1970, 48:2.

Mayor Lindsay will ask the Board of Estimate for about $5 million to buy the Public Theater from the NYSF and complete its restoration. Papp declares himself very happy with the proposal, but says that the company still needs $200,000 to complete the season in Central Park. If the Board of Estimate responds favorably to the Mayor's funding request, Papp hopes the Yorke Construction Corporation will delay imposing a lien against the theater building. Even after the popularity and media attention of the marathon performance of *Henry VI* and *Richard III* the only gift received was $500 from Actors Equity. If the Board of Estimate approves the Mayor's request more money will be forthcoming, as Governor Rockefeller has offered $250,000 in state matching funds if the city acquires the Public Theater.

609. "Papp's Theater Getting $100,000 in State Funds." *New York Times*, July 2, 1970, 28:1.
The State Council on the Arts will give the NYSF at least $100,000 immediately, thus allowing at least four more weeks of free performances in Central Park.

610. "Mayor Postpones Proposal for Buying Papp Theater." *New York Times*, July 3, 1970, 12:1.
Mayor Lindsay will submit his proposal to the Board of Estimate for the city's purchase of the Public Theater on July 23, instead of July 9 as he originally intended, because of a crowded agenda on the earlier date. Papp will, meanwhile, lobby the members of the Board of Estimate and City Council to appraise them of the NYSF's financial crisis and the danger to the landmark building.

611. "Papp Theater Deal Delayed." *New York Times*, July 23, 1970, 27:1.
Mayor Lindsay will not submit the budget modification for the proposed city purchase of the Public Theater to the Board of Estimate until September now. The proposal is still being drawn up by the Bureau of the Budget. Papp said 5,000 supporters of the NYSF would turn out today at City Hall in support of the Mayor's budget amendment.

612. "Jazz Used to Press Papp's Plea for Aid." *New York Times*, July 24, 1970, 20:1.

The NYSF sponsors a jazz concert with excerpts from the musical *Samba* to make a public plea for $100,000 to complete its summer program.

613. "Arts Council Authorizes $50,000 More to Papp." *New York Times*, July 31, 1970, 15:1.

The New York State Council on the Arts will give the NYSF another $50,000, in addition to the $100,000 committed to the Festival by the council last month.

614. Calta, Louis. "'Wars' in Park Get a Reprieve." *New York Times*, Aug. 1, 1970, 13:1.

The NYSF rescinded the August 9 closing date for *The War of the Roses* after the New York State Council on the Arts contributed a further $50,000 to the Festival. The run is extended through August 22. Papp thanked the council, but also expressed disappointment over the rejection of his request for $100,000 towards the company's upcoming season at the Public Theater. For next year Papp proposed that the city contribute $500,000 for an eight week season in Central Park and four weeks of touring the boroughs with the mobile unit.

615. Kisselgoff, Anna. "Feld Work Stands Out as Ballet in Park Begins." *New York Times*, Aug. 27, 1970, 41:5.

The ninth annual *New York Dance Festival* presented by the NYSF opened its run at the Delacorte Theater.

616. Silver, Lee. "Bard Sets New Play, Theater and Director." *New York Daily News*, Sep. 2, 1970, 72.

On September 29 the NYSF will open a second new theater at the Public. The Estelle R. Newman Theater, which has 299 seats, is named after a former trustee of the Festival board. The play that will inaugurate the Newman is *The Happiness Cage* by Dennis Reardon. It will be directed by Tom Aldredge.

617. Barnes, Clive. "Theater Here and in London Separated by Money." *New York Times*, Sep. 29, 1970, 37:1.

The main difference between British and American theater is not the productions, but the financial support given to theater in Britain by the government. Barnes uses the NYSF as an example of this argument. Papp is, as usual, trying to get financial support for his company. He is relatively lucky as it looks as if New York will accept responsibility for his building. The great danger to Papp, in Barnes' opinion, is that he has shown such a remarkable ability for escaping financial peril that one day his skill may be taken for granted and no help will be forthcoming.

618. Barnes, Clive. "Stage: Promising New Playwright in New Theater." *New York Times*, Oct. 5, 1970, 56:4.

The NYSF has opened the new Estelle R. Newman Theater in the Public Theater complex. It was designed by Georgio Cavaglieri and holds 300 people. The first production in the new theater is a new play *The Happiness Cage*, by a young playwright Dennis Reardon.

619. "Jail and Theater Plans." *New York Times*, Oct. 15, 1970, 50:1.

A public hearing is set for November 4 on the proposal that the city buy the Public Theater for $5.1 million.

620. "Shakespeare Theater Gets $250,000 Matching Grant." *New York Times*, Oct. 31, 1970, 59:4.

Governor Rockefeller announces that the NYSF will receive $250,000 in matching grants to aid historic sites. The grants will be used for the acquisition and restoration of the Public Theater by New York City.

621. Ranzal, Edward. "McGrath Asks New Light-Security Jail." *New York Times*, Nov. 5, 1970, 54:3.

The New York City Planning Commission approves a $5.1 million budget amendment for the city to purchase the Public Theater from the NYSF. Papp says that his company has spent $2.6 million in the acquisition and restoration of the building, and that $1 million is owed to the contractors. He also says that a further $2.5 million is needed to complete the restoration of the building, which houses a small cinema, four theaters and two concert halls. Papp expects the city to give him a long-term lease on the theater if the purchase goes through.

622. Canby, Vincent. "Now You Can See Invisible Cinema." *New York Times*, Nov. 29, 1970, sec. 2, 1:1.

The Anthology Film Archives, a museum devoted to "the film as art" is opening at the Public Theater. The NYSF is one of the sponsors of the project. The museum will include a 90-seat theater called the Invisible Cinema because the whole auditorium is black. The non-profit organization will be run by a board chosen jointly by the Film Art Fund and the NYSF.

623. Burks, Edward C. "Board of Estimate Rejects Plan to Aid Shakespeare Theater." *New York Times*, Dec. 4, 1970, 40:4.

The Board of Estimate voted yesterday against the plan to purchase the Public Theater from the NYSF for $5.1 million. The plan to assist the Festival included leasing the building back to them for a nominal sum. Papp said last night that he would submit the purchase plan to the city for the reduced price of $2.1 million, as he had no hope of finding a private buyer.

624. "Papp Has a Cutrate Program." *New York Post*, Dec. 4, 1970, 11:1.

Papp will submit a proposal to the Board of Estimate that the city buy the Public Theater for $2.1 million. This is $3 million less than the plan rejected yesterday by the board. City Council President Sanford Garelik called the Lindsay endorsed plan exorbitant. Both plans would have the city lease the theater to Papp for a nominal sum. Financial problems that include a debt of $500,000 to the contractor and a $360,000 mortgage are forcing Papp to find a buyer.

625. Calta, Louis. "Papp Cuts Bid to City for Theater Fund." *New York Times*, Dec. 15, 1970, 52:1.

Papp is now willing to sell the Public Theater for $2.6 million, almost half the original asking price. According to Papp the elimination of $2.5 million is based on the city's taking over the building in its present state of repair, which he claims is 90% operable. One million dollars of the purchase price would be used to pay off outstanding debts. The balance of $1.6 million would keep the NYSF afloat for two years. Papp also talks about his remuneration. His salary is $494.61 a week, determined by the Festival's board of trustees. From 1954, when the company was established, until 1960 he received no salary, but worked at CBS to support himself. In the last 10 years he had been offered many lucrative positions, but "the Public Theater and the Festival is my life—not a job."

626. Barnes, Clive. "A Plea to Save Papp's Public Theater." *New York Times*, Dec. 18, 1970, 49:1.

A Committee to Save the New York Shakespeare Festival has been formed under the leadership of Roger L. Stevens. Among those who have agreed to serve on it are Julie Harris, Basil Paterson and George C. Scott. Acceptances from other political and theatrical figures are expected. Papp says that if the Public Theater is lost the free Shakespeare in the Park will be badly affected. The actors would have nowhere to rehearse, the backstage facilities and workshops would be lost and the morale of the company greatly impaired.

627. "State Is Petitioned to Help Preserve Shakespeare Fete." *New York Times*, Dec. 23, 1970, 12:1.

The recently formed Committee to Save the New York Shakespeare Festival sent a telegram to Governor Rockefeller, asking him to help save the company and its Public Theater.

1971

628. Huxtable, Ada Louise. "Missing the Point (and Boat) at City Hall." *New York Times*, Jan. 3, 1971, sec. 2, 22:4.

The old Astor Library, now the NYSF's Public Theater, was entered in the National Register of Historic Places by the federal government at the end of December. At the same time the Board of Estimate decided not to purchase the theater. The city is about to lose an important creative resource and a wonderful theater.

629. "Theater Quarterly and Monthly Bow; Published by Papp." *New York Times*, Jan. 5, 1971, 43:1.

Two new theater magazines, *Performance* and *Scripts*, published by the NYSF are now available. *Performance*, a quarterly, contains contributions from playwrights, directors, drama critics and producers. *Scripts*, a monthly of plays and theater pieces, is edited by Erika Munk. The first issue offers plays by unknown as well as established writers. Papp says that the two publications are "feeding the development of a national theater."

630. Calta, Louis. "Kennedy Center Use Gets Mixed Review at Critic's Meeting." *New York Times*, Feb. 8, 1971, 23:5.

The question of whether the John F. Kennedy Center for the Performing Arts is suffering from an "identity crisis" was discussed at the monthly meeting of the Drama Desk, the association of New York theater critics, editors and reporters. Papp was present and said that "the greatest enemies of culture are those people in culture who have access to the media. I believe all artistic leaders should be left alone." Papp also said that he had been discussing with Roger L. Stevens, the Kennedy Center's board of trustees chairman, the possibility of creating a national theater. He had also asked for a meeting with President Nixon on the subject.

631. Calta, Louis. "Papp Shakespeare Unit to Offer Four New Works." *New York Times*, Feb. 13, 1971, 12:1.

The NYSF has an ambitious program this season. During the next two weeks it will offer four new works at the Public Theater simultaneously. It will also present a concert, a puppet show, a cycle of films on the history of motion pictures, and photographic workshops.

The Festival is still in danger though, as the Board of Estimate has not yet voted on Mayor Lindsay's proposal to buy the Public Theater for $2.6 million. The new amendment to be submitted to the Board was drawn up by August Heckscher, the

Parks, Recreation and Cultural Affairs Administrator. The company had also faced a January deadline for the final payment of the mortgage, $360,000, to the Hebrew Immigrant Aid Society. The mortgage holder has agreed however to extend the payment for one more year for $25,000 interest. To reduce the threat of a lien against the building Papp has also reached an agreement with the Yorke Construction Company to pay a construction bill of $400,000 over five years.

632. Henahan, Donal. "They've Gotta be Free." *New York Times*, Feb. 28, 1971, sec. 2, 15:4.

The Free Music Store, which has been giving free musical performances for three years, was performing in the Public Theater's Martinson Hall this season until the NYSF needed the space for a new production. The performances and enthusiasm of the crowd are described.

633. Burks, Edward C. "City Unit Backs Aid for Theater." *New York Times*, Mar. 11, 1971, 32:4.

The City Planning Commission approves the proposed city purchase of the Public Theater in a 5-0 vote. The next step is to get approval by the Board of Estimate, which is holding a public hearing today. The Board's approval is still not assured.

634. "Papp is Named Winner of Margo Jones Award." *New York Times*, Mar. 11, 1971, 32:4.

Papp has been named the winner of the tenth annual Margo Jones Award "for having made the most significant contribution to the dramatic art with hitherto unproduced plays." Papp has presented 35 new plays at the Public Theater.

635. Carroll, Maurice. "Papp Walks Out on City Talks about Buying Festival Theater." *New York Times*, Mar. 12, 1971, 26:1.

Papp walked out of a Board of Estimate meeting while 40 or more supporters stood and applauded. He was there to testify on behalf of the Lindsay administration's proposal that the city buy the Public Theater. Papp had tangled with the Queens Borough President, Sidney Leviss, who claimed that Papp's enterprise was Manhattan oriented. Papp denied the charge vigorously, then stalked out and sat on the stairway in the City Hall rotunda while the meeting continued. The Board voted to defer action until March 25.

636. Burks, Edward C. "Papp Doth Win Battle of Public Theater." *New York Times*, Mar. 26, 1971, 24:1.

The Board of Estimate votes unanimously to buy the Public Theater for $2.6 million and lease it back to the NYSF for one dollar a year. The proposal still needs ratification by the City Council. The Queens Borough President Sidney Leviss, who had argued with Papp at the last Board of Estimate meeting on March 11, voted in favor of the plan. The two shook hands after the meeting.

637. Kupferberg, Herbert. "Mr. Papp Presides Over a Theatrical Warren." *National Observer*, Mar. 29, 1971, 20.

The Public Theater is alive with activity. Since 12 to 15 plays are presented in a season there are constant changes. Even plays that are doing well in box office terms have to be moved out to make room for upcoming productions. Although Papp has a reputation for staging modern and outrageous plays he also puts on popular works, since his audience is diverse and ranges from students to regular Broadway patrons.

638. Carroll, Maurice. "City Purchasing Public Theater." *New York Times*, Apr. 28, 1971, 34:1.

The City Council has voted to buy the Public Theater for $2.6 million. At the Council's finance committee hearing Papp apologized for the absence of actor George C. Scott who was scheduled to testify for the plan. The committee sent the plan to the council floor where it was approved 27 to 10. Now a lease-back agreement must be negotiated. Eight hundred thousand dollars of the city's purchase price will be used to pay off debts on the building. The remainder will finance the continuing renovations.

639. Tallmer, Jerry. "At Home with Peggy Papp." *New York Post*, May 15, 1971, 33:1.

Papp met Peggy Bennion in 1951 when she was an actress and he was stage manager and understudy in a touring company. Married for 20 years, she has since given up acting and become a therapist. The article includes her recipe for red wine shrimp.

640. Calta, Louis. "Papp Altering Central Park Theater." *New York Times*, May 20, 1971, 46:1.

The Delacorte Theater in Central Park is being altered from its fan-like design to a horseshoe form to bring the audience closer to the stage action. The alterations will cost $40,000. George Delacorte, the publisher, has pledged $25,000. The remainder will be raised by the NYSF.

641. "Papp Will Publish Theater Magazine." *New York Times*, June 4, 1971, 21:2.

Papp announces that the NYSF will publish two new magazines, *Performance* and *Scripts*, at the Public Theater. The editor for both will be Erika Munk. *Scripts* is a monthly of plays and theater pieces. *Performance*, a quarterly journal, will "document, analyze and provide an impetus for new ideas in theater, dance, film and music."

642. Silver, Lee. "Shakespeare Festival Sets Actors' Workshop." *New York Daily News*, June 5, 1971, 23:1.

An actors' workshop organized by Papp and named the Five O'Clock Theater, will begin meeting in September. The purpose of the group is to give regularly employed actors the opportunity to try out unfamiliar roles. Another Papp enterprise will be the publishing of two theater magazines. *Scripts* will be a monthly of plays and theater pieces. *Performance* will be a quarterly devoted to performing arts criticism.

643. "City Bestows on Papp Its Handel Medallion." *New York Times*, June 30, 1971, 36:8.

The Handel Medallion, the city's highest award for cultural achievement, was presented to Papp by

Mayor Lindsay before the start of a benefit performance of *Timon of Athens* in Central Park.

644. Bongartz, Roy. "Pitchman for Free (And Freewheeling) Theater." *New York Times*, Aug. 15, 1971, Magazine sec., 12+.

Papp has reached his "culminating moment." The city has finally acknowledged that the Public Theater is an essential service by purchasing it. In this wide-ranging article Papp talks about the conflict between his political militancy and his art. He would have difficulty heading an anti-Vietnam war committee while he is getting federal funding for his theater, although he frequently goes on anti-war marches. His poverty-stricken background is recounted as the origin of his radicalism. It has caused him trouble, not only during the McCarthy era, but Papp believes that it has stopped him getting grants from the Ford and Mellon Foundations.

Papp recalls that he has acted in only one Shakespeare play, *Romeo and Juliet*, at the Emmanuel Presbyterian Church. He also comments on the other two major Shakespearean troupes in North America. He thinks that the Stratford, Ontario, company is better than the NYSF, but feels that the American Shakespeare Festival follows British tradition too much. He does not like the British influence on Shakespeare, and thinks that Americans "have a better comic speech than Cockney for the low characters." Papp also takes critics such as Walter Kerr and John Simon, who pan his shows, to task.

645. "Papp Grant Tops U.S. Arts Awards." *New York Times*, Sep. 15, 1971, 38:1.

The National Endowment for the Arts announces grants of $1.6 million to 36 theaters across the country, with the biggest award of $125,000 going to the NYSF. The grant is to support the company's entire operation, including its Shakespeare in the Park, Mobile Theater and Public Theater. Papp says that he will use the grant to raise actors' wages.

646. Calta, Louis. "Schary Is Seeking To Save Beaumont." *New York Times*, Sep. 18, 1971, 17:5.

Dore Schary, the playwright and the city's former Commissioner of Cultural Affairs, agrees to head a committee of theater people, including Papp, to fight plans to alter the Vivian Beaumont Theater at Lincoln Center for the purpose of providing facilities for the Henri Langlois film collection and creating three additional small theaters.

647. "Broadway to Get Papp Production." *New York Times*, Sep. 27, 1971, 42:5.

The NYSF's musical production of *The Two Gentlemen of Verona*, one of three presentations this summer in Central Park, will open December 1 at the St. James Theater on Broadway. The musical will be presented by the NYSF, with an anonymous $400,000 gift from a board member, with the condition that all earnings go to the company to be used for the production of other plays at the Public Theater and in Central Park. Papp believes that "this may be the first time in theater history where a nonprofit organization is producing a Broadway play with all profits to be returned to it for nonprofit purposes."

648. "Unit to Report on Forum Step." *New York Times*, Sep. 28, 1971, 46:4.

Papp, Dore Schary and Jo Mielziner will give a progress report, at Sardi's Belasco Room, on the campaign to prevent the relocation of the Forum Theater from the basement to the backstage area of the Vivian Beaumont Theater. The relocation is part of a plan that includes the proposed purchase of the Beaumont by the city for one dollar. The theater complex would then be turned over to the New York City Center of Music and Drama for operation and remodelling with city funds at a cost of $5.2 million.

649. Gussow, Mel. "Burden Supports Plan for Beaumont." *New York Times*, Sep. 30, 1971, 56:1.

Carter Burden, a member of the City Council, has announced that he is very much in favor of the reorganization of the Vivian Beaumont Theater as he believes it is the only financial solution. He feels that Dore Schary and other theater people, such as Papp, who are on the Committee to Save Theater at Lincoln Center "have the obligation to come up with an economic solution." He claims that the group has done little lobbying of the City Council.

650. Calta, Louis. "Plans Aim to Salvage the Forum." *New York Times*, Oct. 5, 1971, 46:4.

At a meeting of the Drama Desk on October 4, Papp recommended that the Vivian Beaumont

Theater at Lincoln Center be sold to the City Center organization for $5 million and that the money be used to subsidize the theater's deficit operation.

651. "Shakespeare Fete Tickets Surpass Producer's Goal." *New York Times*, Oct. 28, 1971, 50:2.

The NYSF will not sell any more Public Theater passes which allow admission to at least eight productions for a cost of $15. Papp says that the pass sales have exceeded 12,000, surpassing the original goal of 10,000. The concept was designed to ensure continuous audience support, while still leaving available tickets for patrons at the box office.

652. Beaufort, John. "New York Shakespeare Festival Public Theater: The Difference Between Creative Vision and Wishfulness." *Christian Science Monitor*, Dec. 10, 1971, sec. 2, 1:1.

Papp is busy working on the transfer of the musical *Two Gentlemen of Verona* to Broadway after its success in Central Park. The continuing success of the musical is vital to the NYSF. Profits from this first Broadway venture will help finance an expanded program.

653. Carroll, Maurice. "Plan Panel Sends Mayor a Budget of $2.2 Billion." *New York Times*, Dec. 31, 1971, 23:1.

The proposed 1972-73 city fiscal budget includes $250,000 for the Public Theater. The city Planning Commission says that the NYSF had asked for $800,000 for renovations to the building.

1972

654. Oster, Jerry. "Joe Papp to Shift *Sticks* to Broadway." *New York Daily News*, Jan. 29, 1972, 23:1.

In order to free up one of the four theaters at the Public for a new production, Papp is moving *Sticks and Bones* to Broadway's Golden Theater. The move will be financed by private gifts totaling $75,000. The play, which is about a Vietnam veteran's homecoming, will open on March 1.

655. Phillips, McCandlish. "State Art Grants: Less Money for More Groups." *New York Times*, Mar. 26, 1972, 50:3.

The New York State Council on the Arts gave $200,000 to the NYSF in support of its work in the Delacorte Theater, its Mobile Theater and the Public Theater, as part of $1.5 million in drama grants to 144 companies this year.

656. Funke, Lewis. "Hall, Hall, the Gang's All There." *New York Times*, Apr. 9, 1972, sec. 2, 1:5.

There is a plan to place a Theater Hall of Fame and Museum in the new Uris Theater. Papp has been appointed to the executive committee to run it. The project has received criticism over the method used to select members. Papp says "there has to be an over-all responsible organization to handle this thing or I will be against it."

657. Phillips, McCandlish. "*Sticks and Bones*, *Verona* Win Tonys." *New York Times*, Apr. 24, 1972, 40:1.

Two Papp productions received the top Antoinette Perry Awards this year. *Two Gentlemen of Verona*, which was presented in Central Park last summer and reopened on Broadway on December 2, was judged the best musical. *Sticks and Bones*, which opened at the Public Theater in October and moved to Broadway March 1, won the best play award. It was the first time that any producer had won in both categories in a single year.

658. Seigel, Max H. "Troy Unit Tables Furlough Plans." *New York Times*, May 5, 1972, 22:1.

The City Council voted to allow the NYSF to lease the Public Theater for one dollar a year for 10 years.

659. Tallmer, Jerry. "Joseph Papp: 2 Theaters, 2 Tonys & 75 Drachmas." *New York Post*, May 6, 1972, sec. 2, 15.

A week after winning a Tony for *Sticks and Bones*, and one for *Two Gentlemen of Verona*, Papp told the interviewer that it was a "pyrrhic victory." *Sticks and Bones* has been losing $10,000 a week and Papp does not think that any serious play can make money on Broadway. He believes that the federal government should give a direct subsidy of $1 or $2 million to New York for its theater. He is committed to the idea of a national theater, which would consist of numerous touring groups bringing theater to communities throughout the country.

660. Nachman, Gerald. "And Now National Theater." *New York Daily News*, May 7, 1972, Leisure sec., 3.

Papp's latest fight is for a national theater to tour new plays by American writers. Regional theaters do only classics and Broadway revivals. He wants to reach blue-collar audiences with radical new plays paid for with federal money. Government censorship does not worry him.

661. "*Ti-Jean and His Brothers*." *New York Times*, May 19, 1972, 19:1.

For the first time in its 16 year history the NYSF will perform a contemporary play, *Ti-Jean and His Brothers* by Derek Walcott, in Central Park.

662. Phillips, McCandlish. "Pappian Way Leads to Theater Heights." *New York Times*, May 22, 1972, 41:1.

This article describes the busy lifestyle of Papp. He is seemingly inexhaustible, working from 10 to 16 hours a day. At this particular moment in time he has nine productions either on stage or in the works. It would have been 10, but he killed his all-male production of *Antony and Cleopatra* which didn't work.

Papp is now the top producer in New York, but he is aware of how tenuous his position is. The annual budget for his productions is $2.6 million and as the NYSF loses money he has to constantly raise subsidies. His ambition to conquer more territory still exists though. He would like to help form what he calls a National Theater Service Agency, for the distribution of theater all over the country. He believes that the agency should be part of the National Endowment for the Arts, with a policy board drawn from participating theaters.

663. Belsky, Dick. "Honor Papp in Absentia." *New York Post*, May 26, 1972, 56;1.

Papp was unable to accept a New York State Award for Cultural Contributions from Governor Rockefeller yesterday because he was under arrest in Washington D.C. Papp, along with other prominent show business people, was taken into custody two days ago during an anti-war protest at the Capitol. He was charged with unlawful entry of a government building and fined $25.

664. Gent, George. "Arts Award Goes to Absent Papp." *New York Times*, May 26, 1972, 20:1.

Papp was one of eight recipients of the 1972 New York State Awards for Cultural Contributions. He was, however, unable to receive his award from Governor Rockefeller at the Whitney Museum, because he was one of a 100 antiwar protesters arrested the day before in Washington D.C. He was detained for arraignment on charges of unlawful entry, a misdemeanor punishable by a fine of up to $100 or up to six months in jail, or both. Papp's award was accepted by his wife Peggy and David Rabe, author of the Tony Award-winning play *Sticks and Bones* which Papp produced.

665. Narvaez, Alfonso A. "Rockefeller Signs Runoff Vote Bill." *New York Times*, June 10, 1972, 36:4.

Governor Rockefeller approved a bill which would permit New York to lease the Public Theater to the NYSF for one dollar a year for the next 10 years.

666. Rabe,David. "So We Got Papp in to See a Run Through." *New York Times*, June 14, 1972, sec. 2, 1:1.

Rabe describes how he and director Jeff Bleckner called Papp in to see the rehearsals for his first production *The Basic Training of Pavlo Hummel* because things were not going well. At first Rabe resented Papp's criticisms, but agreed to try and make changes to the play. On the opening night Papp told the playwright he was pleased with the play and would stage future productions by him.

Rabe was also not enthusiastic about Papp's decision to move *Sticks and Bones* to Broadway. However, Papp convinced him that the play would be better in an uptown proscenium theater than in the semi-arena situation at the Public Theater, and that it would appeal to a Broadway-type audience.

667. Oppenheimer, George. "Man in the Eye of the Storm." *Newsday*, June 25, 1972, sec. 2, 9.

Since 1967 Papp has produced 87 plays including some of Broadway's biggest hits. During an interview at the Public Theater, critic Oppenheimer found Papp personable, friendly and respected by a large staff. Papp is less interested in plays than playwrights, whom he treats as friends and proteges, working with them on their scripts and giving advice when needed.

668. "Papp on Go On and Off Broadway." *New York Daily News*, July 9, 1972, Leisure sec., 8:2.

That Championship Season, Papp's latest hit, will move from the Public Theater to Broadway's Booth Theater in September. Papp is doing this to free up the Newman Theater for new productions. *Sticks and Bones* was moved to Broadway for the same reason. Any profits made on Broadway are plowed back into financing more plays.

669. "Six Groups Share $2 Million in Grants for Aid to Theater." *New York Times*, July 13, 1972, 29:3.

The Rockefeller Foundation gave grants totalling more than $2 million to six organizations, including $480,000 to the NYSF. The Festival plans to use part of the money to link theaters all over the country into a network that would exchange actors, directors and scripts.

670. Beaufort, John. "When Three Actors Play Six Roles in Four Theaters." *Christian Science Monitor*, July 14, 1972, 4:1.

Actors Tom Aldredge, Charles Durning and Raul Julia are in the unusual position of playing more than one role every evening at different playhouses. All three actors are playing in *Hamlet* at the Delacorte Theater and in other NYSF productions. Aldredge is in *Sticks and Bones*, Durning in *That Championship Season*, and Julia in *Two Gentlemen of Verona*.

671. Phillips, McCandlish. "Papp Will Produce 13 Plays for CBS in 4 Years." *New York Times*, Aug. 1, 1972, 71:1.

The NYSF has entered into an agreement with the Columbia Broadcasting System to produce a series of full-length plays for network television. The agreement calls for a minimum of 13 productions, classical as well as contemporary, over a four year period at an estimated cost of over $7 million. Robert D. Wood, the president of CBS television, called the alliance with Papp "a venture in prestige rather than in profit-making." Papp is looking forward to moving into the area of television and has set up a television department at the Public Theater. The NYSF will deliver completed productions to the network on videotape. Papp has to submit scripts to CBS for its approval prior to taping though. Papp says, "We will try not to offend gratuitously, but we will risk offending if the theme is meaningful and serious."

672. "Exile's Return." Editorial. *New York Times*, Aug. 2, 1972, 36:2.

The editor hails the plan for Papp to produce 13 plays over four years on CBS Television. Papp was fired by that company during the McCarthy era, so his return to network television is "a sign of maturity for CBS both in its respect for civil liberties and its willingness to raise the standards of taste for its millions of viewers."

673. "Light Up the Tube." Editorial. *New York Post*, Aug. 2, 1972, 34.

Calls Papp a "daring and prolific producer" who now has the opportunity to produce 13 Shakespeare plays on CBS.

674. "Papp Gives Share of *Verona* Profits to City in Thanks." *New York Times*, Aug. 23, 1972, 30:4.

Papp gave $5,750 to Mayor Lindsay, the city's first share of profits of *Two Gentlemen of Verona.*

The check represents 5% of the show's profits from its opening on Broadway last December through August 19. The city will also receive 5% of the profits of a telecast of *Much Ado About Nothing* this winter. Papp has received almost $5 million from the city since 1961 to help subsidize his company, including $2.85 million for the purchase and renovation of the Public Theater.

675. Watt, Douglas. "Festival Gets a Fair Shake on Broadway." *New York Daily News*, Sep. 24, 1972, Leisure sec., 3.

When *Much Ado about Nothing* opens at the Winter Garden in November, the NYSF will have a total of four productions on Broadway. The other three are: *Two Gentlemen of Verona*, *That Championship Season*, and *Sticks and Bones*. This is an uncommon accomplishment that only a few producers, among them Florenz Ziegfeld and David Merrick, have managed. Watt concludes his article by attacking the Delacorte Theater in Central Park as an eyesore and a violation of the idea of preserving the park as a large and restful wooded area.

676. Gussow, Mel. "Repertory Theater Battles Deficit Woes." *New York Times*, Nov. 22, 1972, 26:1.

The Vivian Beaumont Theater is suffering a severe economic crisis because of its deficit. It has led to the resignation of Jules Irving as the artistic director. Papp is mentioned as a possible successor. Papp says that if he were the artistic director he would ask the theater board to resign if they were unable to raise funds. He also says that he thinks

Michael Langham of Minneapolis' Tyrone Guthrie Theater the best candidate for the post.

677. Watt, Douglas. "Big Question: What about *Much Ado*?" *New York Daily News*, Nov. 26, 1972, 3.

Papp says that even if every show is sold out through January 13, when it is scheduled to end its run, *Much Ado about Nothing* will lose $150,000. The problem is the exceptionally low ticket prices that Papp refuses to raise. The author gives Papp's production of the play a favorable review and urges readers to see it before it closes.

678. Krebs, Albin. "Papp *Much Ado* Coming to TV on CBS for Three Hours on Feb. 2." *New York Times*, Dec. 13, 1972, 107:3.

An IBM spokesman announced that the corporation will sponsor the NYSF production of *Much Ado about Nothing* on CBS television. He says that the purchase of the program and the 8 p.m. to 11 p.m. prime-time period represents an investment of less than $1 million.

1973

679. Gent, George. "Papp Repudiates U.S.I.A. Film on Him." *New York Times*, Jan. 18, 1973, 48:1.

Papp repudiates the 13 minute film about him, *One Man: Joseph Papp*, set for foreign distribution by the United States Information Service. He says that the film leaves the impression that the Public Theater consists mainly of singers and dancers, and ignores the fact that it has also produced serious works. The head of the USIA film section, Hugh Woodward, says that he believes that the difficulty arises from a misunderstanding of the nature of the film, which had never been intended as a film on the festival, but rather as a study of Papp. Since he thinks that the film is honest and "depicts a very positive aspect of our country and people," USIA will release it for distribution abroad.

680. "Casts of 17 Shows Give $10,000 for Bach Mai." *New York Times*, Jan. 23, 1973, 47:6..

Cast members of 17 Broadway and Off-Broadway shows gave up their pay for last Saturday, Inauguration Day, as a contribution to rebuild Hanoi's bombed-out Bach-Mai Hospital. More than $10,000 was raised in this protest against U.S. bombing in North Vietnam. The campaign was organized by Papp and fellow producer Andre Gregory. Papp also pledged to raise the equivalent of the proceeds for one performance of each of his three Broadway shows, *Two Gentlemen of Verona*, *That Championship Season* and *Much Ado about Nothing*. The figure could approach $20,000.

681. Gardella, Kay. "Papp Brings His Public Theater to TV." *New York Daily News*, Jan. 28, 1973, Leisure sec., 17+.

The NYSF's three hour *Much Ado about Nothing*, the first of 13 full length productions by Papp, will be presented on CBS this week. Papp will receive $7 million under the terms of his contract with CBS. The controversial *Sticks and Bones* will be the second in the series and Papp predicts that the network will have problems with the Nixon administration and many viewers over this one. Papp has yet to find a sponsor for *Sticks and Bones*, but he is hoping to convince IBM to pick up the tab.

682. Knight, Michael. "*Much Ado* of TV Dooms Stage Version." *New York Times*, Feb. 7, 1973, 30:1.

Papp disclosed that the NYSF production of *Much Ado about Nothing* will close on February 11 after 116 performances. He says that the CBS nationwide telecast of the play reached an estimated two million people in the New York metropolitan area and drastically cut box office receipts. He says that the show had already incurred losses of $165,000 and the sudden drop in ticket sales dealt the final blow. CBS gave the NYSF $775,000 for the television production, but he says it cost $810,000.

683. "Much Ado about Box Office." *New York Post*, Feb. 7, 1973, 47.

The nationwide television production of the NYSF's modernized *Much Ado about Nothing* hurt the sales at the Broadway box office so badly that the show must close at the end of the week. Papp had hoped that the CBS telecast would help sell tickets to the live performance. Instead, ticket sales plunged to only $500 on Monday. About 20 million people watched the TV production.

684. McMorrow, Tom. "Papp Bids "Much" Adieu; Play Went Down the Tube." *New York Daily News*, Feb. 12, 1973, 43.

Much Ado about Nothing closed last night because of plummeting ticket sales. The drop at the box office began after the play was televised on CBS. Ironically Papp believed that ticket buying would be stimulated by the television production. He said that he would never again put a current play on TV, unless it was ready to close. His next TV venture will be *Sticks and Bones*.

685. "*Sticks and Bones* on CBS March 9." *New York Times*, Feb. 21, 1973, 87:4.

CBS announces that *Sticks and Bones*, the second NYSF production to be shown on television, has been scheduled for March 9.

686. Koenenn, Joseph C. "War Drama Is Postponed." *Newsday*, Mar. 7, 1973, 5.

Because of its affiliates' refusal to carry the anti-war play *Sticks and Bones*, CBS has decided to postpone the show. Of 184 affiliates, 69 have refused to air the drama of a blinded Vietnam veteran's return home. In retaliation, Papp has cancelled his four year agreement to produce 13 plays for CBS.

687. "Papp's *Sticks and Bones* Put Off by CBS." *New York Times*, Mar. 7, 1973, 87:1.

CBS Television president Robert D. Wood announced yesterday that the network had postponed indefinitely the scheduled March 9 telecast of the NYSF production of *Sticks and Bones*, a play about a blinded Vietnam veteran's homecoming. He said the action was taken because the presentation of the play "at this time" might be "unnecessarily abrasive to the feelings of millions of Americans whose lives are emotionally dominated by returning POWs." Papp contends that the postponement is a cowardly "cop-out" and "rotten affront to freedom of speech." He vows he will not honor the terms of his four year contract with CBS. CBS said that 69 of 184 network affiliates refused to carry the program.

688. Seligsohn, Leo. "Joseph Papp: Off-Off Broadway to Lincoln Center." *Newsday*, Mar. 7, 1973, part II, 3A.

Amyas Ames, chairman of the board of Lincoln Center, announced at a press conference that Papp had agreed to take over the Vivian Beaumont theater and its small downstairs adjunct, the Forum. Since it opened 10 years ago, the theater has suffered artistic and financial headaches. Papp's new role is contingent on raising $5 million over the next six to eight weeks from private, foundation and government sources. Starting in October, Papp plans to present new works by American playwrights at the Beaumont and Shakespeare plays at the Forum. Ironically, in 1963 Papp proposed bringing the NYSF to Lincoln Center, but was turned down.

689. Krebs, Albin. "ACLU Decries CBS Over Play." *New York Times*, Mar. 9, 1973, 75:4.

The American Civil Liberties Union branded as "corporate cowardice" the CBS decision to postpone the scheduled March 9 telecast of *Sticks and Bones*. It said the CBS decision violated the First Amendment. Papp charged that CBS "became the creature of its affiliates" when it bowed to their pressure. A *New York Times* spot telephone check of 12 television stations revealed that managers were overwhelmingly opposed to showing the play at a time when Vietnam prisoners of war were returning home.

690. Gardella, Kay. "Papp's Waiting for CBS to Make April Resolution." *New York Daily News*, Mar. 10, 1973, 10.

Papp is threatening to break his contract with CBS if they do not show *Sticks and Bones* within the next few weeks. Last week Robert D. Wood, president of CBS Television, told Papp that the play would not be televised because 69 affiliated stations are refusing to carry it. The play, by David Rabe, is about the Vietnam war and CBS fears that it might be abrasive to millions of viewers. The contract between CBS and Papp is for four years, but is subject to renewal each year.

691. Weisman, Steven R. "City Club at 80 in Busiest Year." *New York Times*, Mar. 10, 1973, 17:3.

The City Club of New York, a civic organization, commemorated its 80th anniversary by giving 23 "For New York" awards to residents who had "devoted energy, skill and talent to improvement of the quality of life in New York." Papp was one of the recipients.

692. Funke, Lewis. "Papp Pushes On." *New York Times*, Mar. 11, 1973, sec. 2, 21:5.

Papp's NYSF will join Lincoln Center as the theatrical component replacing the Repertory Theater. Papp will produce new American plays at the

Beaumont Theater, while the Forum will be devoted to presenting Shakespeare plays.

693. O'Connor, John J. "How About Some Backbone?" *New York Times*, Mar. 18, 1973, sec. 2, 19:1.
Comments on CBS's decision not to televise Papp's production of David Rabe's controversial anti-war play *Sticks and Bones*. CBS reached its decision when over a third of its affiliates refused to carry the production. The critic contends that commercial networks must demonstrate that they can deal with provocative and abrasive subjects. He says that CBS should recover the courage of its original convictions and air *Sticks and Bones*.

694. Krebs, Albin. "Paley, CBS Chairman Personally Vetoed Showing of *Sticks and Bones*." *New York Times*, Mar. 20, 1973, 78:3.
CBS board chairman William S. Paley personally vetoed the showing of *Sticks and Bones*. He reportedly arranged to view the play when 71 of 184 affiliate stations informed CBS that they would not accept it.

695. Ashby, Neal. "'Don't Get the Idea This Is a One-Man Operation' Says Joe Papp..." *New York Daily News*, Apr. 15, 1973, Magazine sec., 22+.
A narrative pictorial essay of a day in the life of Papp. The author followed him around the Public Theater as he looked in on rehearsals and auditions, and advised some young playwrights.

696. Corry, John. "For Joseph Papp, Fund-Raising Is an Art Surpassed Only by His Stage Skills." *New York Times*, Apr. 19, 1973, 45:1.

The author characterizes Papp as the "the hottest money raiser in town." Papp himself believes he provides a service, like garbage collecting, and believes it should be funded accordingly. Meanwhile, he is attempting to raise $2 million in the next two months to enable the NYSF to take up residence at Lincoln Center in place of the Repertory Theater. He is asking the National Endowment for the Arts, the New York State Arts Council and the Ford Foundation for $500,000 respectively, New York City for $1 million, and the Rockefeller and Mellon Foundations for $350,000 each.

697. "5 in Various Fields Chosen for Awards by Einstein College." *New York Times*, May 4, 1973, 27:1.

Papp is one of the five recipients of the 1973 Albert Einstein Commemorative Awards given by the Albert Einstein College of Medicine at Yeshiva University. He was given the award "for developing his free theater into multiple dramatic activities unmatched in number, excellence, originality and public access."

698. Gent, George. "Papp Gets Threatening Letters Charging Bias Against Latins." *New York Times*, May 19, 1973, 28:1.

Papp turned over to the police threatening letters and posters that were plastered on the Public Theater accusing him of discrimination against Puerto Rican and other Latin actors. He made public an exchange of letters between himself and the Puerto Rican

Actors Guild, in which the organization expressed outrage over the dismissal of four Puerto Rican and Latin performers by the NYSF. Papp says that it is absurd to assert that he discriminated against Hispanics in view of his public record on employing minorities.

699. "Equity Investigates the Dismissal of Latin Actress from *Verona*." *New York Times*, May 22, 1973, 46:3.

Actors Equity confirmed on May 21 that it was investigating the dismissal of a Puerto Rican actress from the cast of the Los Angeles production of *Two Gentlemen of Verona*. The Puerto Rican Actors Guild had alleged that the action represented a pattern of discrimination agaist Puerto Rican and other Hispanic performers. Guild spokesmen said that Papp had refused to meet with them to discuss the case.

700. Krebs, Albin. "CBS Chief Defends Decision to Postpone *Sticks and Bones*." *New York Times*, May 24, 1973, 91:3.

CBS president Arthur R. Taylor defends the network's decision in March to postpone the showing of *Sticks and Bones* indefinitely. He says "such nontangibles as taste, timeliness and context in which a program is shown enter deeply into our decisions." Papp, who charged CBS with being cowardly in bowing to the wishes of a large number of its affiliate stations, says that the network continues to "run scared."

701. "Notes on People." *New York Times*, May 25, 1973, 40:8.

The Salvation Army presented its annual Golden Doughnut Award to Papp. Helen Hayes said at the presentation, "Two forces irresistible to me met here today—the Salvation Army that stands for God and humanity, and Joe, who stands for the City of New York."

702. Gussow, Mel. "Mrs. Newhouse Gives Papp $1 Million." *New York Times*, May 31, 1973, 50:1.

On May 30 Papp agreed to make the NYSF the theater constituent at Lincoln Center and signed a 25 year lease with the board to operate the Vivian Beaumont and Forum Theaters. His action was prompted by a contribution of $1 million from Mrs Samuel I. Newhouse, which eases the Festival's burden of having to raise $10 million over a five year period to operate the complex. A ceremony marking Papp's plans was held at Alice Tully Hall during which a news conference was held by Papp and Amyas Ames, the Lincoln Center board chairman. Mrs Newhouse's gift is reportedly the largest single sum ever given to an operating theater.

703. Beaufort, John. "Brave Start for Joe Papp's Lincoln Center Connection." *Christian Science Monitor*, June 9, 1973, 14:5.

Starting in the fall Papp will add the Vivian Beaumont Theater at Lincoln Center to his theatrical domain, which presently consists of five playhouses at the Public, the Delacorte in Central Park and the Mobile Theater. Papp signed a 25 year lease for the

Beaumont with Lincoln Center chairman Amyas Ames. Although some of Papp's detractors think he is overextending himself by taking on the Beaumont, this author advises the wisdom of suspending judgement because of Papp's ability to always land on his feet.

704. "Statue in Park Dedicated to Papp." *New York Times*, June 26, 1973, 54:1.

A bronze statue of Prospero and Miranda, two characters in *The Tempest*, was dedicated on June 25 to Papp. The statue was commissioned by George T. Delacorte, the chairman of Dell Publishing, and executed by sculpter, Milton Hebald. The statue stands at the entrance to the Delacorte Theater in Central Park.

705. "Papp and CBS End Contract to Produce Dramatic Specials." *New York Times*, June 27, 1973, 111:4.

Papp's much-publicized contract to produce dramatic specials for the CBS television network was ended on June 26 by both Papp and the company. Papp says he is now talking with other networks about producing classical and contemporary works for them. He has been critical of CBS ever since it postponed the scheduled March broadcast of his television version of *Sticks and Bones*.

706. "Woman at Theater in Park Shot." *New York Post*, July 5, 1973, 38:1.

A 22-year-old woman was shot in the wrist last night as she watched a performance of *As You Like It* at the Delacorte Theater.

707. Gent, George. "CBS Reschedules *Sticks and Bones*." *New York Times*, July 14, 1973, 55:1.

CBS television president Robert D. Wood announced that the network has rescheduled its previously postponed showing of *Sticks and Bones* for August 17.

708. Phillips, McCandlish. "Papp's Plays to Get Philadelphia Tryout." *New York Times*, July 27, 1973, 16:1.

Papp announced that he has entered into an agreement with the University of Pennsylvania to use its Zellerbach Theater to stage various plays for two week runs before they are brought to the Beaumont Theater at Lincoln Center. This gives him a chance to try out and improve new plays with a live audience before they have to face the New York critics.

709. Krebs, Albin. "CBS Stations Balk on *Sticks and Bones*." *New York Times*, Aug. 17, 1973, 63:2.

CBS affiliate stations have massively defected from showing the anti-war play *Sticks and Bones* tonight. The number of stations refusing to air the award-winning play is unprecedented in the history of network television, far exceeding the number that declined to run the program when it was originally scheduled for March 9. The number of stations failing to carry the program will probably exceed one hundred.

710. "*Sticks and Bones*." Editorial. *New York Times*, Aug. 17, 1973, 30:2.

This editorial was published the day that CBS was to show the delayed NYSF production, *Sticks and Bones*. The editor said that the original excuse for delaying the show, that it would be tasteless to air it while prisoners of war from North Vietnam were being welcomed home, had some plausibility. There was a possibility, however, that the network and its affiliates might have been bowing to pressure from the White House.

711. "Papp's Festival Wins Ford Grant." *New York Times*, Aug. 21, 1973, 40:2.

Papp announced that the Ford Foundation has awarded a $1.5 million grant to the NYSF. The funding is divided into an outright grant of $500,000 and a challenge grant of up to $1 million, with one dollar for every three raised by the Festival over a three year period.

712. "Forum Theater Now the Newhouse." *New York Times*, Sep. 11, 1973, 53:1.

Papp announced that the Forum Theater at Lincoln Center has been renamed the Mitzi E. Newhouse Theater in honor of Mrs.Newhouse, who donated $1 million to enable Papp to start operating the Beaumont and Forum Theaters.

713. "For City's Next Mayor, Words of Advice, Wisdom and Warning." *New York Times*, Nov. 6, 1973, 39:1.

On Election Day prominent New Yorkers are asked what advice they would give to the next mayor. Papp says that the new mayor should deal with social problems of blacks and Hispanics.

714. Watt, Douglas. "Despite an Early Misfire Papp's Work Is Booming." *New York Daily News*, Nov. 18, 1973, 3:1.

In the current Beaumont program Papp explains that he is concerned for the survival of the theater. He therefore feels that the production of new works must take priority over revivals. He believes that new writers are the public conscience and provide insights into our society. In this way he justifies his policy of showing mainly new plays at Lincoln Center.

715. Brown, Les. "Joseph Papp Signs an Exclusive Contract with ABC." *New York Times*, Nov. 20, 1973, 79:1.

Papp signs a contract with ABC television to produce a minimum of two contemporary dramas for prime-time television and to develop programs for the Saturday morning children's schedule and "Wide World of Entertainment," ABC's late-evening program. The prime-time programs will be television adaptations of shows he has produced for the stage. Papp welcomes the contract as a source of funding for his stage plays, and a way to reach a much larger audience.

716. Bosworth, Patricia. "Joseph Papp at the Zenith—Was It Boom or Bust?" *New York Times*, Nov. 25, 1973, sec. 2, 1:2.

On the opening night of David Rabe's *Boom Boom Room*, the first production by the NYSF at Lincoln Center, the play received some bad reviews, particularly from the *New York Times* critic Clive Barnes. Papp believes it was a personal vendetta against him by Barnes, who wanted to see a classical theater on the lines of Britain's National Theatre at Lincoln Center. However, the production had problems from the beginning, which resulted in the firing of actress Julie Newmar and director Julie Bovasso. Papp took over the direction himself just three weeks before the play opened.

1974

717. Gardella, Kay. "Papp's Cynicism of Masses No Bar to Rating Courtship." *New York Daily News*, Jan. 21, 1974, 33.

Papp has signed a contract with ABC for two productions. The first is *Wedding Band*, which will be aired in April. The play, by black writer Alice Childress, is about a love affair between a young black woman and a white southern man before World War II. Papp, who has said that the public is "usually stupid," wants the largest audience he can get for *Wedding Band*. His interest is in reaching people with art not morality or political ideas.

718. Gussow, Mel. "Goldman Sworn In As Culture Chief." *New York Times*, Mar. 7, 1974, 52:1.

Mayor Abraham Beame swore in Irving Goldman, head of the Shubert theater empire, as New York City Cultural Affairs Commissioner. Papp attended the ceremony and announced his support of the appointment.

719. Brown, Les. "8 ABC Affiliates Bar Papp TV Play." *New York Times*, Apr. 23, 1974, 83:4.

Eight stations in the ABC television network declined to carry *Wedding Band*, the Alice Chidress play with a miscegenation theme. Most of the stations are in the south. The play is the first one that Papp has produced for ABC.

720. Watts, Janet. "Am I Corrupt?" *Guardian* [Manchester U.K.], May 14, 1974, 14:1.

Watts interviewed Papp, whom she calls "the most important man on Broadway off Broadway." Papp himself thinks that he is doing the most important work in the American theater today. The article recounts his background as the son of a Polish-Jewish trunkmaker in Brooklyn. Papp was one of only 28 applicants chosen from 500 for a place at the Actors' Laboratory in Los Angeles. He began producing Shakespearean plays in a New York basement in 1953. Papp prides himself on his creativity and on recognising a good play. He also explains what he believes makes a good playwright.

721. "Papp's Bow in Celluloid." *New York Times*, May 19, 1974, 56:6.

It has been announced that Papp is to direct a film version of David Rabe's play *Boom Boom Room*.

722. "Drama Congress Weighs Problems." *New York Times*, June 3, 1974, 39:3.

FACT, the First American Congress of Theater, is holding a four day conference at Princeton "to discuss the common artistic and economic concerns of the commercial and institutional theater." Papp is to be one of the speakers.

723. Brustein, Robert. "News Theater." *New York Times*, June 16, 1974, Magazine sec., 7+.

Brustein writes about the "collaboration between newsworthy personalities, a vast public, and the visual or print media." Papp is one of the examples he gives. Because the commercial theater is in virtual collapse, while Papp's is vibrant, he has become a newsworthy personality. His young playwrights and directors are "invested with expectations far beyond their immediate capacity to fulfil" by the news media. Brustein believes that this pressure made Papp ambitious to expand, so he took on the disastrous Lincoln Center. He is also beginning to get negative treatment from the media. "Confirmation of the fact that the only thing as newsworthy as success is...failure."

724. "City, Papp Agree on a Theater." *New York Post*, Aug. 7, 1974, 50:1.

The Parks Department has agreed to build a $3 million, 2,500 seat open-air theater to replace the Delacorte Theater in Central Park. The architect is Georgio Cavalieri.

725. Goldberger, Paul. "New Theater in Park Is Planned to Replace Delacorte." *New York Times*, Aug. 7, 1974, 1:1.

Parks Department officials and Papp have reached a tentative agreement on plans for building a new 2,500 seat open-air theater in Central Park. It will probably cause some controversy among park preservationists. George Delacorte will provide some of the financing for the project.

726. "Shakespeare Goes Beyond Boroughs." *New York Times*, Aug. 18, 1974, 40:4.

The NYSF Mobile Theater will perform outside New York City for the first time in its 11 year history. It will give six free performances in Manhasset, New Rochelle, Mount Vernon, Buffalo, Rochester and Syracuse.

727. Goldberger, Paul. "Parks Chief Is Now Opposing New Theater for Papp Festival." *New York Times*, Sep. 4, 1974, 1:5.

Parks Commissioner Edwin L. Weisl, Jr. announced his opposition to the permanent concrete theater in Central Park proposed by Papp as a replacement for the deteriorating Delacorte Theater. His opposition follows negative public reaction after the disclosure of the plan in August. In a letter to Mayor Beame, Papp argues the cause of a new theater, calling Weisl's suggestion of rehabilitating the present structure at an estimated cost of $250,000, "short-sighted." He estimates the overhaul would cost $1 million. The new building is estimated to cost three to four million dollars.

728. Lieberman, Mark. "Peeved Papp May Relocate Shakespeare." *New York Daily News*, Sep. 4, 1974, 38:1.

Papp is threatening to move his free Shakespeare productions from the Delacorte Theater in Central Park to the Beaumont Theater, unless the city comes up with enough money to either construct a new theater in the park, or completely overhaul the old one. Papp would prefer a new theater because the Delacorte, which opened in 1962, is "falling apart."

The city has offered $250,000 to repair the old theater, but Papp says at least $1 million is needed.

729. "Papp to Give Course in Directing at Yale." *New York Times*, Sep. 4, 1974, 53:1.

Robert Brustein, the dean of Yale Drama School, announced that Papp has been named Visiting Critic in Directing by the school for the 1974-75 academic year.

730. "Feld Ballet Named for Papp Festival." *New York Times*, Sep. 5, 1974, 45:2.

Papp named the Eliot Feld Ballet as the resident ballet company of the NYSF. The company will stage a four week winter season with choreographer Glen Tetley.

731. "Too Solid Concrete." Editorial. *New York Times*, Sep. 6, 1974, 32:2.

The $1 million for the renovation of the old Delacorte Theater, or the $3 million for a new structure, are both irresponsible when the total budget for Central park is only $4.5 million for the year. The fact that the park is in desperate need of drainage, erosion control and horticultural improvement should be taken into account and attended to first.

1975

732. Gussow, Mel. "The Classics, Lincoln Center and Papp." *New York Times*, Mar. 17, 1975, 36:1.

An analysis of Papp's decision to renounce his policy of presenting new American plays at the Beaumont Theater, and switch to revivals of classics with guest stars. Notes the negative reception by both audiences and critics to his past season. Some critics feel that Papp has remained too faithful to his favorite directors and playwrights, and at the same time refused many other good new plays. Subscriber reaction to the new plan has been positive.

733. "Notes on People." *New York Times*, Apr. 8, 1975, 74:2.

Papp and actors Peter Boyle and Richard Dreyfuss were among a group of theatrical and film figures representing the Safe Return organization, who lobbied in congress for unconditional amnesty for war resisters.

734. Calta, Louis. "Henry St. Stage and Papp to Develop Plays Jointly." *New York Times*, Apr. 26, 1975, 13:1.

Papp and Henry Street Settlement executive director, Bertram Black, have agreed to develop plays that would be presented first at Henry Street and then at Lincoln Center or the Public Theater, in an effort to spur black and Hispanic participation in drama.

735. Barnes, Clive. "Critic's Notebook: Perils of a Dancer—or a Producer." *New York Times*, May 13, 1975, 30:1.

Papp is worried by rumors about his forthcoming musical, *A Chorus Line*. Surprisingly, he is concerned because the reports are that the production is very good. He hopes that the show will not disappoint the critics' expectations when they finally see it.

736. Topor, Tom. "Broadway Next for Joe Papp." *New York Post*, May 23, 1975, 29:3.

Papp is planning to take over the Booth Theater in the fall for a full season of new American plays. The American plays that Papp has produced at the Vivian Beaumont Theater have lost the NYSF 5,000 subscribers in two years. In March Papp announced that he was ending the policy of showing only Shakespeare plays at the Mitzi E. Newhouse Theater.

737. Gussow, Mel. "Papp Sounds Knell for Off Broadway." *New York Times*, May 27, 1975, 36:1.

Papp will take over the Booth Theater on Broadway in the fall to present five new American plays. He will also change his entire Public Theater into Off Off Broadway workshops, probably with no admission charge and with critics invited to most productions.

738. Calta, Louis. "Bargain Preview Tickets Set by Papp at the Booth." *New York Times*, June 18, 1975, 31:1.

When he takes over the Booth Theater in the fall for a season of five new American plays, Papp will offer the lowest priced tickets on Broadway. He wants to attract a new audience. The low prices were made possible by the cooperation of the Shubert organization who own the theater.

739. Little, Stuart. "Can Shakespeare, Ibsen, Shaw and Pinero Save Joseph Papp?" *New York Times*, July 13, 1975, sec. 2, 1:3.

This is a dark period for Papp. He has had to acknowledge defeat in his attempts to bring new plays to Lincoln Center. From a first season high of 27,000, subscriptions slipped to 22,000 in the second year. He has hurriedly arranged a list of classic plays for the next season: *Trelawny of the Wells*, *Hamlet*, *Mrs. Warren's Profession*, and *Peer Gynt* with a black cast. He would like to have a separate black company "to bring the disenfranchised into the mainstream of the culture."

740. Calta, Louis. "New Guides Set Up by Actors Equity." *New York Times*, Aug. 7, 1975, 39: 3.

In a move to protect its members from possible exploitation, Actors Equity has established new guidelines for showcase productions. The guidelines have piqued Papp and Off-Off-Broadway producers. They fear that the code changes will drastically affect small theater activities and also discourage the presentation of new works. After a conference with Donald Grody, the executive secretary of Equity, Papp suspended plans for the presentation of three showcase offerings at the Booth Theater.

741. Vidal, David. "Actors Vote Against New Equity Code." *New York Times*, Aug. 26, 1975, 36:1.

A special membership meeting of Actors Equity voted overwhelmingly against the new code that had come under fire as a threat to Off Off Broadway. Papp came to the meeting by special invitation of equity's ruling council. He had a five page speech ready to deliver against the code, but in the end he only spoke for less than a minute after the vote, to congratulate the membership on its decision.

742. Marowitz, Charles. "The Trouble With Papp." *New York Times*, Sep. 21, 1975, sec. 2, 1:6.

Highly critical review of Papp's accomplishments at Lincoln Center. Critical of Papp's unswerving support of his playwrights, although he has never unearthed any major writing talents. Nor does the author believe that an institutional theater like the Beaumont was the place to produce new, untried plays. Papp's attempt to attract new audiences was at the expense of traditional subscribers, on whom Lincoln Center was dependent. He acted too much like a commercial impresario to create a great theater at Lincoln Center.

743. Fleming, Shirley. "IRS and Music." *New York Times*, Oct. 5, 1975, sec. 2, 17:6.

Contains comments, including Papp's, on the bill proposed by Rep. Fred Richmond, that would allow taxpayers to indicate on their tax forms their willingness to make a contribution, over and above the tax payment, to the National Endowment for the Humanities. The bill is supported by virtually all musicians and others in the arts.

744. "In Defense of Joseph Papp." Letters. *New York Times*, Oct. 5, 1975, sec. 2, 5:7.

A trio of letter writers, including Bernard Gersten, defended Papp and his work against the attack by Charles Marowitz (*New York Times*, Sep.

21, sec. 2, 1:6.). They cited the success of his many projects, and his ability to get funding.

745. Gussow, Mel. "Musicals Hope to Resume This Week." *New York Times*, Oct. 13, 1975, 38:3.
After the end of the almost month-long American Federation of Musicians' strike, Papp said he had lost almost $200,000 in revenue from the closing of *A Chorus Line*, and would have to cancel the fifth and last play in his season of new plays at the Booth Theater.

746. Calta, Louis. "Papp Drops Five Play Series at Booth." *New York Times*, Oct. 21, 1975, 42:1.
Papp announced that he will discontinue his season of five new plays by contemporary American playwrights at the Booth Theater on Broadway, because of "catastrophic financial difficulties." He says that the plays will be relocated at smaller theaters within the Public theater complex and at Lincoln Center. This move should reduce the NYSF's projected deficit for the season from $1.2 million to a more manageable $500,000.

747. Gottfried, Martin. "What's the Matter With Papp?" *New York Post*, Oct. 25, 1975, Entertainment sec., 2.
Papp's luck has run out according to Gottfried. He has been forced to change the orientation at the Beaumont from new plays to classics. Several days ago he announced the cancellation of a series of new plays at the Booth Theater, and the Public Theater has yet to have its first professional production this season. Describes Papp as a man with an obsession

to upset apple carts, and who believes in change for its own sake. Hopes Papp will benefit from his recent setbacks.

748. Gussow, Mel. "A Playwright's Invention Named Papp." *New York Times*, Nov. 9, 1975, Magazine sec., 18+.

The different elements of Papp's theatrical empire are described. His wholehearted support of his playwrights has caused him many problems. Examples are given of the way he constantly changes his mind about what productions to stage. Papp is, however, a master at using the media to benefit his causes ever since his legendary battle with Robert Moses. The author feels that Papp's two chief contributions to American theater have been encouraging minority theater and nurturing new playwrights. Some details about his private life and his family are included at the conclusion of the article.

1976

749. "Notes on People." *New York Times*, Jan. 1, 1976, 18:7.

Papp and Gail Merrifield, who is director of play development at the NYSF, will get married January 18. Ms. Merrifield is the great-great granddaughter of John Wilkes Booth.

750. Trumbull, Robert. "Papp Assails Arts Center in Ottawa." *New York Times*, Jan. 10, 1976, 18:2.

Papp, speaking at a convention of American and Canadian art center directors, described the Ottawa National Arts Center as a "lousy conception whose creator should have been shot." He said, that like the Vivian Beaumont Theater in Lincoln Center, it was "of poor design for the purpose." Canadian newspaper critic Jamie Portman termed Papp's appraisal as "rude, unsubstantiated and ill-mannered" in a syndicated article. The Ottawa Center director, G. Hamilton Southam, praised the building, but Bernard Hopkins, the actor and director, said that he agreed with Papp's criticism.

751. Calta, Louis. "Papp Starts $780,000 Drive for Delacorte." *New York Times*, Feb. 10, 1976, 42:1.

Papp announced the start of a campaign to raise $780,000 for the rehabilitation of the Delacorte Theater in Central Park. He met with about 60 heads of foundations and corporations as well as persons with philanthropic interests. He also disclosed that George T. Delacorte had made a matching grant of $200,000. Papp said that all hopes for a new theater in the park had been abandoned.

752. Dougherty, Philip. "Aid for Delacorte." *New York Times*, Feb. 10, 1976, 62:6.

The Committee to Rebuild Delacorte Theater and Save Free Shakespeare for Central Park is in the midst of a fund-raising effort with the help of the Case & McGrath advertising agency, which created four newspaper advertisements and translated them into direct mail pieces.

753. Brown, Les. "PBS Play Tonight Causes Conflict." *New York Times*, Feb. 18, 1976, 75:4.

Papp is concerned about the loss of audiences for theatrical plays after they have been presented on television. He says he is particularly bothered by British productions "which not only conflict with stage dramas presented here, but can be purchased so cheaply by public television that they reduce opportunities for American production of serious drama on television."

754. Van Gelder, Lawrence. "Why 1976 Is Beginning to Look Like $19.76." *New York Times*, Apr. 3, 1976, 15:4.

This article on the commercialization of the U.S. Bicentennial focuses on some politicians and celebrities who are "turned off" by souvenir buying. Papp is one of those commenting. He does not intend to put on a play to commemorate the occasion.

755. Gussow, Mel. "Despite the Success of *A Chorus Line*, Papp Says He Still Needs Financial Aid." *New York Times*, Apr. 23, 1976, 24:1.

Papp talks about the NYSF's continuing need for funds despite the commercial success of *A Chorus Line*. He says that without that production's revenue the Festival would have only been able to present 20 percent of its plays, because 90 per cent of all its shows do not create revenue.

756. Berkvist, Robert. "Notes: Boom Time for the Bard." *New York Times*, May 16, 1976, sec. 2, 7:1.

Papp describes the research he did for his latest production of *Henry V* at the newly remodelled

Delacorte Theater. He wanted to make the war scenes realistic, so in addition to the cast of 60, the largest number he has ever used at the Delacorte , he's using dummies to create the effect of more bodies.

757. Berkvist, Robert. "Visiting a Papp Workshop." *New York Times*, May 28, 1976, sec. C, 3:1.

Free workshops have been staged at the Public Theater since it first opened. Papp describes the three basic categories of workshop production. Firstly, a play may need work that can be done in a workshop setting. Papp may like a play but be unsure of audience reaction. Finally, some plays have no potential, but Papp stages them for the authors' benefit.

758. "The Shakespeare Tree." Editorial. *New York Times*, June 16, 1976, 38:2.

It is the 20th anniversary of the NYSF's free performances in the city parks. Papp also has a special surprise for the public—a refurbished Delacorte Theater. The company has renovated it without city help.

759. Gold, Sylviane. "Festival Cuts—Papp's Step Toward a National Theater." *New York Post*, Aug. 24, 1976, 17.

Papp is hoping to form a permanent theater company to play classics at the Beaumont. To lay the groundwork for this, the NYSF is curtailing its season at Lincoln Center. Instead of four plays, just two will be presented—*The Cherry Orchard* and one other classic with the same actors and director. Papp has approached a number of his favorite actors, including Irene Worth, Raul Julia, Meryl Streep, Stacy Keach, James Earl Jones and Cicely Tyson, all of whom have expressed an interest in such a company. One of Papp's goals is to have a major American acting company that can compete in the international arena. He says that if we wait for the federal government to start a national theater "our hair will turn gray and our teeth will fall out."

760. Gussow, Mel. "Papp Halves New Season at Beaumont." *New York Times*, Aug. 24, 1976, 20:1.

Papp has changed his theatrical policy at Lincoln Center for the third time in four seasons. He has reduced by half his 1976-77 season at the Vivian Beaumont Theater. The new Beaumont season, originally scheduled for fall, will not begin until February 4 with *The Cherry Orchard. The Threepenny Opera*, a hit from last season, will continue until January. Papp cited financial problems as the reason for the change in program. His financial problems are ironic as he currently has "four palpable hits"—*A Chorus Line* on Broadway; *For Colored Girls Who Have Considered Suicide*, which is moving from the Public Theater to Broadway; *The Threepenny Opera* at the Beaumont and *Streamers* at the Mitzi E. Newhouse Theater. The Lincoln Center plays, although operating at capacity, make no profit. Papp said that during this lull in his activities he would make plans for the creation of "American classical theater company" with "first-class American actors."

761. Barnes, Clive. "Critic's Notebook: Comments, Not Complaints, About Mr. Papp and the Irish." *New York Times*, Dec. 8, 1976, sec. C, 19:1.

Barnes believes that Papp is "the best thing to happen to the American Theater," but wishes that he would accept responsibility for creating a national theater at Lincoln Center. Papp's predecessor, Jules Irving, did try to create one. Barnes feels that at present Papp is not using the Lincoln Center theaters very effectively.

1977

762. "Baking Out the Blues in Your Own Sauna." *New York Times*, Feb. 9, 1977, sec. C, 14:4.

The Papps installed a four feet by six feet sauna in their New York apartment three years ago. They use it as often as twice a day to unwind and get away from the children.

763. "Appeal sent by Writers and Artists." *New York Times*, Feb. 15, 1977, 3:2.

Papp was one of 54 American writers and artists who supported a petition sent to Czechoslovak leader, Gustav Husak, protesting the recent arrests of dissidents.

764. Epstein, Helen. "The N.Y. Shakespeare Festival—Does Biggest Mean Best?" *New York Times*, Feb. 27, 1977, sec. 2, 1:2.

The NYSF is now the largest arts institution in the United States. Its operating budget for 1977 is $30.1 million and the last summer festival employed about 700 people. As well as including a brief history of the company, the article describes the process by which plays are picked for production, and how their directors and actors are chosen. The organization of the company is also explained.

765. Gussow, Mel. "Papp Plans New Look for Beaumont." *New York Times*, Apr. 13, 1977, sec. C, 21:1.

Papp has presented plans to the Lincoln Center Board of Directors for a $6.5 million renovation of the Vivian Beaumont Theater. The theater would be rebuilt as open flexible space and would be redesigned by Giorgio Cavaglieri.

766. Winfrey, Carey. "Papp Quits Lincoln Center, Citing Artistic-Fiscal Trap." *New York Times*, June 10, 1977, sec. A, 1:1.

Papp announced that the NYSF would vacate the Lincoln Center theaters at the conclusion of the return engagement of the Chekhov play *The Cherry Orchard*, which will begin June 28. Papp said he felt trapped in the institutional structure at Lincoln Center, but now he would be free to focus on developing new plays for his Public Theater. He planned to create a cabaret and 650 seat theater, as well as expand his television production activities. He would continue summer productions in Central Park. Papp said that he believed no theater could operate at Lincoln Center and make a profit. Even a successful season resulted in a $2 million deficit. He said that even without the fiscal problems he would have left. He was unhappy that the poor design of the Beaumont and the unreceptive, middle class audience forced him to stage mainly classics. The history of the NYSF's tenure at Lincoln Center is recalled.

767. Eder, Richard. "Beaumont's Future: Papp Withdrawal Raises Question of Subsidy and of What Kind of Theater it Should Be." *New York Times*, June 11, 1977, 10:1.

Papp said no theater company could make a profit at Lincoln Center, when he announced his withdrawal from it. He was subsidizing about 20 percent of the budget even when the box office did well. He was unhappy having to use the profits from *A Chorus Line* to subsidize classics instead of new plays, which are his real interest.

768. Winfrey, Carey. "Theater Men React to Papp Departure." *New York Times*, June 11, 1977, 10:3.

Papp's announcement that he was leaving Lincoln Center took most theater people by surprise. Different personalities were asked to comment on how the Vivian Beaumont Theater should be used in the future. The underlying problem most agreed was the inability to make Lincoln Center economically viable without more federal financing. However, more aid from that source seems unlikely. Michael Straight, deputy chairman of the National Endowment for the Arts, said that last year the Endowment gave Papp a grant of $155,000 for his Lincoln Center operation, the most authorized to a single institution under present legislative ceilings.

769. "After Joseph Papp, What Next for Lincoln Center?" *New York Times*, June 26, 1977, sec. 2, 1:3.

The *New York Times* invited a number of leading theatrical figures to comment on the future of the theaters at Lincoln Center after Papp's departure. Irene Worth , the star of the NYSF's final production at Lincoln Center, *The Cherry Orchard*, said that she was sad Papp was leaving. However, she could understand why he was doing so, as the architectural limitations of the Vivian Beaumont made it a difficult theater to work in.

770. "What Now for Lincoln Center?" Editorial. *New York Times*, June 26, 1977, sec. 4, 18:1.

Papp tried new plays, revivals, star-studded productions and classics, but finally concluded that no theater company could operate profitably at Lincoln Center. Supports idea that Vivian Beaumont Theater should house a national repertory company. The project would need a lot more financial support though than the $730,000 Papp received last year in government and foundation grants. Commends Papp for trying very hard to make Lincoln Center viable. Glad he will still be creating exciting theater downtown at the Public Theater.

771. Ferretti, Fred. "Shakespeare in the Park Opens Without the Bard of Avon." *New York Times*, June 28, 1977, 33:3.

The 21st season of NYSF performances in Central Park contains no Shakespeare. *The Threepenny Opera* and *Agamemnon* are the plays being performed. Papp denies that it was a shortage of money that forced him to repeat plays already produced at the Vivian Beaumont Theater the previous winter. He says he wants people who could not afford to pay for tickets to see these plays as well. The Delacorte theater is newly refurbished for this season.

772. Eder, Richard. "The Vivian Beaumont Concept—Was It an Impossible Dream?" *New York Times*, July 17, 1977, sec. 2, 1:1.

The history of failure at Lincoln Center and speculation on its future. Does not blame Papp for leaving, as he was very unhappy with the productions he had to stage there. He was also losing money and putting his Public Theater in jeopardy. Even Papp himself agrees that only a middle-of-the-road company performing classics can succeed at Lincoln Center.

773. Pace, Eric. "Beaumont May Be Shut 2 Years." *New York Times*, Aug. 6, 1977, 9:1.

The Vivian Beaumont may be shut for as long as one or two years after *The Cherry Orchard* ends its run tomorrow, four weeks earlier than originally planned. Papp is leaving Lincoln Center because he felt he had been "trapped in an institutional structure both artistically and fiscally" and wanted to be free "to focus his energies and assets on developing new plays for his Public Theater." The Lincoln Center board has no immediate plans for the building, while looking for a successor to Papp.

774. Beaufort, John. "What's Needed to Reopen the Beaumont: Lincoln Center Head Talks of Two

Year Delay." *Christian Science Monitor*, Aug. 11, 1977, 23:1.

Papp was the wrong choice for Lincoln Center, as he alienated many subscribers with his policy of presenting only new plays. He subsequently reverted to the classics. The 1976-77 deficit was met with profits from *A Chorus Line* and Papp did not want to have to support the Beaumont any more, when he could make better use of the money at the Public Theater.

775. "Seminar Discusses Ways to Assist." *New York Times*, Sep. 12, 1977, 71:4.

Papp was one of the speakers at a seminar on the future of the arts in New Jersey, in which ways to increase government support of artistic endeavors were discussed. Papp said he felt that the government should increase its financing of the arts. He did not think, as some people did, that subsidies were in some way subversive. Another speaker was Rep. Andrew Maguire, who has sponsored a bill which gives taxpayers the right to designate a dollar of their annual tax bill for support of the arts. This support could total $1.7 billion. Papp said that in the way the arts are organized, he did not think that it was possible to spend all that money.

776. Henry, Gerrit. "Will Cabaret Catch On in New York?" *New York Times*, Nov. 6, 1977, sec. 2, 1:3.

When Papp pulled out of Lincoln Center he turned his attention "to a renewed effort to realise his dream of making the Public Theater the center of theatrical creativity in New York." A major element of the program is converting Martinson Hall into a cabaret. The "club" will seat 208 patrons at tables. Papp said he chose a cabaret because he wanted to create an informal, intimate atmosphere between the performers and audience. Music is to be an important part of the shows.

777. Cummings, Judith. "Agency to Renovate Arts Facilities Proposed by State Senator." *New York Times*, Nov. 23, 1977, sec. C, 10:3.

Papp testified at a hearing of the New York State Senate subcommittee on the Future of the Motion Picture and Entertainment Industry in New York State. He said that New York City and the state should set up a special school to train high school dropouts in the technical aspects of theater work. "The theater district can't be an oasis. The most pressing problem facing the city is teenage unemployment."

778. Fraser, C. Gerald. "Arts Leaders Back Call for White House Meeting." *New York Times*, Dec. 18, 1977, sec. 1, 25:1.

Government officials and arts leaders, including Papp, gathered at the Juilliard School of Music to testify in favor of a congressional resolution calling for a White House conference on the arts in 1979.

1978

779. "Papp Fights Plan to Air BBC's Bard over PBS." *New York Times*, Feb. 10, 1978, 26:1.

Papp criticised PBS' plan to televise a BBC series of all the plays of Shakespeare over a six year period. He said it would make it impossible for a Shakespeare production to be done on television by an American company for six years. He advocated an exchange of television programs with England. Papp felt that American theater companies could put on just as good productions of Shakespeare. He said that with some financial aid from the government and private industry he would be prepared to be responsible for half of the 36 programs. Henry Loomis, the president of PBS said that the BBC programs were going to be produced anyway and "all PBS is doing is getting the American rights."

780. Popkin, Henry. "Joseph Papp...Public Theater Brings His Visions to Stage." *New York Herald Tribune*, Feb. 14, 1978, 25.

Papp is astonishing and a "true revolutionary," whose abrupt changes of policy are his trademark. For example, several years ago Papp mixed black actors with white actors in Shakespearean roles, but now he favors separate black projects at the Public. In another turnabout, Papp is thinking of going back to the Beaumont after leaving it less than a year ago. He feels that the Beaumont is the only major facility for repertory.

781. "Papp Assails WNET Plan." *New York Times*, Feb. 16, 1978, sec. C, 24:1.

Papp opposes the WNET public television station plan to use American actors in a series of programs to introduce BBC productions of Shakespeare plays on PBS. Papp was asked to be a consultant for the series, "Shakespeare for Everyone." He believes it is insulting to ask American theatrical figures "to serve as a warm-up for the British series," when they had demanded that American companies be allowed to make 18 of the 36 proposed productions.

782. "Radio City Debated by Landmarks Unit." *New York Times*, Mar. 15, 1978, sec. B, 3:6.

The New York City Landmarks Commission held a debate on a proposal to designate the interior of Radio City Music Hall as a historic landmark. Supporters hope that this will save the theater from being closed by the Rockefeller Center, which owns it. Papp urged the commission to make the designation. He also called for the management to produce different shows than the traditional entertainment format, in order to make the Music Hall economically viable.

783. "Papp: Now, Movies, Too." *New York Post*, Mar. 24, 1978, 31.

Papp is starting a film program today at the Little Theater at the Public. He plans to show films that failed in commercial theater for a variety of non-artistic reasons, such as poor publicity. The opening film will be *High Street*, which received good reviews last year but closed after five weeks because its single print was in tatters and there was no money to make another. Papp plans to subsidize these films but envisions government subsidies in the future.

784. Brown, Les. "Papp and Lear Fight On for Better TV Theater." *New York Times*, Mar. 31, 1978, sec. B, 28:1.

Papp and Norman Lear propose to team up in an ambitious television project that would involve the presentation of a weekly play on a commercial network. Nothing has come of their plan so far as none of the three commercial networks have been willing to do it, but the producers have not abandoned the idea.

785. Eder, Richard. "Papp Proves Less is More." *New York Times*, Apr. 2, 1978, sec. 2, 1:1.

When Papp left Lincoln Center it seemed as if he was suffering a serious defeat, but the NYSF has proved itself more vibrant than ever since then. The quality of the past season at the Public Theater has been very high. The company still has serious problems, however, with its box office earnings accounting for less than a fifth of its budget.

786. "Yale Troupe to Play at Papp Theater." *New York Times*, Apr. 5, 1978, sec. 2, 21:1.

The Yale Repertory Theater is to take up residence at the Public Theater for six weeks, at the invitation of Papp.

787. "New Crisis Over Actors' Pay Off-Off Broadway." *New York Times*, Apr. 21, 1978, sec. C, 28:1.

Actors' Equity is asking its members to ratify new pay regulations for Off-Off Broadway theaters that have been evolving for several years. Papp says that at the heart of the regulations are financial restrictions that he believes will kill many theaters.

788. Tuck, Lon. "Chutzpah—That's What You Need to Get Grants." *New York Post*, May 29, 1978, 13:1.

A history of Papp's success at grantmanship. He got his first grant in 1956 from the Doris Duke Foundation, which had never before granted money to theater. Although the Ford Foundation officers ignored his requests for 15 years, in 1973 they finally granted him $1.5 million. His NYSF, which once operated on a shoestring, grossed $30 million in 1977 and employed 300 people.

789. Palmer, Robert. "New Jazz Thrives at the Public." *New York Times*, June 2, 1978, sec. C, 11:1.

Papp is presenting a jazz concert series entitled *New Jazz at the Public* at the Public Theater.

790. Shepard, Richard F. "Friends of Papp Produce a Party." *New York Times*, June 23, 1978, sec. C, 4:1.

A surprise party, attended by 1,500, was held at the Delacorte Theater to celebrate Papp's 57th birthday and the 25th anniversary of the issuing of a provisional charter by the state to the Shakespearean Theater Workshop, the original name of the Festival. President Carter sent Papp a telegram congratulating him on his birthday and his "brilliant work with the Festival."

791. Barnes, Clive. "In Praise of Shakespeare in the Park." *New York Times*, June 29, 1978, 38:3.

Barnes calls the NYSF possibly the most active theater in the United States, and credits Papp's love of Shakespeare as the reason for its growth. A history of the Festival is given.

792. Brewster, Townsend. "A Rapp with Joe Papp." *New York Amsterdam News*, Aug. 5, 1978, sec. D, 1.

One of Papp's theatrical achievements has been his support of black actors, playwrights and directors. Beginning with his use of black actors in the early days of Shakespeare in the Park, he has gone on to produce plays by black dramatists, including Adrienne Kennedy, Alice Childress, Charles Gordone, Ntozabe Shange, Derek Walcott and Aishah Rahman. Papp laments the decline of black theater since the early 1970's and blames the economic depression, the waning of the civil rights movement and the loss of black talent from the stage to television and films. He believes that the basic elements on which to build a national theater are to be found in the black population, since its culture is intact.

793. Peck, Seymour. Untitled. *New York Times*, Sep. 12, 1978, 112.

Bernard Gersten, Papp's close friend and associate producer for 17 years, has left the NYSF because he disagreed with Papp's decision to sever his connection with *Ballroom*, the new musical by Michael Bennett, who created *A Chorus Line*. Papp felt that the musical was an inappropriate project for a nonprofit organization like the Festival. Gersten will probably join Bennett and the Shubert organization to bring *Ballroom* to Broadway.

794. Corry, John. "Papp Sees a 'Terrific' Papp Year." *City News* [New York], Sep. 15, 1978, 53.

Papp discusses his new season and says that theater people should have a sense of social importance. He gives as an example Meryl Streep, who has often worked for him for little pay. One of the most interesting plays planned for this season is E. L. Doctorow's new drama, *Drinks before Dinner*. Mike Nichols will direct and Christopher Plummer has been cast as the lead.

795. Judge, Diane. "Joe Papp May Be a Monster but He's Sacred." *New York Post*, Nov. 4, 1978, 13.

An interview with Papp at the Public Theater. Most of the plays produced at the Public cannot be moved to Broadway because they are not commercial. The only time Papp thinks of Broadway is when he thinks it can make money to keep the Public operating. *A Chorus Line* has been paying all of the Public's debt for several years. Papp needs $6 million a year to support his theatrical enterprises, and the government contributes only $800,000. He also discusses his newly formed black Shakespeare company.

796. Lask, Thomas. "Publishing: $2.25 Million for 'Love Sign' Rights." *New York Times*, Dec. 1, 1978, sec. C, 24:2.

Papp seems to be including all the arts at the Public Theater. Having presented a jazz series, a film series and several seasons of ballet featuring the Eliot Feld Ballet, he is now inaugurating a monthly poetry series. The series will begin with readings by David Mamet and Marvin Cohen.

797. Heilpern, John. "Joe's Show." *Observer* [London], Dec. 3, 1978, Magazine sec., 39+.

Written for an English audience, this review of Papp's career and successes starts with Clive Barnes' negative review of the play *The Boom Boom Room* on the opening night of the NYSF at Lincoln Center. Papp's background is recounted; his childhood in Brooklyn, socialist leanings, wartime service in the navy, where he organized vaudeville shows, and his training at the Actors' Laboratory in Hollywood, where he became managing director after two years. This led to his campaign for a free Shakespeare festival in Central Park. "I felt the masses would like Shakespeare because I did, and I had the same tastes as the masses. I was one of them." This in turn led to the famous battle known as "The Robert Moses Affair."

798. Pace, Eric. "New Stage Panel Plans O'Neill Celebrations." *New York Times*, Dec. 22, 1978, sec. C, 3:1.

A committee of professional theater people and noted admirers of the plays of Eugene O'Neill has been formed to mount annual observances in his honor, which will culminate in 1988 in nationwide celebrations of the 100th anniversary of his birth. Papp and his wife, Gail Merrifield, are both members of the committee.

1979

799. "Political Party for Papp." *New York Times*, Jan. 9, 1979, sec. C, 8:5.

The New York County Democratic Party announced it was breaking with tradition by honoring a non-politician, Joseph Papp, at its annual dinner February 1. Papp said he considered himself a politician. He said, "I spend more time at city hall than at the Metropolitan Opera."

800. Blau, Eleanor. "Papp Starts a Shakespearean Repertory Troupe Made Up Entirely of Black and Hispanic Actors." *New York Times*, Jan. 21, 1979, 55:1.

A Shakespearean repertory company made up entirely of black and Hispanic actors will present its first production, *Julius Caesar*, on January 25 at the Public Theater. It was founded by Papp and is probably the first such company.

801. Gussow, Mel. "Can a Committee Revive the Beaumont?" *New York Times*, Jan. 21, 1979, sec. 2, 1:1.

The Vivian Beaumont Theater at Lincoln Center is to be used in late 1979 or early 1980 for the first time since the NYSF vacated it. Instead of operating in the traditional fashion under one or two artistic directors, it will have five directors, Woody Allen, Sarah Caldwell, Liviu Ciulei, Robin Phillips and Ellis Rabb, and one playwright Edward Albee. Papp was critical of the new arrangement because he saw "no theatrical precedent or justification" for rule by a committee. He also wondered where the power would lie. His other concern was the continuing lack of financing for the theater.

802. "Democrats Give Papp $125-a-Ticket Dinner in Honor of His Work." *New York Times*, Feb. 2, 1979, sec. B, 3:2.

About 900 Democrats paid $125 to attend the annual dinner of the New York County Democratic Party and to honor Papp for his "contribution to the life and lifestyle of New York City." Papp has no direct ties with the Democratic Party.

803. Lawson, Carol. "Papp Pushes Minority Troupe." *New York Times*, Feb. 14, 1979, sec. B, 15:4.

Papp talks about his commitment to his new black and Hispanic Shakespeare company "which has been criticized for its racial composition, its inexperience in Shakespeare and its difficulty with classical speech." Papp defends it by saying that you can only have integration if you have equal opportunity, which he is providing to blacks and Hispanics. He says "they can't get power out of politics, but they can develop it in the theater."

804. Fraser, C. Gerald. "Asian-American Actors Get Pledge from Papp." *New York Times*, Feb. 22, 1979, sec. C, 26:1.

A group of Asian-American actors, picketing outside the Public Theater, was assured by Papp that the NYSF will employ significant numbers of Asian-American actors, playwrights and directors in future productions. The actors claimed that 10 or fewer Asian-American actors have worked at the Public Theater in the last 10 years.

805. Fenichell, Stephen. "The Perfect Setting for Theater and Art." *New York Post*, Feb. 27, 1979, Magazine sec., 19.

The transformation of Central Park into a cultural resource for the City of New York began with Papp's production of *Romeo and Juliet* from the top of a flatbed truck that broke down near Belvedere Lake. The great park, from the beginning, was intended to be a sylvan retreat for relaxation and contemplation, not a place for plays and concerts. Responding to the enthusiastic reception of New Yorkers to Papp's group, George Delacorte offered to pay for the construction of a theater. Within several years, the New York Philharmonic and the Metropolitan Opera Company were performing in the park.

806. "Ay, There's the Rub." *New York Times*, Mar. 12, 1979, sec. C, 21:4.

The NYSF will encourage playgoers in Central Park next summer to make a "suggested contribution" of five dollars, because the city will make no financial contribution to the season. Only a single production, *The Pirates of Penzance* with Linda Ronstadt and Raul Julia, will be offered.

807. Gussow, Mel. "Papp's Third World Troupe to Be Classics Repertory." *New York Times*, Mar. 23, 1979, sec. C, 4:5.

Papp is expanding his black and Hispanic Shakespeare company into a third world repertory classical acting company. The company will begin with a budget of $1.2 million a year, which will eventually rise to $2.5-$3 million a year, approximately half of the entire budget of the NYSF. The organization will also include Asian-Americans, and will be the nucleus of what Papp envisions as a year-round repertory theater.

808. Whitney, Craig R. "Papp Says Moscow Shows Interest in U.S. Musical." *New York Times*, May 20, 1979, 8:1.

Papp wants to bring the Broadway musical *A Chorus Line* to Moscow, where he has just paid a five day visit. He says that the Soviet authorities have shown interest in the proposal. He also says that he asked the Russians to encourage the development of a new Yiddish musical theater company, that has been formed in the U.S.S.R., so that it might visit the United States in two years.

809. Gussow, Mel. "Papp Plans Five Play Soviet Swap." *New York Times*, May 30, 1979, sec. C, 17:1.

Papp is negotiating with the U.S.S.R. for the exchange of five American and five Russian plays. This could follow a six month tour by *A Chorus Line* of Russia and Eastern Europe. Papp and his wife have recently returned from a 10 day journey to Moscow and Leningrad that they made at the invitation of the Soviet Ministry of Culture.

810. Sullivan, Joseph F. "Princeton Confers 1,589 Degrees on Its 232d Commencement Day." *New York Times*, June 13, 1979, sec. B, 7:3.

Papp was awarded the honorary degree of Doctor of Fine Arts at Princeton's 232d commencement day.

811. Lawson, Carol. "Two-City Productions." *New York Times*, June 27, 1979, sec. C, 28:4.

Papp and the Kennedy Center director Roger L. Stevens have made a deal to co-produce plays that will originate at the Public Theater and move to the Kennedy Center's Eisenhower Theater. The production and operating costs, as well as the income, will be shared.

812. Mason, Clifford. "A New Black Theater." *New York Times*, July 22 1979, Magazine sec., 28.

This history of black classical theater in America includes Papp's third world company of blacks, Asians and Hispanics. It is an unusual group in that only a few white actors will be invited to work with the company on occasion. Papp realizes that its creation is regarded as a political statement on his part, and acknowledges this is true. He believes that minorities are so discriminated against in New York City that they only have a cultural outlet.

813. Shepard, Richard F. "300 at Picnic to Assist Shakespeare Festival." *New York Times*, Aug. 1, 1979, sec. C, 19:1.

A fund-raising picnic for the NYSF was held near the Delacorte Theater. The guests paid $150 a couple. The free Central Park and Mobile Theater performances cost over $1 million a year. *A Chorus Line* pays a third of the cost (though its revenues are starting to decline). Another third comes from the city, and the final third from private donations. Papp says the Festival is particularly interested in getting corporate support, which it has never had. He believes this is due to the misconception that theater can pay for itself when it is successful.

814. Lawson, Carol. "News of the Theater." *New York Times*, Aug. 8, 1979, sec. C, 17:4..

A Chorus Line will play in Kiev for two weeks starting April 1, 1980. It will then transfer to Leningrad for two weeks, and to Moscow for four weeks. The Moscow Art Theater will appear simultaneously in New York, then in Boston and Washington D.C. The American part of the exchange is expected to cost $1.5 million, which Papp will try to raise from large American companies.

815. Crossette, Barbara. "Mobile Theater Stages *Mighty Gents* at Pier 84." *New York Times*, Aug. 17, 1979, sec. C, 17:1.

The play *The Mighty Gents* opened the 1979 Mobile Theater season. Its first performance was held on the city's newly rehabilitated Pier 84. This is the 16th season of the Mobile Theater. Over the years the choice of plays has moved away from pure Shakespeare to works of contemporary writers that neighborhood audiences can relate to. Attempts are made to bring the theater into areas where playgoing is hardly a normal activity. If possible, neutral turf is selected that does not belong to one neighborhood or another.

816. "Public Theater Will Show Mizoguchi Film Festival." *New York Times*, Sep. 23, 1979, 58:3.

The Saga of Kenji Mizoguchi, a three week festival, will be presented by Papp's Film at the Public program.

817. "Joseph Papp Will Sponsor *Evening for the Boat People*." *New York Times*, Sep. 29, 1979, 12:6.

Papp and the International Rescue Committee will sponsor *An Evening for the Boat People* theater benefit on October 15 at the Public Theater to aid South East Asian refugees.

818. "Benefit Is Held Here to Aid Boat People." *New York Times*, Oct. 16, 1979, sec. B, 6:3..

The Public Theater held a special benefit performance to raise funds for the Vietmanese boat people. The benefit was presented by Papp and the International Rescué Committee.

819. "Marchers Protest in New York." *New York Times*, Oct. 25, 1979, 3:4.

A group of Americans, including Papp, Arthur Miller and Kurt Vonnegut, demonstrated in front of Czechoslovakia's mission to the United Nations in New York, demanding the release of dissidents.

820. "Theaters to Collect for Cambodia." *New York Times*, Nov. 8, 1979, sec. D, 21:3.

Papp has founded the Theater Committee for Relief to Cambodian Refugees. He says that for the first time legitimate theaters will allow the collection of funds from audiences for a cause other that the Actors' Fund. The committee, headed by Papp, Michael Moriarty, Mike Nichols and Liv Ullman, will try to raise $100,000 in the next two weeks for medical teams and supplies for refugee camps along the Thai-Cambodian border. As well as 24 Broadway theaters, 18 Off-Broadway houses and two regional theaters will participate. The funds raised will be sent to Cambodia through the International Rescue Committee.

821. "An Offer that Joseph Papp Couldn't Refuse." *New York Times*, Nov. 14, 1979, sec. B, 5:1.
The Edward R. Murrow High School in New York will establish an actors studio named the Joseph Papp Theater. Papp will attend the dedication ceremony. Papp's daughter, Susan Papp Lipman, is the school's librarian.

822. Alston, Blanche Cordelia. "Papp and Olivier Win $18,250 Drama Awards." *New York Times*, Nov. 30, 1979, sec. C, 4:5.
Papp and Lawrence Olivier have received $18,250 each in the first presentation of the Common Wealth Awards of Distinguished Serice for their contributions to the dramatic arts. The awards were given by the Bank of Delaware under a trust established by Ralph Hayes. They were presented at a luncheon at the Players Club. Papp intends to give his award money to the Theater Committee for Cambodian Relief.

823. "Stage Folk Give $192,841 for Cambodian Relief." *New York Times*, Dec. 6, 1979, sec. C, 19:1.
Actress Liv Ullman presented a check for $192,841 for Cambodian relief to the International Rescue Committee chairman. The funds were

collected by the Theater Committee for Cambodian Relief. Papp, who organized the committee, attended the ceremony.

824. Lawson, Carol. "Lack of Cash Perils Soviet Exchange." *New York Times*, Dec. 19, 1979, sec. C, 23:4.

The proposed American-Soviet cultural exchange, involving the musical *A Chorus Line* and the Moscow Art Theater, is on the verge of being cancelled because there is no financing available for the American side of the venture. Papp has notified the U.S.S.R. that his efforts to raise $1 million have failed. Papp has set a January 15 deadline for raising the money. The 30 companies Papp approached refused to help him. He blamed poor United States-Soviet trade relations for the corporations' lack of interest in sponsoring this cultural exchange. He also failed to get governmental financial support.

825. Fraser, C. Gerald. "*Chorus Line* Trip Halted." *New York Times*, Dec. 28, 1979, sec. C, 11:5.

The exchange between the U.S.S.R. and the NYSF has been cancelled because Papp could not raise the $1 million needed to send a company to Russia. Papp said that he hoped Congress would increase appropriations to the International Communications Agency, a branch of the Department of State, so that it could fund more such projects. He said "unless more cultural exchanges are effected, we will appear only as a military machine although we are a profoundly cultural country."

1980

826. Blau, Eleanor. "Arts Face Drastic Cuts in Koch Budget Plan." *New York Times*, Jan. 18, 1980, sec. C, 6:5.

New York City Cultural Affairs Commissioner Henry Geldzahler reported that city financing for cultural programs would be almost eliminated under Mayor Koch's proposed budget. It would include a reduction from $1.6 million in the current fiscal year to $150,000 for free performances in Central Park by the NYSF, the New York Philharmonic Orchestra and the Metropolitan Opera. Papp said that even if there was no cut the NYSF could probably put on only one play in Central Park, because of a decline in revenues from *A Chorus Line*, which has provided most of the financing for the Festival in recent years.

827. Lawson, Carol. "Top Stars Join New Papp Venture." *New York Times*, Feb 13, 1980, sec. C, 24:1.

Meryl Streep, Robert De Niro, Jill Clayburgh and Raul Julia have all decided to spend six months working Off-Broadway next season for $225 a week. They have agreed to join a new repertory company being formed by Papp at the Public Theater. To lure such stars back to the stage is a great coup for Papp, but the company will cost about $1.4 million, so he is approaching government agencies and foundations for funds. Papp's last repertory company, consisting of minority actors, was not a critical success and has been disbanded.

828. Lask, Thomas. "Poetry: Reading Yiddish." *New York Times*, Feb. 27, 1980, sec. C, 15:5.

A Yiddish poetry reading was held at the Public Theater. Papp was one of the readers.

829. Shepard, Richard F. "300 Arts Leaders Rally to Protest Budget Cuts." *New York Times*, Mar. 4, 1980, sec. C, 7:1.

Papp was one of the speakers at a protest rally at Lincoln Center, attended by 300 representatives from New York cultural groups, to lobby for more support for the arts from New York City, the state and the federal government.

830. Corry, John. "O'Casey Centenary Fans Flames of His Works." *New York Times*, Mar. 26, 1980, 26:5.

The NYSF will stage a show on April 17 of readings, films, photographs and recordings as part of the centenary celebrations of the birth of the playwright Sean O'Casey.

831. "The Bard and His Heritage." *New York Times*, Apr. 24, 1980, sec. B, 12:1.

Papp addressed school children at the board of education headquarters during Jewish Heritage Week in New York schools and on the anniversary of Shakespeare's birth.

832. Oyama, David. "Asian-Americans Take Center Stage at the Public." *New York Times*, Apr. 27, 1980, sec. 2, 3:1.

After a group of Asian-American actors picketed the Public Theater to protest Papp's failure to use Asian actors or produce plays by Asian playwrights,

Papp began to look for such actors and plays. The first performance of *The Music Lessons* by the Japanese-American playwright Wakako Yamauchi will open shortly, followed by *FOB* by Chinese-American David Hwang.

833. "Manhattan Cites Twelve for Aid to Cultural Life." *New York Times*, Apr. 29, 1980, sec. B, 16:6.

Twelve certificates were awarded by the Manhattan borough president's office to individuals and organizations who "most contributed to the cultural vitality of the Borough of Manhattan during the current period of fiscal crisis." Papp was one of the recipients.

834. "Bank Aids Festival." *New York Times*, May 14, 1980, sec. C, 21:2.

A gap of $323,000 in the NYSF budget, created by a cut in city funds, has been largely restored by a grant from Citibank. Papp announced that the Festival has received $150,000 from the bank to help finance the free performances in Central Park. The bank has also promised to provide the Festival with $100,000 on a matching basis. Papp said the grant is the largest single corporate gift ever received by the Festival.

835. Nelsen, Don. "Bank Bucks for Papp Players." *New York Daily News*, May 14, 1980, 23.

Citibank came to the rescue of the NYSF when the city cut off funding for the park performances. For the first time Delacorte Theater audiences will also be asked to donate five dollars to be used toward meeting the matching grant from the bank. Instead of the usual Shakespeare program, the Festival will present *The Pirates of Penzance* this summer.

836. Ferretti, Fred. "Free Shakespeare in Central Park? That Is the Question." *New York Times*, July 13, 1980, sec. 2, 1:1.

Papp refused to put on Shakespeare in the Park this year because the city would not fund it. Papp believes that arts institutions should be funded on an annual basis through the city budget. He could have gotten some public money through the Summer Arts Fund, a collection of private and public financing, but refused to accept it from this source as he wants permanent funding. He did, however, accept funding from Citibank for a production of *The Pirates of Penzance* instead. This new battle is not the first time that Papp has challenged the city government. He had earlier battles with Robert Moses and the Board of Estimate.

837. Fraser, C. Gerald. "Board Vote Approves Portman Hotel." *New York Times*, July 18, 1980, sec. C, 15:3.

Papp leads the fight against the demolition of three theaters—the Helen Hayes, the Morosco and the Bijou—in order to build a large convention hotel, the Portman, on the site at Times Square. Papp called the theater district a "major historical district."

838. Shepard, Richard F. "Two Arts Festivals in Town." *New York Times*, Aug. 15, 1980, sec. C, 19:5.

Papp is one of the co-sponsors of the second Latin American Popular Theater Festival being held at the Public Theater. Plays by six theatrical groups from South America and the United States will be performed.

839. Johnston, Laurie. "Theater Turns to a Rich Past to Aid Library." *New York Times*, Oct. 20, 1980, sec. B, 2:1.

Papp was one of the personalities who helped to conduct an auction of arts memorabilia at Lincoln Center for the benefit of the Performing Arts Research Center of New York Public Library. The auction netted $9,000.

840. "Papp-Stevens Plans Off." *New York Times*, Oct. 22, 1980, sec. C, 22:5.

Papp and Roger L. Stevens have cancelled their plan to produce plays together. Under the agreement jointly produced plays would have been presented at both the Public Theater and at Kennedy Center.

841. Ferretti, Fred. "Joseph Papp: A 'Divisive Force' or a 'Healing' One?" *New York Times*, Dec. 20, 1980, 16:1.

Playwright Sam Shepard and Papp have quarrelled over the casting of Shepard's play *True West*. Papp was also dissatisfied with the play's director, Robert Woodruff, who resigned. Shepard supported Woodruff in the dispute. He said Papp would never get another of his plays to produce.

1981

842. Ferretti, Fred. "Mr. Papp's Treasure Chest Moves to the Great Indoors." *New York Times*, Jan. 3, 1981, 12:1.

Papp's production of *The Pirates of Penzance* is opening on Broadway at the Uris theater. Papp hopes that like *A Chorus Line* it will be a source of funds to subsidize his Off-Broadway experiments. Since 1975 *A Chorus Line* has made $32 million. Papp is also talking about a cast record of *The Pirates of Penzance* and co-producing it as a film with Francis Ford Coppola.

843. "Evening of Love Songs to Honor Harold Clurman." *New York Times*, Feb. 19, 1981, sec. C, 21:2.

Papp will be one of the performers in *An Evening of Love Songs* in memory of Harold Clurman and to benefit the Harold Clurman Theater.

844. Lawson, Carol. "Papp Urges Replacing U.S. Arts Endowment with State Agencies." *New York Times*, Feb. 21, 1981, 9:6.

After President Reagan proposed a 50% cut in appropriations for the arts, Papp called for the abolition of the National Endowment for the Arts. He proposed that federal money for the arts be channeled instead to state arts councils to administer the funds. He believes that decisions affecting the arts in New York should be made closer to home. Noting that the arts stimulate $2 billion in business in New York City, he called on the state and city governments to increase their own budgets for arts projects.

845. "Re-Creation and Recreation in Santa Fe." *New York Times*, Mar. 27, 1981, sec. C, 22:5.

Papp will appear in *Medicine Show*, a benefit at the Shubert Theater for the Santa Fe Festival. He will make brief remarks about the American theater scene.

846. Baker, Rob. "Joe Papp, a Gambling Man Plans for the Future." *New York Daily News*, Apr. 1, 1981, Manhattan sec., M2.

A long article on Papp's current theatrical plans and projects. Baker says no one has done more to influence New York theater than Papp in the past 20 years. He has almost single-handedly built the most controversial theatrical empire in the country. Papp worries about the future of the Public Theater without him, and to ensure its existence is putting most of the money from *The Pirates of Penzance*, currently a hit on Broadway, into an endowment fund. Papp denies interfering with playwrights and directors at the Public, although he admits that he attends rehearsals and makes suggestions. The Public Theater is his whole life. He is not interested in producing directly for Broadway or television, although many Public productions have been seen on both.

847. "Papp May Stage Operas." *New York Times*, Apr. 2, 1981, sec. C, 16:4.

Papp has been considering the production of popular operas by the NYSF. Francis Ford Coppola has expressed an interest in directing *La Boheme*.

848. "Twenty-six in Stage Hall of Fame." *New York Times*, Apr. 6, 1981, sec. C, 16:3.

The first L. Arnold Weissberger Award, given for outstanding theatrical achievement, was presented to Papp at the Uris Theater in a program entitled *A Tribute to Broadway*. A total of 26 people were inducted into the Theater Hall of Fame during the ceremony.

849. Lawson, Carol. "Broadway." *New York Times*, Apr. 24, 1981, sec. C, 2:4.

Public Television will air Elizabeth Swados's Passover cantata *The Hagaddah* live from the Public Theater, in a show entitled *Live from the Public Theater*. The NYSF is paying $125,000 to finance it. Papp sees this as an investment in the NYSF's eventual involvement in cable television.

850. Blau, Eleanor. "Papp and Pressman to film *Pirates*." *New York Times*, May 6, 1981, sec. C, 23:3.

Papp has sold the film rights to *The Pirates of Penzance* to Edward R. Pressman Productions. The film will be made in England. Papp originally intended to make the film with Francis Coppola, but the plan did not work out. He will join Pressman in planning the film. The NYSF will also receive 5% of the gross of the film and 10% of the profits.

851. McDowell, Edwin. "American Academy Medals Given to Cowley and Soyer." *New York Times*, May 21, 1981, sec. C, 14:3.

Papp was given an award for distinguished service to the arts by the American Academy and Institute of Arts and Letters at its 40th awards ceremony. He is the first theatrical producer to be so honored.

852. Heilpern, John. "Another Victory for Joseph Papp, and New York Theatre Lives Again." *Times* [London], Sep. 7, 1981, 7:1.

Heilpern believes that Papp has created "the finest example of a vital popular theatre to be found on either side of the Atlantic." Papp possesses the Midas touch as well, somehow managing to get his company bailed out of insolvency each year. At the same time he periodically produces a huge commercial hit, whose vast profits are used to keep his theaters alive. His latest blockbuster *The Pirates of Penzance* came at a desperate time for Papp. For the first time in 26 years New York City said it could not afford to subsidise free Shakespeare in the Park. Papp argued that it was the city's duty to support the arts. He seems to have won his case. Shakespeare is back in Central Park and the city has officially recognized the Public Theater as a city institution, with a permanent subsidy of $589,000 a year.

853. "Theater Piece Studies Children of Immigrants." *New York Times*, Nov. 16, 1981, sec. C, 19:2.

Papp was a participant in a performance called *Children in a New Land.* This theater anthology about the children of Jewish immigrants was sponsored by YIVO, the Institute for Jewish Research.

854. Perlez, Jane. "Joseph Papp's Big New Project Is Finding Himself." *New York Times*, Dec. 13, 1981, sec. 2, 1:3.

Written at a time of great financial success for Papp and the NYSF. Papp had established an endowment, which now stood at over $12 million.

About 95% of it came from *A Chorus Line*, and the remainder from *The Pirates of Penzance.*

Many details about Papp's personal life and personality are included. In the last 10 years he has increasingly acknowledged his Jewishness publicly, culminating in a recent trip to Israel. He has also had stormy relationships with writers, directors, politicians, wives, friends and institutions. Quarrels with Sam Shepard, Bernard Gersten and David Rabe, in particular, are chronicled.

855. Higgins, John. "A Very Promising Plank for 'Pirate' Papp." *Times* [London], Dec. 23, 1981, 8:2.

Not until he was 60 years old did Papp have any commercial contact with the cinema. *The Pirates of Penzance* has changed all that. The popular New York show is being made into a film, using most of the original stage cast. It is being filmed at Shepperton Studios near London. Papp is the producer. The NYSF got $1.5 million for the film rights. Papp has finally entered the cinema world because he wants to reach a larger audience. How the film is being made is described.

1982

856. Corry, John. "Broadway Stages a Drama to Save Two Theaters." *New York Times*, Mar. 5, 1982, 1:2.

Actors and playwrights demonstrated in front of the Morosco Theater in an attempt to prevent its demolition to make way for the Portman Hotel. Papp was one of the demonstration organizers. Readings were staged from eight Pulitzer Prize plays.

857. "Judge Extends a Ban on Razing Theaters; Protest Is Called Off." *New York Times*, Mar. 6, 1982, 1:1.

An injunction against the demolition of the Morosco and Helen Hayes theaters was extended until March 22. Papp ended the 24 hour demonstration in front of the Morosco and called the court decision a victory.

858. Prial, Frank J. "Top State Court Refuses to Block Theater Razing." *New York Times*, Mar. 17, 1982, sec. B, 1:6.

The New York State Court of Appeals refused to hear an appeal to delay the demolition of the Morosco and Helen Hayes theaters. Papp vowed to "lie in front of the wrecking equipment if necessary."

859. Prial, Frank J. "Court Stay Lifted and Demolition Begins at Two Broadway Theaters." *New York Times*, Mar. 23, 1982, 1:1.

About 170 demonstrators, including Papp, prevented the demolition of the Helen Hayes and Morosco theaters, which was to begin immediately after the United States Supreme Court lifted a stay. They demonstrated in an empty lot adjoining the Morosco. By prior arrangement with the police they were arrested and taken away in 13 police vans.

860. "Judge Drops Charges in Portman Protests." *New York Times*, Apr. 20, 1982, 8:5.

A judge in Manhattan Criminal Court dismissed trespass charges against Papp and 164 other theater people and supporters who were arrested on March 22 for protesting against the razing of the Helen Hayes and Morosco Theaters.

861. Lawson, Carol. "Joseph Papp Goes Abstract." *New York Times*, May 2, 1982, sec. 2, 1:1.

In this interview, Papp describes how he is focusing on what he calls "abstract plays" that suggest "the confusion and complexity in the world." He is disappointed with the failure of contemporary theater to deal with major social and political issues.

Papp has been increasingly involved in social causes and activities outside the theater, such as the fight to save the Helen Hayes and Morosco Theaters. On the day of this interview he is to lead a march of the Greater New York Conference on Soviet Jewry. He is also a member of Performing Artists for Nuclear Disarmament, and is going to Vietnam to search for information about American soldiers missing in action. Always searching for sources of funding for his theatrical enterprises, he is making deals for several of his Public Theater productions to appear on cable television.

862. "Papp, Vietnam-Bound, to Aid Veterans." *New York Times*, May 27, 1982, sec. B, 15:1.

Papp is going to Vietnam with a veterans' delegation that will try to trace missing servicemen and study the effects of the defoliant Agent Orange. He also hopes to arrange an American concert tour for Dang Thai Son, an acclaimed Vietmanese pianist, while he is there. The United States has no diplomatic ties with Vietnam and Papp says that when he broached the idea with a State Department official, he was told such a concert tour would be "inappropriate." Papp says he will press for the tour anyway.

863. "Japanese Film Series Opens at Public Today." *New York Times*, June 22, 1982, sec. C, 7:5.
The Public Theater's summer film program will consist of 12 Japanese films.

864. Fraser, C. Gerald. "Papp Thanks Patrons of His Park Theater." *New York Times*, July 22, 1982, sec. C, 13:3.
Citibank sponsored a supper and performance at the Delacorte Theater in Central Park for grant givers from 45 corporations and foundations, to thank them for their support and encourage those who don't already contribute. Papp said that corporate and foundation fund-raising were essential, but not the most important income for his $8 million operation. The greatest source of income has been successful shows like *A Chorus Line* and *The Pirates of Penzance*.

865. Lawson, Carol. "Latin American Theater to be Star of a Festival." *New York Times*, July 31, 1982, 9:5.
The NYSF is hosting the Third Latin American Popular Theater Festival. As many as 15 companies from Latin America and the United States will participate in the two week festival. The first one was held in 1976, and a second one in 1980. The experimental theater companies who take part are

community-based and collective in structure. Their plays deal with political and social issues.

866. Bennetts, Leslie. "Broadway Producers and Dramatists Lock Horns Over Antitrust Lawsuit." *New York Times*, Aug. 21, 1982, 17:1.

The League of New York Theaters and Producers filed an antitrust suit against the Dramatists Guild. The suit claimed that the Guild fixes the minimum shares of royalties that a playwright has to be paid, and prevents negotiations with producers. Papp is a member of the League, but objects to the lawsuit. He believes that the theater industry depends on playwrights, and new ones need to be defended from exploitation. He also thinks that writers have the right to organize themselves.

867. Corry, John. "Anspacher to Reopen Oct. 26." *New York Times*, Sep. 16, 1982, sec. C, 25:2.

The Anspacher Theater is being reconstructed with a new stage and seating arrangement. About a third of the 299 seats will be moveable.

868. "Papp Plans Programs for ABC Arts Station." *New York Times*, Sep. 24, 1982, sec. C, 24:6.

Papp has signed an agreement for six hours of programming to be broadcast on Hearst/ABC ARTS, the ABC cable station devoted to cultural programs. Two of the programs have already been completed, *A Midsummer Night's Dream* and *Swan Lake, Minnesota*, a spoof of the classical ballet.

869. Lawson, Carol. "Year-Round Shakespeare Is Among Papp's Plans." *New York Times*, Oct. 4, 1982, sec. C, 20:1.

Papp plans to present Shakespeare plays year-round in the Public Theater's Anspacher Hall. The first production will be *Hamlet* with Diane Venora in the title role. He is also planning an exchange with the Royal Court Theater of London.

This year the Public Theater's $7 million budget will suffer from a sharp decline in profits from *A Chorus Line* and *The Pirates of Penzance*. The theater will be able to make up most of the deficit from other sources, including $1.4 million in interest earned from its $17 million endowment.

870. Bennetts, Leslie. "Why Not a Woman As Hamlet?" *New York Times*, Nov. 28, 1982, sec. 2, 5:1.

Papp's fourth production of *Hamlet* has a woman, Diane Venora, playing Hamlet. There is a long tradition dating back to the 18th century of women playing the role, but Papp still expects his production to be controversial.

871. Barnes, Clive. "The World's an Empty Stage Without the Bard." *New York Post*, Dec. 11, 1982, Movie page.

The New York stage needs more Shakespeare. Only three or four Shakespeare plays a year are presented in the city. Since Papp opened the Public Theater in 1967, he has emphasized contemporary drama over Shakespeare. This season he has suggested that he might start a new policy of having at least one Shakespeare play in production at all times at the Public. Barnes suggests using the empty

Vivian Beaumont Theater for Shakespeare plays. He thinks that the obvious candidate to run the program is Michael Langham.

1983

872. Lawson, Carol. "Broadway." *New York Times*, Jan. 21, 1983, sec. C, 2:1.

Papp plans to spend $10 million for the development of new musicals and plays at the Public Theater over the next five years. He hopes to pep up New York theater and at the same time produce some successful Broadway productions that will help finance his $9 million a year operation.

873. Nelsen, Don. "Meet Joseph Papp, Promoter Extraordinaire." *New York Daily News*, Feb. 9, 1983, 57.

Discusses Papp's radio commercials for the Public Theater. Although he is "an insufferable egotist," he is one of the few "personalities" left among theater producers today.

874. Conroy, Sarah Booth. "*Pirates* and Plaudits: Papp Receives Coe Award at Kennedy Center." *Washington Post*, Feb 21, 1983, sec. C, 1:1.

Papp was given the third Richard L. Coe Award at a ceremony at the Kennedy Center to benefit the New Playwrights Theater. The first film Papp has produced, *The Pirates of Penzance*, was also shown.

875. Blau, Eleanor. "Papp's Play Deal with British Stirs Happy Ripple Effect." *New York Times*, Mar. 4, 1983, sec. C, 2:2.

Papp has arranged an exchange of plays between the NYSF and the Royal Court Theatre in London. The first British play in the exchange program, Caryl Churchill's *Top Girls*, did so well in New York that an American cast took over when the British cast went home. Thomas Babe's *Buried Inside Extra* will be the first play to go to England. The plan is not only to continue the exchanges, but also to commission plays specifically for the program. Papp hopes it will also encourage more American play-writing.

876. Blau, Eleanor. "Pickets Assail Cuts for Arts." *New York Times*, Mar. 4, 1983, sec. C, 4:6..

Papp and other leaders of the New York arts world gathered in front of the Lincoln Center Plaza to protest Governor Cuomo's proposed cut of $4.5 million in arts aid. Papp said that it was a mistake because the arts are income producing.

877. O'Haire, Patricia. "For Shakespeare, Just Dial (212) 861-PAPP." *New York Daily News*, June 11, 1983, 11.

The New York Telephone Company has given Papp $200,000 for his Shakespeare in the Park program. This is approximately 10% of the estimated $2 million needed to fund the summer program. The remainder comes from the profits of *A Chorus Line*, the National Endowment for the Arts, the New York State Council on the Arts, and private contributions from corporations and individuals.

878. Gilliatt, Penelope. "What Have *A Chorus Line*, *The Cherry Orchard*, Mozart and Shakespeare Got in Common? Answer: Joe Papp." *Sunday Times* [London], June 12, 1983, 13.

This is an overview of the energetic schedule and career of Papp. It covers the variety of his productions, from classical to experimental, both on and off Broadway. Papp has a public reputation of being ruthless, but after having interviewed him for this article the writer finds this difficult to believe. He greatly admires theater in Britain, particularly the Royal Court Theatre, the two national companies and the tradition of ensemble acting.

879. Billington, Michael. "A Bold Thrust on Broadway." *Guardian* [Manchester U.K.], June 17, 1983, 16.

Papp was in London at the time of this interview to re-stage his production of Thomas Babe's *Buried Inside Extra* as part of an exchange program with the Royal Court Theater. He is on the Mayor's Advisory Committee on the Zoning of the New York Theater District. Its aim is to protect theaters from demolition. Papp realizes that it is not enough to put a preservation order on them. You also have to ensure their continued use. So he came up with the idea of a trust fund for the theater district to be paid for by the sale of air rights (the building space above the theaters) to developers. Papp would also like to set up a fund to take over the running of five Broadway houses and use them for the presentation of subsidized short-run new works.

880. Lawson, Carol. "Broadway." *New York Times*, June 17, 1983, sec. C, 2:2.

Papp is trying to get either Liza Minelli or Cher to star in *Non Pasquale*, a pop version of Donizetti's opera *Don Pasquale*, at the Delacorte Theater in Central Park. Papp has also announced a new hotline for information about performances in the park: 861-PAPP. He is also singing radio commercials for the Public Theater.

881. Rabin, Victoria. "The Hard-Nosed Idealist." *Observer* [London], June 19, 1983, 34:1.

Papp is in London for the opening of the NYSF's production of *Buried Inside Extra*. This is the second stage in an exchange between the Public Theater and the Royal Court Theatre. The English play *Top Girls* was taken to New York first. The playwright of *Buried Inside Extra*, Thomas Babe, is one of Papp's prodigies. Papp is proud of having helped many young people, particularly minorities. "The key to his motivation—and to his success—lies in his championing of the underdog."

882. Nelsen, Don. "Joe Papp Going the Distance for New York Theater." *New York Daily News*, June 26, 1983, Leisure sec., 3.

Calls Papp "the most imaginative and exasperating man on the New York theater scene." Contemporary playwrights are more important to Papp than plays. Lately he has been showing an interest in British playwrights. He produced David Hare's *Plenty* at the Public last year and two plays by Caryl Churchill this season. Papp's relationships with playwrights and directors have been stormy. He broke with Sam Shepard and David Rabe after well publicized fights. Bernard Gersten, Papp's closest associate for 18 years, was fired in 1978. After a reconciliation, however, Gersten is one of Papp's most loyal supporters.

883. Reiter, Susan. "The Delacorte Theater: Papp and Shakespeare in Central Park." *New York Daily News*, June 26, 1983, Leisure sec., 7:1.

Chronicles the history of the Delacorte Theater and its summer programs over the past 21 years. Nearly every play in the Shakespeare canon has been presented in the 2300 seat theater. Despite the growth and complexities of the NYSF's operations, the Delacorte remains a model of simplicity. Theatergoers with picnic baskets still wait patiently for the distribution of tickets just before show time. This summer the Festival will present *Richard III*, directed by Britisher Jane Howell, and starring Kevin Kline in the title role.

884. Eder, Richard. "Will Show Go On at Beaumont?" *Los Angeles Times*, July 31, 1983, sec. C, 55:2.

The NYSF gave up a performance in Central Park of *Richard III* for a concert by Diana Ross, but the event was rained out. Papp objected to having to give up another performance the following night when the concert was rescheduled. A compromise was reached and he agreed to delay his performance until the Ross concert ended.

885. Mitgang, Herbert. "U.S. Denies Visas to Italian Political Satirists." *New York Times*, Aug. 27, 1983, 8:5.

The United States consulate in Milan denied visas to Dario Fo and Franca Rame, two of Italy's best-known political satirists. Both were scheduled to come to the United States for the first time to perform at the NYSF and to lecture at New York University and Yale. Papp appealed to President Reagan for a reversal of the decision, calling the denial a form of censorship.

886. Richards, David. "U.S. Denies Visas to Playwrights." *Washington Post*, Aug. 27, 1983, sec. C, 7:1.

Italian playwright and performer Dario Fo and his wife and collaborator Franca Rame have been denied visas to enter the United States on the grounds that they have engaged in fundraising and related activities on behalf of Italian terrorist organizations. Papp had engaged them to perform material at the Public Theater. He protested the decision by sending a telegram to President Reagan asking him to intervene to reverse the decision.

887. Freedman, Samuel G. "332 Dance on a Record 3,389th *Chorus Line*." *New York Times*, Sep. 30, 1983, 1:3.

A Chorus Line has become the longest running show in the history of Broadway. It has won a Pulitzer Prize, the New York Drama Critics Circle Award and nine Tony awards. It has also played to 14 million people and earned $75 million.

888. Freedman, Samuel G. "Broadway Waits to See What Develops." *New York Times*, Oct. 2, 1983, sec. 4, 9:1.

After the failure to save the Morosco and Helen Hayes Theaters, Papp has joined the Mayor's Advisory Council appointed to find ways of sustaining Broadway's remaining 44 legitimate theaters. One plan, which appears to have the support of the Theater Advisory Council, would try to save the theaters by allowing their owners to sell their development rights—the difference between the existing theater and the largest structure legally permitted on the site—to builders who could apply them to projects on Manhattan's West Side. These rights are estimated to be worth a total of 40 to 160 million dollars. Papp's proposal is to use some of the income from the development rights to finance a national theater company that would stage new American dramas in some of the older theaters in financial jeopardy.

889. Nelsen, Don. "Papp's Tonic for a Sick Theater." *New York Daily News*, Oct. 5, 1983, 51.

Broadway has become an inhospitable arena for dramatic presentations. Theater audiences are dwindling and producers want to invest in sure successes. Playwrights have turned to Off-Broadway and Off-Off Broadway. Papp is urging the city to subsidize new playwrights and save theaters like the Belasco and Cort.

890. Freedman, Samuel G. "Papp Urges a National Theater on Broadway." *New York Times*, Oct. 6, 1983, sec. C, 31:1.

In a draft report to the Theater Advisory Committee, Papp proposed that a national theater be created on Broadway. The committee was appointed by Mayor Koch to determine ways of saving the 44 legitimate Broadway theaters. Papp said that the smaller theaters most suitable for serious dramas were those most in jeopardy because of the lack of suitable productions. His goal is to bring new American dramas to Broadway, supporting the shows' playwrights, producers and audiences with subsidies drawn from a $10 million fund financed both by the city and Broadway theater owners. His proposal also calls for the city to become the purchaser of last resort of any Broadway theaters threatened with demolition.

891. Freedman, Samuel G. "National Theater Waits in the Wings." *New York Times*, Nov. 13, 1983, sec. 4, 11:1.

Papp has a plan for a national theater on Broadway. He and his supporters want New York City and Broadway's commercial producers and theater owners to financially support theaters facing closure by subsidizing new plays in them. His philosophy is that a livelier Broadway would ultimately generate more money for all theaters and the city.

892. Gussow, Mel. "Broadway." *New York Times*, Dec. 23, 1983, sec. C, 2:4.

The year 1984 marks the 30th anniversary season of the NYSF. Papp will present a series of gala events beginning with a benefit featuring a rock group, Crime and Punishment, formed by three former Pirates of Penzance: Kevin Kline, Rex Smith and Treat Williams.

1984

893. O'Haire, Patricia. "N.Y. Shakespeare Festival Turns 30." *New York Daily News*, Jan. 9, 1984, 35.

Papp held a benefit on January 5 to celebrate the 30th anniversary of the NYSF. Tickets to the party, which took place at the Public Theater, were $50.

894. O'Haire, Patricia. "Joe Papp: Best Man for Promo." *New York Daily News*, Jan. 23, 1984, 19.

Story on the making of a television commercial for the NYSF production of Saroyan's *The Human Comedy*. Although Papp has made many radio commercials for his plays, this is his first one for television. The 30 second film shows Papp dressed as a Bogart-type character. The cost of the promotion was only $35,000.

895. Freedman, Samuel G. "Financial Problems Are Compromising Non-Profit Theaters." *New York Times*, Mar. 14, 1984, sec. A, 1:1.

Leaders of many of the country's nonprofit theaters say they are having to make artistic compromises to remain solvent. The NYSF is facing a dropoff in royalties from *A Chorus Line*, which when it was selling out tickets on Broadway and had spawned several road shows, made $7 million a year for the company. This year Papp said it would make only $500,000 at best. Papp says he has had to become very cautious. He cannot spend so much on plays, nor let them run as long as he would like.

896. Freedman, Samuel G. "*Human Comedy* Moves to Broadway." *New York Times*, Apr. 5, 1984, sec. C, 17:1.

The story of the transfer of the musical *The Human Comedy* to Broadway from the Public Theater in order to make money for the NYSF. It was quite a gamble, however, as it involved a commitment of $400,000. Papp has rarely been so involved in a show, he even did all the radio and television commercials for it himself. Papp says he was initially attracted to the show because it reminded him of his youth.

897. Freedman, Samuel G. "Tomorrow's Playwrights Today." *New York Times*, May 5, 1984, 15:1.

The NYSF donated theater space and its casting services for the Young Playwrights Festival, to which writers under the age of 19 submitted 1,160 plays. Eleven plays were chosen for performance. Papp also sang about the festival on his latest radio commercial.

898. "Blowstein Says State Schools Are Becoming More Important." *New York Times*, May 25, 1984, sec. B, 3:3.

Papp was awarded an honorary degree by Rutgers University for having "immeasurably enriched the theater and expanded the horizons of theatrical art."

899. Shepard, Richard F. "Papp Goes Latin at the Public." *New York Times*, Aug. 10, 1984, sec. C, 1:4.

The fourth Festival Latino de Nueva York at the Public Theater is bigger in size than its predecessors. In addition to Latin American plays, there will also be 20 films, subtitled in English, representing the National Latino Film and Video Festival. The festival will cost $250,000, and the largest share of the expense will be borne by the NYSF.

900. Page, Tim. "Latin Festival Accused of 'Ideological Bias'." *New York Times*, Aug 11, 1984, 9:5.

A group of Cuban-American artists and writers charge that the Public Theater's Festival Latino de Nueva York is practising discrimination and ideological censorship by excluding them. Papp denies the charges. He says, "Our idea was to sponsor collective endeavors rather than single artists."

901. Blair, David. "Latino Canard in the Name of the Bard." *Wall Street Journal*, Aug. 29, 1984, 22:4.

Claims that the NYSF's latest Festival Latino was biased in favor of the governments of Cuba and Nicaragua and left wing organizations in South America. Eighty-two Cuban-American writers, film makers and artists wrote an open letter to Papp complaining about the exclusion of anti-Castro Cubans.

902. Nemy, Enid. "Public Theater Names Susan Stein Shriva Unit." *New York Times*, Oct. 30, 1984, sec. C, 13:1.

The NYSF dedicated its experimental theater to the memory of Susan Stein Shriva, a member of the Festival's board of directors for more than 15 years. The family of Mrs. Shriva also gave the Festival a gift of $1 million. Papp said that half of the money would be added to the endowment fund of $17 million. The rest would be used to help finance the 14 works the NYSF would produce this season.

903. Bennetts, Leslie. "Papp's New *Boheme* Might Surprise Puccini." *New York Times*, Nov. 3, 1984, 13:1.

The NYSF is producing an updated version of Puccini's opera *La Bohème* starring Linda Ronstadt. Papp says this is a continuation of his policy "which is to make a great classical work more accessible by having it in English." The production is expected to be controversial because none of the singers has operatic training, and it is not what people are used to seeing when they go to an opera.

904. Freedman, Samuel G. "*Chorus Line* Vs. Hollywood —a Saga." *New York Times*, Nov. 11, 1984, sec. 2, 1:2.

A history of the attempts to make *A Chorus Line* into a film. Papp received his first offer, $150,000, for the film rights to the musical in May 1975, while it was still only in previews at the Public Theater. Universal bought the film rights later that year for $5.5 million and agreed not to release the movie version for five years, so as not to hurt the show's ticket sales. Yet the film was not made for nine years. The main problem was the question of royalties because the show had many creators. There were also artistic problems which delayed its production. Papp himself considered making the film in 1981, but due to studio politics the project was dropped. Finally in 1983 English director Richard Attenborough agreed to make the film version.

905. Bennetts, Leslie. "In Swap by Papp, Two Plays for Public and Two for London." *New York Times*, Nov. 16, 1984, sec. C, 2:2.

Papp plans to continue his exchange program with the Royal Court Theatre in London. He will send two plays to London, *Aunt Dan and Lemon* and *Coming of Age in Soho*. The English productions coming to the Public Theater will be *Tom and Viv* and *Rat in the Skull*.

906. Holland, Bernard. "Linda Ronstadt Reaches for an Operatic High Note." *New York Times*, Nov. 25, sec. 2, 1:5.

In this article focusing on Linda Ronstadt, the star of the NYSF's version of *La Bohème*, the preparations for the production are described.

1985

907. "Crises and the Muses." *New York Times*, Feb. 14, 1985, sec. B, 3:1.

The organization PACT, Performing Arts for Crisis Training, honored Papp by establishing a scholarship in his name at New York University. He is a member of the group's board. In the presentation ceremony at the Tavern on the Green he also appeared in a skit with members of the organization and helped demonstrate their purpose: training people to handle potentially explosive confrontations using theatrical techniques.

908. Nemy, Enid. "Broadway." *New York Times*, Feb. 22, 1985, sec. C, 2:3.

Papp offered to form an American Friends of the Royal Court organization to raise $50,000 a year for that theater, if it could raise a similar amount on its own. Papp is also involved in organizing a benefit evening for Oxfam America and famine aid for Africa, which will take place March 10 at the Shubert Theater.

909. Freedman, Samuel G. "Reshaping a Play to Reveal Its True Nature." *New York Times*, Feb. 24, 1985, sec. 2, 1:1.

After Albert Innaurato's play *Coming of Age in Soho* seemed to have problems during the previews, the official opening was postponed. With Papp's support the playwright virtually rewrote the play in nine days, changing the romantic theme from heterosexual to homosexual and making the work more autobiographical.

910. Hogrefe, Jeffrey. "Papp's Parade of Hits: Four Winners in a Dismal Theater Season." *Washington Post*, Mar. 5, 1985, sec. C, 7:1.

Papp has four successful plays running at one time at the Public Theater: *Coming of Age in Soho*, *Tom and Viv*, *Virginia*, and *Tracers* produced by the Vietnam Veterans Ensemble. Three television networks intend to use clips from the latter production to commemorate the 20th anniversary of the first major installment of American troops in Vietnam.

911. Lawson, Carol. "The Evening Hours." *New York Times*, Apr. 5, 1985, sec. B, 6:1.
Invited to a party at the Steuben Glass Galleries, Papp read excerpts from Shakespeare as part of a showing of new glassware sculpture called "A Shakespeare Garden at Steuben." He admitted that he was really there to raise money from the wealthy guests.

912. Rothstein, Mervyn. "37 Documentary Films at the Public." *New York Times*, Apr. 12, 1985, sec. C, 4:3.
The NYSF is presenting the Global Village 11th Annual Documentary Festival at the Public Theater. It consists of 37 films.

913. Nemy, Enid. "Broadway: At *Edwin Drood* the Audience Will Choose the Ending." *New York Times*, May 3, 1985, sec. C, 2:1.
A description of the unusual open-ended production of *The Mystery of Edwin Drood*, which will be the second show of the Central Park season. It will be presented as though performed in a 19th century English music hall.

914. O'Haire, Patricia. "Joe and Will: Together Forever." *New York Daily News*, June 16, 1985, Leisure sec., 3:3.

On the eve of the opening of Papp's 30th season of free outdoor theater, the author looks back at some of the memorable earlier productions and lists the many famous actors who have worked for Papp.

915. Kakutani, Michiko. "The Public and Private Joe Papp." *New York Times*, June 23, 1985, Magazine sec., 14+.

The NYSF is starting its 30th summer season with *Measure for Measure*, the 41st production Papp has directed himself. He is also active on nearly a dozen cultural and social committees, ranging from the Mayor's Theater Advisory Council to Planned Parenthood.

Papp is the NYSF. Publicity campaigns "have increasingly played up his role as figurehead of the institution." He makes all the major decisions involving the company personally. At the time this article was written NYSF productions had won 23 Tonys, 91 Obies and three Pulitzer Prizes.

Much information is given about Papp's personal life. He has re-embraced his family's Judaism. There are also details about his relations with his five children, playwrights and colleagues.

916. "Thank You, Mr. Delacorte." *New York Times*, June 28, 1985, sec. B, 4:3.

The NYSF threw a party in Central Park for George Delacorte on his 92nd birthday. He is a member of the company's board and one of its chief philanthropists.

917. Brin, Douglas. "Joe Papp." *New York Daily News*, June 30, 1985, People sec., 3.

In this interview on his life and love of the theater, Papp comes across as a man totally in control of his organization. He selects the plays, the directors and the cast, and then keeps his eye on all of them.

Steve Cohen, his associate producer, says Papp knows where every dollar goes and that he is involved in every Festival production, making suggestions to playwrights, directors and actors. Papp has 150 employees and a $13 million annual budget.

918. "Latino Prize for Gallardo Play." *New York Times*, July 2, 1985, sec. C, 13:1.

Edward Gallardo's *Women Without Men* won the NYSF's National Contest for Latino Plays. The prize is $5,000 and production of the winning play during the annual Festival Latino en Nueva York. Gail Merrifield was one of the competition's judges.

919. Nemy, Enid. "Broadway." *New York Times*, July 19, 1985, sec. C, 2:3.

William C. Ferguson, the president of New York Telephone, presented Papp with a check for $250,000 at a reception to celebrate 30 years of free Shakespeare in the Park. This was the third season the telephone company had sponsored free park performances.

920. Blau, Eleanor. "Where Plays Are Wrapped in the Stuff of Magic." *New York Times*, July 21, 1985, sec. B, 4:1.

Milo Morrow has run the NYSF's costume shop for 18 years. His career with the company, and the role and organization of the costume shop are described.

921. Holden, Stephen. "New York in August a Feast of Festivals." *New York Times*, Aug. 9, 1985, sec. C, 5:1.

This year's Festival Latino in New York will be held at various indoor and outdoor sites. It will present award-winning theater, film and dance events "representing a wide cross-section of Latin culture the world over." Some of the productions at the Public Theater are described.

922. Karp, Jonathan. "Musical Mystery Tour: Rupert Holme's *Drood* Vibrations." *Washington Post*, Aug. 11, 1985, sec. H, 1:5.

Rupert Holmes, an obscure pop star, wrote the music, lyrics and libretto for the NYSF's musical *The Mystery of Edwin Drood.* The project started in 1983 when Gail Merrifield, Papp's wife and director of the play selection department at the Public Theater, saw Holmes in a night-club act. She asked him if he was interested in writing for the theater. Holmes presented 10 ideas to Merrifield and Papp. They decided that Edwin Drood was the strongest, so he started work on the production. The musical will be presented in Central Park and, if successful, will transfer to Broadway.

923. Nightingale, Benedict. "Why Dickens Plays so Well on Stage." *New York Times*, Aug. 18, 1985, sec. 2, 1:2.

As the NYSF's Central Park production of *The Mystery of Edwin Drood* is about to open, the author gives a history of theatrical productions of Dicken's works, and attempts to account for their continuing popularity.

924. Freedman, Samuel G. "Evolution of *Drood* as Musical." *New York Times*, Aug. 28, 1985, sec. C, 17:1.

Gail Merrifield asked Rupert Holmes to write a musical for the NYSF. He created *The Mystery of Edwin Drood*, based on Dicken's unfinished novel. The audience gets to vote on whether or not Drood is dead and who killed him. Papp was not sure the audience would like this aspect of the show, but Merrifield persuaded him it was a good idea.

925. "Papp's Rx: Change Theater Structure." *New York Daily News*, Oct. 7, 1985, 4.

In an interview Papp talks on one of his favorite themes: government-subsidized theaters. There are seven or eight empty theaters on Broadway that the city could buy, and then support productions of plays not ordinarily seen on the Broadway stage.

926. Holden, Stephen. "An All-Star Cabaret to Benefit YIVO Institute." *New York Times*, Nov. 17, 1985, 73:1.

Papp is to sing in a cabaret gala at the Public Theater to benefit the YIVO Institute for Jewish Research. He hopes to raise $60,000 for the organization on its 60th anniversary.

927. Fein, Esther B. "Refitting *Edwin Drood* for Its Broadway Run." *New York Times*, Nov. 29, 1985, sec. C, 4:3.

The Delacorte production of *The Mystery of Edwin Drood* is being moved to Broadway. To achieve the informality that made the outdoors show so popular it has been cut in length and a longer opening number added. The interaction between the cast and audience has also been increased.

928. "Centre Street Role for Papp." *New York Times*, Dec. 16, 1985, sec. B, 4:5.

While a juror in the State Supreme Court, Papp got the jury to read parts of *King Lear*. The jurors had finished their deliberations before the judge was ready for them, so this was a way of biding time in the jury room.

929. Ferretti, Fred. "A Year's Worth of Travel Wishes." *New York Times*, Dec. 29, 1985, sec. 10, 15:1.

The writer asked a number of public people, including Papp, where they would like to go in 1986. Papp said that he would like to take a week's camping trip into the Sinai desert where he would have "no obligation to anyone but God."

1986

930. Freedman, Samuel G. "Students to Meet Bard on Broadway." *New York Times*, Jan. 6, 1986, sec. C, 11:4.

The NYSF is forming a multiracial acting company to present Shakespeare on Broadway for school audiences. The new ensemble will be directed by Estelle Parsons. The company requires a budget of $2.2 million for its first year of operation. The

Festival will raise $1.2 million if the Board of Estimate contributes the other $1 million, which has been requested by the school board. Papp has already approached the Ford Foundation for a grant, and will be asking major corporations to give money by "adopting a school" and paying for its students to attend the performances. The Shubert Organization has agreed to let Papp have the use of the Belasco Theater free of rent and maintenance charges.

931. Lawson, Carol. "The Evening Hours." *New York Times*, Feb. 28, 1986, sec. B, 6:1.

New York Telephone invited supporters of the Public Theater to cocktails, dinner and a preview of *Hamlet* with Kevin Kline in the leading role. At the party the rumor was spread that the Wall Street arbitrager Ivan Boesky had fulfilled a fantasy of being an actor when he took part in a reading of *The Man in the Glass Booth* at the Public Theater.

932. Freedman, Samuel G. "Portrait of a Playwright As An Enemy of the State." *New York Times*, Mar. 23, 1986, sec. 2, 1:6.

Article on playwright Vaclav Havel, whose plays have been banned in his native Czechoslovakia since 1969. Papp has produced a number of Havel's plays—*Memorandum* in 1968, *A Private View* in 1983, and next week *Largo Desolato.*

933. Brady, James. "In Step with: Joseph Papp." *New York Daily News*, Apr. 20, 1986, Magazine sec., 22.

Papp has put up more than one million dollars for his latest project. Starting this month and continuing until the money runs out, he will be bringing 10,000 school children a week to the Belasco Theater to watch *Romeo and Juliet* and *As You Like It*. Estelle Parsons is directing a company of 16 young black, Hispanic, Asian-American and white actors in both plays.

934. Schellhardt, Timothy and Carol Hymowitz. "Visions of the Future." *Wall Street Journal*, Apr. 21, 1986, sec. 4, 6:1.

Prominent figures were asked how they envision leisure activities in the year 2011. Papp predicts that, in spite of great technological changes, people will still want to see living human beings performing on stage. There will still be a production of *Hamlet* playing somewhere.

935. Kleiman, Dena. "Happy Birthday, Will: The World's Still a Stage." *New York Times*, Apr. 24, 1986, sec. C, 21:1.

The NYSF celebrated Shakespeare's 422nd birthday with a cake and a performance of *As You Like It* for 400 high school students at the Public Theater. It was part of a new program by a recently formed minority company to introduce Shakespeare to students around the city. Ten thousand children are expected to see *As You Like It* and *Romeo and Juliet* before the school year ends. Papp hopes that a $1 million budget will be approved by the Board of Estimate so that the program can be expanded to 200,000 students throughout the city next fall. The Shubert organization has offered the use of the Belasco Theater on Broadway for this purpose.

936. Freedman, Samuel G. "Two Shakespeare Troupes Vie for Scant Donations." *New York Times*, Apr. 30, 1986, sec. C, 19:5.

Papp's new Shakespeare theater for high school students threatens an older program, Theater for a New Audience, because of a shortage of potential funding. The fame of the Public Theater makes it easier for the NYSF to attract funds. Papp's program, which will cost $2.5 million, will get $1 million of this money from the Board of Education budget. The Theater for a New Audience will only get just over $20,000 of its $250,000 operating costs from this source. The programs are very different though. Papp's 20 member Shakespeare troupe will put on plays in the Belasco Theater on Broadway for 200,000 high school students. The Theater for a New Audience performs generally in smaller theaters for elementary as well as high school students.

937. Dunning, Jennifer. "Reader's Digest Awards $3 Million to Arts Groups." *New York Times*, May 9, 1986, sec. C, 36:1.

Reader's Digest announced an award of $3 million to 49 dance and theater companies across the country for the creation and production of new works. The grants would come from the Wallace Fund established by the founders of the magazine. The NYSF was one of four theater and three dance companies receiving the biggest grants of $150,000 each over three years.

938. Anderson, Susan Heller and David W. Dunlap. "For Shakespeare Festival." *New York Times*, May 30, 1986, sec. B, 2:6.

Two thousand people from the theater, magazine publishing, and advertising gathered at the Seventh Regiment Armory to honor Joseph Papp as founder of the NYSF. *People Magazine* hosted the party, whose main purpose was to raise money for the Festival. Papp entertained the guests with a rendition of "Brother, Can You Spare a Dime?"

939. Nemy, Enid. "Five Tonys Are Won by *Drood*" *New York Times*, June 2, 1986, sec. C, 13:1.

The Mystery of Edwin Drood won the annual Tony award for best musical. George Rose, star of the show, was voted best actor in a musical. The show also received awards for best book, best original score, and best direction of a musical.

940. "Business for Best Plays Increases After Tonys." *New York Times*, June 6, 1986, sec. C, 24:6.

Before winning five Tony awards the average daily sales of tickets for *Drood* were $53,000. Two days after the awards were given, sales climbed to $110,252.

941. Robertson, Nan. "De Niro Takes Cut for Cuba." *New York Times*, June 12, 1986, sec. C, 15;1.

Robert De Niro and his co-stars in *Cuba and His Teddy Bear* have agreed to work for minimum salaries, $700 a week, in order to bring the play to Broadway. The play closes at the Public in two days and will open at the Longacre Theater on July 16 for a 10 week run. Tickets for the second balcony will be sold for only 10 dollars. Papp hopes to bring other new plays to endangered Broadway theaters at low ticket prices.

942. "*Twelfth Night* as Jazz." *New York Times*, June 27, 1986, sec. C, 1:2.

An operatic adaptation of *Twelfth Night*, composed by David Amram with libretto by Papp, will be performed this coming weekend at New York University.

943. Holland, Bernard. "Opera: Amram-Papp Version of *Twelfth Night*." *New York Times*, June 29, 1986, 66:3.

Critical article on the 15 year old opera *Twelfth Night*, composed by David Amram with libretto by Papp. In Holland's opinion the opera, although "unfailingly gracious and often lyrical," is "clumsy" when compared to the Shakespeare play.

944. Solway, Diane. "An Actor Prepares for Malvolio." *New York Times*, June 29, 1986, sec. 2, 1:1.

Murray Abraham will open the NYSF's 31st season of free Shakespeare in the Park as Malvolio in *Twelfth Night*. Papp said the actor "has an air of comedy about him."

945. Kleiman, Dena. "Festival Latino Adds Shows at the Delacorte." *New York Times*, July 9, 1986, sec. C, 17:1.

In this 10th annual festival, Papp will present plays, films, dance and musical events from Latin America, the Caribbean, Spain, and Italy at both the Public and Delacorte theaters. The program will run from August 6 to August 31.

946. Goldberger, Paul. "*Danny Rosales* Named Latino Play Winner." *New York Times*, July 17, 1986, sec. C, 18:6.

Carlos Morton will receive $5,000 for his play *The Many Deaths of Danny Rosales*, which was picked as the winner in the NYSF's National Contest for Latino Plays.

947. Herman, Jan. "The People's Shakespeare." *New York Daily News*, July 20, 1986, Magazine sec., 8.

Under the direction of Estelle Parsons, a multiracial troupe of young actors has been performing Shakespeare at the Public Theater throughout the spring. The group, created by Papp and known as the Festival Players, has been playing before city students brought to the theater by their teachers. This summer Parsons and company are taking Shakespeare directly to the people. They will perform throughout the five boroughs in parks and school yards. In the fall the company will offer workshops in the schools to familiarize teachers and students with Shakespeare's plays.

948. Kleiman, Dena. "All-Male Japanese Cast to Do *Medea* in Park." *New York Times*, July 24, 1986, sec. C, 19:2.

The last play of the NYSF's 31st season of free plays in Central Park will be *Medea*. The production will include 25 Japanese actors of the Toho company.

949. Robertson, Nan. "Outdoor Theater Blooms Amid Joys and Hardships." *New York Times*, Aug. 1, 1986, sec. C, 5:1.

Estelle Parsons, who is directing a multiracial troupe of actors under the auspices of the NYSF, discusses the problems of contending with rain, noise and sunburn during outdoor performances. The company has been performing *As You Like It* and *Romeo and Juliet* throughout the city. Last spring the troupe was in residence at the Public Theater for six weeks and played before more than 15,000 high school students as part of a continuing program developed by Papp and the New York City Board of Education.

950. Shepard, Richard F. "Extravaganza Offers a Feast of Latin Events." *New York Times*, Aug. 8, 1986, sec. C, 1:2.

The 10th anniversary of the Festival Latino will present more than 400 performers from 31 countries at the Delacorte and Public Theaters. The program will run for 26 days and will include six musical, four dance, and twenty four theatrical companies along with more than twenty films.

Papp has been the life support of the Festival Latino since 1980. He helps with fund raising and provides space at both his theaters.

951. Mirabella, Alan. "Papp Wants to Make Broadway Cheap, but It Won't be Easy." *New York Daily News*, Aug. 12, 1986, 67.

Papp has a plan for opening three or four dark Broadway theaters, such as the Belasco and Lyceum, and keeping ticket prices down. If actors, technicians, musicians and stage hands are willing to work below minimum some tickets could be sold for ten dollars. Actors' Equity has agreed to participate in such a plan but other unions have not. The Federation of Musicians has flatly rejected Papp's project. Papp would also encourage theater owners to give him a break or pick up the entire tab for the use of their houses.

952. Blau, Eleanor. "Latin Film Series Opening Tonight at the Public." *New York Times*, Aug. 15, 1986, sec. C, 5:5.

Festival Latino, Papp's annual Latin American festival, will include a film series. The first film will be a four hour documentary on Chile. More than 20 films will be shown during the two week series.

953. Robertson, Nan. "Broadway." *New York Times*, Aug. 15, 1986, sec. C, 2:3.

A new black musical, *Colored Museum*, is scheduled for the Public Theater this season. Papp will also present two plays by Strindberg, who Papp believes had a "most extraordinary understanding of women."

954. "Aid for Shakespeare Project." *New York Times*, Oct. 8, 1986, sec. C, 19:5.

Mayor Koch announced that the NYSF has been given a grant of $525,000 to bring free performances of Shakespeare's plays to city high school students. The project, called the Belasco Project, will present daily performances at the Belasco Theater starting next month. *Newsday* has agreed to provide $500,000 for the project.

955. Gerard, Jeremy. "Dancers Resist Papp Plan." *New York Times*, Oct. 26, 1986, 64:1.

Papp offered to join the campaign to convert a building at 890 Broadway into a non-profit arts center in order to preserve theater rehearsal facilities and an Off-Broadway theater there. The building was sold two weeks before by the producer and director Michael Bennett to Lawrence Wien, a real estate developer and philanthropist. Wien was acting on behalf of the Eliot Feld Ballet and the American Ballet Theater. The Alvin Ailey American dance Theater also plans to move into the building. The ballet companies think that Papp should have acted earlier if he wanted to retain the building for theatrical purposes, as they have their own plans for it. They have already incorporated as the New York Dance Center.

956. Lohr, Steve. "Old Money Woes Hinder New British Theater." *New York Times*, Nov. 10, 1986, sec. C, 17:1.

The English Stage Company, one of Britain's leading forums for the works of new playwrights, has received a grant of $50,000 from Papp to help them through current financial problems. Papp has had an exchange program with the company, which occupies the Royal Court Theatre, since 1982 when Caryl Churchill's *Top Girls* was brought to the Public Theater. The company's problems stem from decreased government spending on the arts in Britain.

957. "Festival Will Mount 3 Shakespeare Plays." *New York Times*, Nov. 20, 1986, sec. C, 25:1.

The NYSF will present *Titus Andronicus*, *Much Ado About Nothing*, and *Love Labour's Lost* at the Delacorte Theater next summer. Papp says that it is the first time the Festival has produced three Shakespeare plays in the summer series.

CHRONOLOGY OF MAJOR PRODUCTIONS

1951

The Curious Savage
Emmanuel Presbyterian Church — no review

One-Act Play Company (Papp produced and directed)
Lake Arrowhead, N.Y. — no review

1952

Hall of Healing
Yugoslav-American Hall (N.Y.C) — May 8, 35:6

Bedtime Story
Yugoslav-American Hall (N.Y.C) — May 8, 35:6

Time to Go
Yugoslav-American Hall (N.Y.C.) — May 8, 35:6

Deep Are the Roots
Lenox Hill Playhouse (N.Y.C.) — no review

1954

"An Evening with Shakespeare and Marlowe"
Emmanuel Presbyterian Church — no review

1955

As You Like It	
Emmanuel Presbyterian Church	Oct. 29, 12:2
Romeo and Juliet	
Emmanuel Presbyterian Church	Dec. 16, 36:3
Cymbeline	
Emmanuel Presbyterian Church	no review
Much Ado About Nothing	
Emmanuel Presbyterian Church	no review
"Shakespeare's Women" (readings)	
Emmanuel Presbyterian Church	no review
The Two Gentlemen of Verona	
Emmanuel Presbyterian Church	no review

1956

The Changeling	
Emmanuel Presbyterian Church	May 4, 20:3
Julius Caesar	
East River Amphitheater	June 30, 19:6
The Taming of the Shrew	
East River Amphitheater	Aug. 2, sec. 2, 1:1
Titus Andronicus	
Emmanuel Presbyterian Church	Dec. 3, 40:2
Much Ado About Nothing	
Emmanuel Presbyterian Church	no review

1957

Romeo and Juliet
Central Park and the Mobile Theater — June 28, 30:2

The Two Gentlemen of Verona
Central Park — July 23, 21:5

Macbeth
Central Park — Aug. 16, 11:2

Richard III
Heckscher Theater — Nov. 26, 41:1

1958

As You Like It
Heckscher Theater — Jan. 21, 33:6

Othello
Central Park — July 4, 16:1

Twelfth Night
Central Park — Aug. 7, 21:4

1959

Antony and Cleopatra
Heckscher Theater — Jan. 14, 28:1

Julius Caesar
Central Park — Aug. 4, 30:1

1960

Henry V
Central Park — June 29, 23:1

Measure for Measure
Central Park — July 27, 33:1

The Taming of the Shrew
Central Park — Aug. 20, 17:1

1961

Romeo and Juliet
Heckscher Theater and school tour — Feb. 24, 24:1

Much Ado About Nothing
Wollman Memorial Rink — July 7, 17:1

A Midsummer Night's Dream
Wollman Memorial Rink — Aug. 3, 13:1

Richard II
Wollman Memorial Rink — Aug. 30, 25:1

1962

Julius Caesar
Heckscher Theater and school tour — Feb. 22, 19:6

The Merchant of Venice
Delacorte Theater — June 22, 14:1
Telecast on CBS, June 21

The Tempest
Delacorte Theater — July 17, 18:2

King Lear
Delacorte Theater — Aug. 14, 35:1

Hamlet (opera by Sergiuskagen, Papp directed)
Peabody Institute (Baltimore) — Nov. 11, 83:3

Macbeth
Heckscher Theater — Nov. 17, 16:2

1963

Antony and Cleopatra
Delacorte Theater — June 21, 33:1

As You Like It
Delacorte Theater — July 17, 19:2

The Winter's Tale
Delacorte Theater — Aug. 16, 14:1

Twelfth Night
Heckscher Theater and school tour — Oct. 9, 47:1

Idomeneo (directed by Papp on Nov. 22)
Peabody Institute (Baltimore) — no review

1964

Hamlet
Delacorte Theater — June 18, 28:2

A Midsummer Night's Dream
Mobile Theater and school tour — June 30 23:2

Othello
Delacorte Theater — July 15, 29:1

Electra
Delacorte Theater — Aug. 12, 42:1

Puppet Theater of Don Cristobal
Mobile Theater — Sep. 3, 23:2

The Shoemaker's Prodigious Wife
Mobile Theater — Sep. 3, 23:2

1965

Love's Labour's Lost
Delacorte Theater — June 16, 46:1

Henry V
Mobile Theater and school tour — June 29, 27:2

The Taming of the Shrew
Mobile Theater — July 3, 10:5

We Real Cool
Mobile Theater — July 3, 10:5

Coriolanus
Delacorte Theater — July 15, 23:1

Troilus and Cressida
Delacorte Theater — Aug. 13, 17:1

Romeo and Juliet (in Spanish)
Mobile Theater — Aug. 28, 13:3

1966

All's Well that Ends Well
Delacorte Theater — June 17, 39:1

Macbeth
Mobile Theater — June 29, 38:1

Measure for Measure
Delacorte Theater — July 14, 27:1

Richard III
Delacorte Theater — Aug. 11, 26:1

Macbeth (in Spanish)
Mobile Theater — Aug. 29, 23:4

Potluck!
Mobile Theater — no review

1967

Stock Up on Pepper 'Cause Turkey's Going to War (directed by Papp)
La Mamma (N.Y.C.) — no *N.Y.T.* review *Village Voice,* Feb. 9, 1967, 25.

The Comedy of Errors
Delacorte Theater — June 15, 58:4

Volpone
Mobile Theater — June 30, 29:1

Lallapalooza
Mobile Theater — July 12, 28:5

King John
Delacorte Theater — July 14, 19:1

Titus Andronicus
Delacorte Theater — Aug. 10, 43:2

Hair
Public Theater — Oct. 30, 55:1

Hamlet
Public Theater — Dec. 27, 45:1

1968

Ergo	
Public Theater	Mar. 4, 29:1
Memorandum	
Public Theater	May 6, 55:1
Henry IV, part 1	
Delacorte Theater	June 30, 54:7
Henry IV, part 2	
Delacorte Theater	July 2, 33:1
Hamlet	
Mobile Theater and school tour	July 4, 15:1
Take One Step	
Mobile Theater	July 5, 17:1
Romeo and Juliet	
Delacorte Theater	Aug. 16, 19:1
Huui, Huui	
Public Theater	Nov. 25, 58:1

1969

Cities in Bezique (The Owl Answers and A Beast's Story)	
Public Theater	Jan. 13, 26:1
Invitation to a Beheading	
Public Theater	Mar. 18, 36:1
No Place to Be Somebody	
Public Theater	May 5, 53:3
ANTA Theater	Dec. 31, 17:1

Peer Gynt	
Delacorte Theater	July 17, 56:1
Electra	
Mobile Theater	Aug. 8, 14:1
Twelfth Night	
Delacorte Theater	Aug. 14, 29:2
Stomp	
Public Theater	Nov. 23, sec. 2, 1:1
Sambo	
Public Theater	Dec. 22, 42:1

1970

X Has No Value	
Public Theater	Feb. 17, 35:1
The Mod Donna	
Public Theater	May 4, 48:1
Henry VI	
Delacorte Theater	July 2, 30:1
Richard III	
Delacorte Theater	July 4, 11:1
The Happiness Cage	
Public Theater	Oct. 5, 56:4
Trelawny of the Wells	
Public Theater	Oct. 12, 48:1

1971

Subject to Fits	
Public Theater	Feb. 15, 18:1
Slag	
Public Theater	Feb. 22, 22:1
Here Are the Ladies	
Public Theater	Feb. 23, 29:1
Blood	
Public Theater	Mar. 8, 40:3
Candide	
Public Theater	Apr. 15, 38:3
Jazznite	
Public Theater	Apr. 19, 52:1
The Life and Times of J. Walter Smintheus	
Public Theater	Apr. 19, 52:1
The Basic Training of Pavlo Hummel	
Public Theater	May 21, 25:1
Dance Wi' Me	
Public Theater	June 11, 23:1
Timon of Athens	
Delacorte Theater	July 2, 22:1
The Two Gentlemen of Verona	
Delacorte Theater	July 29, 40:1
St. James Theater (Broadway)	Dec. 2, 65:1
Cymbeline	
Delacorte Theater	Aug. 19, 41:1

Sticks and Bones
Public Theater — Nov. 8, 53:1
See 1972 for Broadway production

The Black Terror
Public Theater — Nov. 11, 62:1

The Wedding of Iphigenia
Public Theater — Dec. 17, 28:2

1972

Sticks and Bones
John Golden Theater (Broadway) — Mar. 2, 33:2

Black Visions
Public Theater — Mar. 26, sec. 2, 3:1

That Championship Season
Public Theater — May 3, 34:1
Booth Theater (Broadway) — Sep. 15, 43:2

Older People
Public Theater — May 15, 43:2

The Hunter
Public Theater — May 24, 53:1

The Corner
Public Theater — June 23, 21:1

Hamlet
Delacorte Theater — June 30, 22:1

Ti-Jean and His Brothers
Delacorte Theater — July 28, 20:1

Much Ado About Nothing	
Delacorte Theater	Aug. 18, 13:2
Winter Garden Theater (Broadway)	Nov. 13, 46:1
The Wedding Band	
Public Theater	Oct. 27, 30:1
The Children	
Public Theater	Dec. 18, 54:1

1973

The Cherry Orchard	
Public Theater	Jan. 12, 21:1
Siamese Connections	
Public Theater	Jan. 26, 46:1
The Orphan	
Public Theater	April 19, 51:1
As You Like It	
Delacorte Theater	June 29, 16:1
King Lear	
Delacorte Theater	Aug. 2, 28:1
The Boom Boom Room	
Beaumont (Lincoln Center)	Nov. 9, 31:1
Lotta	
Public Theater	Nov. 23, 42:1
Troilus and Cressida	
Newhouse (Lincoln Center)	Dec. 3, 50:1
The Au Pair Man	
Beaumont (Lincoln Center)	Dec. 28, 18:1

1974

More Than You Deserve	
Public Theater	Jan. 4, 17:4
Barbary Shore	
Public Theater	Jan. 11, 16:1
The Tempest	
Newhouse (Lincoln Center)	Feb. 11, 47:1
What the Wine-Sellers Buy	
Beaumont (Lincoln Center)	Feb. 15, 25:1
Short Eyes	
Public Theater	Mar. 14, 45:1
Les Femmes Noires	
Public Theater	Mar. 18, 40:1
The Killdeer	
Public Theater	Mar. 29, 22:1
The Dance of Death	
Beaumont (Lincoln Center)	Apr. 5, 24:1
Pericles	
Delacorte Theater	July 2, 28:1
The Merry Wives of Windsor	
Delacorte Theater	Aug. 1, 20:1
Richard III	
Newhouse (Lincoln Center)	Oct. 21, 51:1
Where Do We Go From Here?	
Public Theater	Oct. 28, 38:1
Mert and Phil	
Beaumont (Lincoln Center)	Oct. 31, 50:1

The Last Days of British Honduras	
Public Theater	Nov. 6, 64:1
Macbeth	
Newhouse (Lincoln Center)	no review

1975

Black Picture Show	
Beaumont (Lincoln Center)	Jan. 7, 28:1
The Sea Gull	
Public Theater	Jan. 9, 49:1
Our Late Night	
Public Theater	Jan. 10, 20:1
A Midsummer Night's Dream	
Newhouse (Lincoln Center	Jan. 20, 23:1
Fishing	
Public Theater	Feb. 13, 41:1
Kid Champion	
Public Theater	Feb. 20, 38:1
A Doll's House	
Beaumont (Lincoln Center)	Mar. 6, 44:1
The Taking of Miss Janie	
Newhouse (Lincoln Center)	May 5, 40:1
Little Black Sheep	
Beaumont (Lincoln Center)	May 8, 46:1
A Chorus Line	
Public Theater	May 22, 32:1
Shubert Theater (Broadway)	Oct. 20, 44:1

Hamlet
Delacorte Theater — June 27, 26:2

The Comedy of Errors
Delacorte Theater — Aug. 9, 8:4

The Shoeshine Parlor
Mobile Theater — Aug. 10, 41:5

Trelawny of the Wells
Beaumont (Lincoln Center) — Oct. 16, 45:1

Jesse and the Bandit Queen
Public Theater — Nov. 3, 48:1

1976

Jinx's Bridge
Public Theater — Jan. 22, 43:1

The Shortchanged Review
Newhouse (Lincoln Center) — Jan. 23, 17:3

Apple Pie
Public Theater — Feb. 13, 18:1

Mrs. Warren's Profession
Beaumont (Lincoln Center) — Feb. 19, 45:1

Rich and Famous
Public Theater — Feb. 20, 15:1

Woyzeck
Public Theater — Mar. 25, 43:2

Streamers
Newhouse (Lincoln Center) — Apr. 22, 38:5

The Threepenny Opera
Beaumont (Lincoln Center) — May 3, 42:1

So Nice, They Named It Twice
Public Theater — May 27, 31:3

For Colored Girls Who Have Considered Suicide When the Rainbow is Enuf
Public Theater — June 2, 44:4
Booth Theater (Broadway) — Sep. 16, 53:1

Rebel Women
Public Theater — June 4, sec. C, 6:6

Henry V
Delacorte Theater — July 1, 22:1

Measure for Measure
Delacorte Theater — Aug. 13, sec. C, 3:1

Mondonga
Mobile Theater — Aug. 27, sec. C, 4:7

1977

Marco Polo Sings a Solo
Public Theater — Feb. 7, 30:1

The Cherry Orchard
Beaumont (Lincoln Center) — Feb. 18, sec. C, 3:4

Ashes
Public Theater — Feb. 20, sec. 2, 3:1

Hagar's Children
Public Theater — Mar. 24, sec. C, 26:1

On the Lock-In
Public Theater — Apr. 28, sec. C, 23:1
Creditors

Public Theater	May 18, sec. B, 19:1
The Stronger	
Public Theater	May 18, sec. B, 19:1
Agamemnon	
Beaumont (Lincoln Center)	May 19, sec. C, 20:1
Delacorte Theater	Aug. 18, sec. C, 18:5
The Threepenny Opera	
Delacorte Theater	July 8, sec. C, 3:1
Miss Margarda's Way	
Public Theater	Aug. 1, 20:1
Ambassador Theater (Broadway)	Sep. 28, sec. C, 16:5
Unfinished Women Cry in No Man's Land	
Mobile Theater	Aug. 5, sec. C, 8:5
The Landscape of the Body	
Public Theater	Oct. 13, sec. C, 17:1
The Mandrake	
Public Theater	Nov. 18, sec. C, 3:1
The Misanthrope	
Public Theater	Nov. 24, sec. C, 15:1
Where the Mississippi Meets the Amazon	
Public Theater	Dec. 20, 44:1
A Photograph	
Public Theater	Dec. 22, sec. C, 11:1
The Dybbuk	
Public Theater	Dec. 23, sec. C, 3:1

1978

The Water Engine	
Public Theater	Jan. 6, sec. C, 3:1
Plymouth Theater (Broadway)	Mar. 7, 42:1
A Prayer for My Daughter	
Public Theater	Jan. 18, sec. C, 16:3
Museum	
Public Theater	Feb. 28, 28:4
The Curse of the Starving Class	
Public Theater	Mar. 3, sec. C, 3:4
Mr. Happiness	
Plymouth Theater (Broadway)	Mar. 7, 42:1
Runaways	
Public Theater	Mar. 10, sec. C, 3:4
Plymouth Theater (Broadway)	May 15, sec. C, 15:1
Paul Robeson	
Booth Theater (Broadway)	Mar. 12, sec. C, 29:1
Mango Tango	
Public Theater	May 30, sec. C, 6:3
I'm Getting My Act Together and Taking It on the Road	
Public Theater	June 15, sec. C, 17:1
All's Well that Ends Well	
Delacorte Theater	July 7, sec. C, 3:3
The Taming of the Shrew	
Delacorte Theater	Aug. 18, 48:1
The Master and Margarita	
Public Theater	Nov. 21, sec. C, 13:1
Drinks before Dinner	
Public Theater	Nov. 24, sec. C, 4:1

Drinks before Dinner	
Public Theater	Nov. 24, sec. C, 4:1
Fathers and Sons	
Public Theater	Nov. 26, sec. 2, 3:1

1979

Julius Caesar	
Public Theater	Jan. 26, sec. C, 3:1
The Umbrellas of Cherbourg	
Public Theater	Feb. 2, sec. C, 3:4
New Jerusalem	
Public Theater	Feb. 16, sec. C, 3:1
Taken in Marriage	
Public Theater	Feb. 27, sec. C. 7:1
Coriolanus	
Public Theater	Mar. 15, sec. C, 19:1
Delacorte Theater	June 29, sec. C, 3:4
Sancocho	
Public Theater	Mar. 29, sec. C, 15:4
Leave It to the Beaver Is Dead	
Public Theater	April. 4, sec. C, 20:5
Nasty Rumors and Final Remarks	
Public Theater	Apr. 13, sec. C, 3:1
Dispatches	
Public Theater	Apr. 19, sec. C, 17:1
The Woods	
Public Theater	Apr. 26, sec. C, 15:1

Remembrance	
Public Theater	May 10, sec. C, 18:3
Spell #7	
Public Theater	June 4, sec. C, 13:3
Happy Days	
Public Theater	June 8, sec. C, 3:1
Othello	
Delacorte Theater	Aug. 9, sec. C, 15:1
The Mighty Gents	
Mobile Theater	Aug. 17, sec. C, 17:1
Sorrows of Stephen	
Public Theater	Oct. 24, sec. C, 21:3
Savage Love	
Public Theater	Nov. 16, sec. C, 6:5
Tongues	
Public Theater	Nov. 16, sec. C, 6:5
The Art of Dining	
Public Theater	Dec. 7, sec. C, 6:1

1980

Hard Sell	
Public Theater	Jan. 16, sec. C, 20:3
Salt Lake City Skyline	
Public Theater	Jan. 24, sec. C, 15:4
Marie and Bruce	
Public Theater	Feb. 4, sec. C, 13:1
The Haggadah	
Public Theater	Apr. 2, sec. C, 22:4

Sunday Runners in the Rain
Public Theater May 5, sec. C, 17:1

Mother Courage
Public Theater May 14, sec. C, 20:5

The Music Lessons
Public Theater May 16, sec. C, 5:4

Scenes from the Everyday Life
Public Theater June 5, sec. C, 22:1

Fob
Public Theater June 10, sec. C, 6:5

The Pirates of Penzance
Delacorte Theater July 30, sec. C, 15:1
See 1981 for Broadway production

Under Fire
NYSF Touring Theater Aug. 23, 15:1

Girls, Girls, Girls
Public Theater Oct. 1, sec. C, 25:1

You Know Al, He's a Funny Guy
Public Theater Nov. 12, sec. C, 25:1

The Sea Gull
Public Theater Nov. 12, sec. C, 25:1

True West
Public Theater Dec. 24, sec. C, 9:1

1981

Alice in Concert
Public Theater Jan. 8, sec. C, 17:1

The Pirates of Penzance
Uris Theater (Broadway) Jan. 9, sec. C, 3:1

Penguin Touquet
Public Theater Feb. 2, sec. C, 14:3

Mary Stuart
Public Theater Feb. 17, sec. C, 5:4

Texts for Nothing
Public Theater Mar. 9, sec. C, 12:1

The Dance and the Railroad
Public Theater Mar. 31, sec. C, 5:1

Wrong Guys
Public Theater May 15, sec. C, 5:1

The Tempest
Delacorte Theater July 10, sec. C, 3:1

Henry IV, part 1
Delacorte Theater Aug. 21, sec. C, 5:1

Dexter Creed
Public Theater Oct. 7, sec. C, 22:1

Family Devotions
Public Theater Oct. 19, sec. C, 17:1

Twelve Dreams
Public Theater Dec. 23, sec. C, 9:1

1982

Zastrozzi
Public Theater Jan. 18, sec. C, 14:1

Lullabye and Goodnight
Public Theater Feb. 10, sec. C, 24:1

Three Acts of Recognition
Public Theater — Apr. 8, sec. C, 11:2

Antigone
Public Theater — Apr. 28, sec. C, 19:1

Goose and Tomtom
Public Theater — May 8, 17:4

Red and Blue
Public Theater — May 12, sec. C, 28:3

Don Juan
Delacorte Theater — July 2, sec. C, 3:1

The Death of von Richthofen
As Witnessed from Earth
Public Theater — July 30, sec. C, 3:1

A Midsummer Night's Dream
Delacorte Theater — Aug. 16, sec. C, 14:3

Plenty
Public Theater — Oct. 22, sec. C, 3:1
See 1983 for Broadway production

Hamlet
Public Theater — Dec. 3, sec. C, 3:1

Top Girls
Public Theater — Dec. 29, sec. C, 17:1

1983

Plenty
Plymouth Theater (Broadway) — Jan. 13, sec. C, 15:1

Cold Harbor
Public Theater — Mar. 9, sec. C, 15:5

Buried Inside Extra	
Public Theater	May 5, sec. C, 19:1
Egyptology	
Public Theater	May 18, sec. C, 17:5
Fen	
Public Theater	June 12, sec. 2, 7:1
Emmett, A One Morman Show	
Public Theater	July 8, sec. C, 3:1
Funhouse	
Public Theater	July 8, sec. C, 3:1
Richard III	
Delacorte Theater	July 15, sec. C, 3:1
Orgasmo Adulto Escapes from the Zoo	
Public Theater	Aug. 5, sec. C, 3:1
Non Pasquale	
Delacorte Theater	Aug. 15, sec. C, 13:1
Sound and Beauty	
Public Theater	Nov. 7, sec. C, 13:1
A Private View	
Public Theater	Nov. 21, sec. C, 16:1
Lenny and the Heartbreakers	
Public Theater	Dec. 23, sec. C, 10:5
The Human Comedy	
Public Theater	Dec. 29, sec. C, 15:1
See 1984 for Broadway production	

1984

Cinders
Public Theater — Feb. 21, sec. C, 18:3

The Human Comedy
Royal Theater (Broadway) — Apr. 15, sec. 2, 9:1

The Nest of the Wood Grouse
Public Theater — June 15, sec. C, 3:1

Found a Peanut
Public Theater — June 18, sec. C, 1:1

Henry V
Delacorte Theater — July 6, sec. C, 1:1

The Golem
Delacorte Theater — Aug. 17, sec. C, 3:4

The Ballad of Soapy Smith
Public Theater — Nov. 13, sec. C, 15:2

La Boheme
Public Theater — Nov. 30, sec. C, 3:1

1985

Tracers
Public Theater — Jan. 22, sec. C, 13:1

Coming of Age in Soho
Public Theater — Feb. 4, sec. C, 14:3

Tom and Viv
Public Theater — Feb. 7, sec. C, 23:1

Salonika
Public Theater — Apr. 3, sec. C, 17:1

The Normal Heart	
Public Theater	Apr. 22, sec. C, 17:1
The Marriage of Bette and Boo	
Public Theater	May 17, sec. C, 3:1
The Rat in the Skull	
Public Theater	May 22, sec. C, 18:4
Measure for Measure	
Delacorte Theater	July 2, sec. C, 8:4
The Mystery of Edwin Drood	
Delacorte Theater	Aug. 23, sec. C, 3:3
Imperial Theater (Broadway)	Dec. 3, sec. C, 21:1
A Map of the World	
Public Theater	Oct. 2, sec. C, 23:1
Aunt Dan and Lemon	
Public Theater	Oct. 29, sec. C, 13:1
Join'	
Public Theater	Dec. 19, sec. C, 17:3

1986

Rum and Coke	
Public Theater	Jan. 28, sec. C, 13:1
Hamlet	
Public Theater	Mar. 10, sec. C, 13:1
Largo Desolato	
Public Theater	Mar. 26, sec. C, 15:1
As You Like It	
Public Theater	Apr. 24, sec. C, 21:1
Mobile Theater	
Belasco Theater (Belasco Project, autumn 1986)	

Romeo and Juliet	
Public Theater	no review
Mobile Theater	
Belasco Theater (Belasco Project, autumn 1986)	
Cuba and His Teddy Bear	
Public Theater	May 19, sec. C, 11:4
Longacre Theater (Broadway)	July 17, sec. C, 17:4
Twelfth Night	
Delacorte Theater	July 3, sec. C, 22:1
Medea	
Delacorte Theater	Sep. 5, sec. C, 3:4
The Colored Museum	
Public Theater	Nov. 3, sec. C, 17:1

MAJOR PRODUCTIONS BY TITLE

Agamemnon, 1977
Alice in Concert, 1981
All's Well that Ends Well, 1966, 1978
Antigone, 1982
Antony and Cleopatra, 1959, 1963
Apple Pie, 1976
Art of Dining, 1979
As You Like It, 1955, 1958, 1963, 1973, 1986
Ashes, 1977
Au Pair Man, 1973
Aunt Dan and Lemon, 1985
Ballad of Soapy Smith, 1984
Barbary Shore, 1974
Basic Training of Pavlo Hummel, 1971
Beast's Story, 1969
Bedtime Story, 1952
Black Picture Show, 1975
Black Terror, 1971
Black Visions, 1972
Blood, 1971
Boheme, 1984
Boom Boom Room, 1973
Buried Inside Extra, 1983
Candide, 1971
Changeling, 1956
Cherry Orchard, 1973, 1977
Children, 1972
Chorus Line, 1975
Cinders, 1984
Cities in Bezique, 1969
Cold Harbor, 1983
Colored Museum, 1986
Comedy of Errors, 1975
Coming of Age in Soho, 1985
Coriolanus, 1965, 1979
Corner, 1972
Creditors, 1977
Cuba and His Teddy Bear, 1986
Curious Savage, 1951
Curse of the Starving Class, 1978
Cymbeline, 1955, 1971
Dance and the Railroad, 1981
Dance of Death, 1974
Dance Wi' Me, 1971
Death of von Richthofen..., 1982
Dexter Creed, 1981
Dispatches, 1979
Doll's House, 1975

Don Juan, 1982

Drinks before Dinner, 1978

Dybbyk, 1977

Egyptology, 1983

Electra, 1964, 1969

Emmett, A One Mormon Show, 1983

Ergo, 1968

"An Evening with Shakespeare and Marlowe," 1954

Family Devotions, 1981

Fathers and Sons, 1978

Femmes Noires, 1974

Fen, 1983

Fishing, 1975

Fob, 1980

For Colored Girls Who Have Considered Suicide..., 1976

Found a Peanut, 1984

Funhouse, 1983

Girls, Girls, Girls, 1980

Golem, 1984

Goose and Tomtom, 1982

Hagar's Children, 1977

Haggadah, 1980

Hair, 1967

Hall of Healing, 1952

Hamlet, 1962, 1964, 1967, 1968, 1972, 1975, 1982, 1986

Happiness Cage, 1970

Happy Days, 1979

Hard Sell, 1980

Henry V, 1960, 1965, 1976, 1984

Henry IV, part I, 1968, 1981

Henry IV, part II, 1968

Henry VI, 1970

Here Are the Ladies, 1971

Human Comedy, 1983, 1984

Hunter, 1972

Huui, Huui, 1968

Idomeneo, 1963

I'm Getting My Act Together..., 1978

Invitation to a Beheading, 1969

Jazznite, 1971

Jesse and the Bandit Queen, 1975

Jinx's Bridge, 1976

Join', 1985

Julius Caesar, 1956, 1959, 1962, 1979

Kid Champion, 1975

Killdeer, 1974

King John, 1967

King Lear, 1962, 1973

Landscape of the Body, 1977

Largo Desolato, 1986

Last Days of British Honduras, 1974

Leave It to the Beaver, 1979

Lenny and the Heartbreakers, 1983

Life and Times of J. Walter Smintheus, 1971

Little Black Sheep, 1975

Lotta, 1973

Love's Labour's Lost, 1965

Lullabye and Goodnight, 1982

Macbeth, 1957, 1962, 1966, 1974
Mandrake, 1977
Mango Tango, 1978
Map of the World, 1985
Marco Polo Sings a Solo, 1977
Marie and Bruce, 1980
Marriage of Bette and Boo, 1985
Mary Stuart, 1981
Master and Margarita, 1978
Measure for Measure, 1960, 1966, 1976, 1985
Medea, 1986
Memorandum, 1968
Merchant of Venice, 1962
Merry Wives of Windsor, 1974
Mert and Phil, 1974
Midsummer Night's Dream, 1961, 1964, 1975, 1982
Mighty Gents, 1979
Misanthrope, 1977
Miss Margarda's Way, 1977
Mrs. Warren's Profession, 1976
Mr. Happiness, 1978
Mod Donna, 1970
Mondonga, 1976
More than You Deserve, 1974
Mother Courage, 1980
Much Ado About Nothing, 1955, 1956, 1961, 1972
Museum, 1978
Music Lessons, 1980
Mystery of Edwin Drood, 1985
Nasty Rumors and Final Remarks, 1979
Nest of Wood Grouse, 1984
New Jerusalem, 1979
No Place to Be Somebody, 1969
Non Pasquale, 1983
Normal Heart, 1985
Older People, 1972
On the Lock-In, 1977
Orgasmo Adulto Escapes from the Zoo, 1983
Orphan, 1973
Othello, 1958, 1964, 1979
Our Late Night, 1975
Owl Answers, 1969
Paul Robeson, 1978
Peer Gynt, 1969
Penguin Touquet, 1981
Pericles, 1974
Photograph, 1977
Pirates of Penzance, 1980, 1981
Plenty, 1982, 1983
Potluck!, 1966
Prayer for My Daughter, 1978
Private View, 1983
Puppet Theater of Don Cristobal, 1964
Rat in the Skull, 1985
Rebel Women, 1976
Red and Blue, 1976
Remembrance, 1979
Rich and Famous, 1976
Richard II, 1961
Richard III, 1957, 1966, 1970, 1974, 1983
Romeo and Juliet, 1955, 1957, 1961, 1965, 1968, 1986

Rum and Coke, 1986
Runaways, 1978
Salonika, 1985
Salt Lake City Skyline, 1980
Sambo, 1969
Sancocho, 1979
Savage love, 1979
Scenes from the Everyday Life, 1980
Sea Gull, 1975, 1980
"Shakespeare's Women," 1955
Shoemaker's Prodigious Wife, 1964
Shoeshine Parlor, 1975
Short Eyes, 1974
Shortchanged Review, 1976
Siamese Connections, 1973
Slag, 1971
So Nice, They Named It Twice, 1976
Sorrows of Stephen, 1979
Sound and Beauty, 1983
Spell #7, 1979
Sticks and Bones, 1971, 1972
Stock Up on Pepper..., 1967
Stomp, 1969
Streamers, 1976
Stronger, 1977
Subject to Fits, 1971
Sunday Runners in the Rain, 1983
Take One Step, 1968
Taken in Marriage, 1979
Taking of Miss Janie, 1975
Taming of the Shrew, 1956, 1960, 1965, 1978
Tempest, 1962, 1974, 1981
Texts for Nothing, 1981
That Championship Season, 1972
Three Acts of Recognition, 1982
Threepenny Opera, 1976, 1977
Ti-Jean and His Brothers, 1972
Time to Go, 1952
Timon of Athens, 1971
Titus Andronicus, 1956, 1967
Tom and Viv, 1985
Tongues, 1979
Top Girls, 1982
Tracers, 1985
Trelawny of the Wells, 1970, 1975
Troilus and Cressida, 1965, 1973
True West, 1980
Twelfth Night, 1958, 1963, 1969, 1986
Twelve Dreams, 1981
Two Gentlemen of Verona, 1955, 1957, 1971
Umbrellas of Cherbourg, 1979
Under Fire, 1980
Unfinished Women Cry..., 1977
Volpone, 1967
Water Engine, 1978
We Real Cool, 1965
Wedding Band, 1972
Wedding of Iphigenia, 1971
What the Wine-Sellers Buy, 1974

Where Do We Go from Here?, 1974
Where the Mississippi Meets the Amazon, 1977
Winter's Tale, 1963
Woods, 1979
Woyzeck, 1976
Wrong Guys, 1981
X Has No Value, 1970
You Know Al, He's a Funny Guy, 1980
Zastrozzi, 1982

AUTHOR INDEX

SUBJECT INDEX